# An Introduction to Changing India

T0352556

# An Introduction to Changing India

## Culture, Politics and Development

Sirpa Tenhunen and Minna Säävälä

ANTHEM PRESS

LONDON · NEW YORK · DELHI

Anthem Press
An imprint of Wimbledon Publishing Company
*www.anthempress.com*

This edition first published in UK and USA 2012
by ANTHEM PRESS
75-76 Blackfriars Road, London SE1 8HA, UK
or PO Box 9779, London SW19 7ZG, UK
and
244 Madison Ave. #116, New York, NY 10016, USA

*British Library Cataloguing-in-Publication Data*
A catalogue record for this book is available from the British Library.

*Library of Congress Cataloging-in-Publication Data*
Tenhunen, Sirpa.
An introduction to changing India : culture, politics and
development / Sirpa Tenhunen and Minna Säävälä.
p. cm.
Includes bibliographical references and index.
ISBN 978-0-85728-805-9 (hbk. : alk. paper) – ISBN 0-85728-805-9
(hbk : alk. paper)
1. India–Economic conditions–1991– 2. India–Politics and
government–21st century. I. Säävälä, Minna. II. Title.
HC435.3.T463 2012
954.05'3–dc23
2012026359

ISBN-13: 978 0 85728 805 9 (Pbk)
ISBN-10: 0 85728 805 9 (Pbk)

Cover image © Sirpa Tenhunen

This title is also available as an eBook.

# CONTENTS

# ACKNOWLEDGMENTS

The expertise that this book builds on has been accumulated during two decades of research in and about India. We would like to acknowledge the guidance and cooperation provided by innumerable colleagues, collaborators and friends in India, Finland, the United States, the Netherlands and other countries, both during our research projects and when writing this book. Among the most important persons to thank are villagers in Janta and Gopalapalli and urbanites in Kolkata and Hyderabad who were our primary guides to Indian realities and without whom this book would never have materialized.

In the academic world, Prof. Emeritus Asko Parpola has been an inspiring and erudite supporter and encouraged us to complete the book. We also like to thank following people for their expertise, granted in interviews and discussions when preparing for this book: Virendra Pal Singh (Assam University), Arul Aram (Anna University, Chennai), Ravinder Kaur (Indian Institute of Technology), Suresh Babu (Centre for Research and Environment), N. S. Siddhartan (Institute of Economic Growth), Nilabja Ghosh (Institute of Economic Growth), Sir Ratan Tata Fellow Parmod Kumar (Institute of Economic Growth), Bharat Karndad (Centre for Policy Research, National Security Studies), Amiya Bagchi (Institute for Development Studies, Kolkata), and Smita Gupta.

We are thankful for Rana Sinha, Kasturi Basu and Marie-Louise Karttunen who have all helped us with English idioms and expression in various stages of the manuscript. Rana Sinha translated the original Finnish manuscript into English which we have further developed and expanded into this book. We would like to thank the Finnish Cultural Foundation for granting us the funding to write a book, *Muuttuva Intia*, on the changing Indian society in 2005. We are thankful for the Academy of Finland where we both have worked as researchers as well as our current employers, the University of Helsinki (Sirpa Tenhunen) and the Population Research Institute in the Family Federation of Finland (Minna Säävälä), for providing us with the necessary intellectual and practical environment for developing and writing this book. Our special thanks go to the editors at Anthem Press for their belief in this book and their useful ideas, hard work and perseverance throughout the editing process.

# Chapter 1

# INTRODUCTION

India has long fascinated Western imagination, and trade routes from Europe have been linked to the Indian subcontinent for millennia. Today India is part of world economy more than ever before. Since the 1990s, India has emerged as one of the leading global economies, continuing to be one of the fastest growing economies. The state has liberated the economy, and infrastructure and communication systems are improving. Yet, despite having its own space flight program, India remains a developing country plagued by widespread child malnutrition, gender discrimination and caste hierarchies. Many features of Indian culture and society continue to be prominent even in the midst of changes, albeit accompanied by new interpretations and tensions.

India is also visible and tangible outside of South Asia. People of Indian origin are among the largest migrant groups in the world, from the Caribbean and Malaysia, to the United States, Europe and the Gulf States. Migrant Indian populations keep up with their Indian identity and cultural practices, even when they have lived in their host societies for centuries. Cultural, social, and political transnational connections of migrant Indians link them with their country of origin and increase the need to understand how India as a nation-state is evolving and making itself recognized globally.

India's growing international importance—economically, politically, and culturally—has been accompanied with a widening need to understand India's diversity, changes, and continuity. The idea for this introductory book evolved from our experiences of teaching diverse audiences about contemporary India from business people and civic organizations, to students of various disciplines. What unites these various audiences is their desire for a holistic understanding of contemporary India. For instance, issues of health and population do not merely concern health professionals but also business people and environmental activists: population issues determine the size of the market and contribute to environmental burden. This book is also intended to be used by students of Asian and Indian studies, development studies, and various social sciences when in need of a wider understanding of development, culture and society in contemporary India.

This book focuses on the intertwining of culture, politics and development in India. By drawing on our own anthropological fieldwork in various settings in rural and urban India we give ordinary Indians a voice by exploring their aspirations for change and continuity, while also describing macro-level processes. We aim to provide a balanced picture of emerging India's many triumphs as well as its lingering problems and the ongoing battle for more inclusive growth. The following chapters deal with politics, economic life, appropriation of new technologies, population and environmental issues, culture, and everyday life, thereby providing the reader the information needed for intercultural encounters between Indians and people from other national backgrounds.

We argue that culture, politics, and development need to be understood as interconnected and interdependent spheres. While cultural connections make daily politics and development efforts intelligible, politics and development efforts themselves mould culture. "Culture" is a multifaceted concept, referring to a rather different phenomenon in everyday parlance than in academic discourse in which it has become highly contested and debated during the last decades. The common sense meaning of "culture" tends to be essentializing and to view the world as a mosaic of separate and clearly demarcated cultures. Culture is often recognized in rituals, festivals, and other phenomena that are easy for an outsider to regard as exotic. Here, our understanding of culture follows the mainstream of current anthropological thinking, and we view culture as socially acquired meaning systems through which people see and understand their worlds but which also enables a contest of meanings. In this book, we aim to bring forward the double nature of culture, having on the one hand continuity and perseverance as naturally occurring, and on the other hand, being susceptible to change. Culture is dynamic through the interplay of social power asymmetries and core symbols that have to be continuously reinterpreted in social praxis in order for them to remain resilient.

We aim to capture cultural dynamism by looking at agents with differing positions and viewpoints—and cultures in motion. When we speak about culture in India, we do not claim an existence of "Indian culture" as a unified and shared totality. Due to very noteworthy regional, religious, social, and other differences which are described throughout the book and more specifically in Chapter 3, such a general abstraction would have no meaning. Thus it is better to speak about "cultures *in* India" than about the "Indian culture." However, we do not consider "culture" only as discourse or as a politically motivated invention, but believe that there are certain temporally resilient, largely taken-for-granted core symbols, emotions, values, and relations that people learn through the process of socialization. These in turn are in constant interplay with politics and development.

According to the socio-cultural anthropological view, well-being and development receive their meaning in a cultural context. Development inevitably touches upon the conceptions of good life which are not universally shared, even if certain basic values such as avoidance of pain or hunger may be universal. Development refers to a positive and desirable change. In the Indian context caste and kinship, despite their wide regional and community wise differences, form the cultural backbone of social relations, and thus are examined in detail in Chapter 4. Culture is inseparable from social and economic relations, and thus is present throughout the book.

One of the basic social values shared by many Indians is the desirability of being maximally interconnected with others. The necessity of interconnectedness is constitutive of a gendered lifecycle, and has particular importance for women's lives in South Asia. Women's identities are more based on their relatedness within the family and kin than on their individual freedoms, which easily leads to using women, particularly young women, as the supporters of the ends of others rather than as ends in their own right (Nussbaum 2000, 5–6). This naturally limits their structural capabilities for individual well-being and development. Gender asymmetries crucially influence issues of population, labor force, politics, rural development, health, and education in India, and consequently we discuss gender throughout the book. Our focus is not solely on women's lives but on how men's and women's roles are interrelated. In India—as elsewhere—development is gendered.

Our national background as descendants of Finland, a nation that experienced one of the fastest structural transformations between 1965 and 1975, from an agrarian, poor country, to a high-tech, post-industrial society together with our shared disciplinary background in social anthropology directs attention in this book more to the potential dynamism in Indian society than to the incapacitating colonial legacies of the past. When the Third World is in focus, the main interest tends to be the various indicators of the level of economic or human development. Such a view that sees development as a state to be compared to and defined by the level of per capita income, national gross domestic product, educational or literacy level, life expectancy or the like, has been widely used but also incessantly criticized. Naturally it is justified to use such parameters to characterize the state of particular national economies or to understand macro-level processes. However, such an aggregated and universalizing view does not help in understanding the developmental challenges of Third World countries like India very well. Here, we understand development broadly as improved well-being and capabilities, drawing from an American philosopher Martha Nussbaum (2000) and Indian Nobel Laureate in Economics Amartya Sen (1999) whose definitions of development take into consideration capabilities, i.e. what people are effectively able to do, instead of merely measuring wealth and poverty levels. Rather than using universal definitions of development, we follow Sen in viewing ideas of development as deriving from contemporary local and global debates.

Nussbaum and Sen point out that development cannot be reached without freedoms and human rights, and rights in turn are not enough if they are not substantial or based on real opportunities. Rights tend to be understood too passively and should be replaced by considerations of freedoms as positive freedoms to act. For instance, the right to vote is ineffectual without securing literacy and access to accurate information on the candidates. In the most philosophical sense, this reading of development as freedom derives from John Rawls's (1971) principle of social justice in which economic development or efficiency should never be acceptable justifications for limitation of basic liberties such as freedom of speech, thought and political liberties. This approach means that when we speak about development, we are inevitably destined to discuss politics and democracy as well, which is central particularly in Chapters 5 and 6. Moreover, development as a positive freedom that makes it possible for people to secure human dignity also points to social justice, equality, and limited socio-economic disparities. A society plagued by constantly widening income differences between the poor and the affluent can hardly be considered as advancing human development, no matter how fast its gross national product is rising. This issue is discussed especially in Chapter 7.

The interconnectedness of basic liberties, development, and well-being is further stressed for example in Len Doyal and Ian Gough's (1991) *A Theory of Human Need*, which points out how in addition to basic freedoms, basic capabilities relating to health are essential for people's ability to participate politically and to reap the benefits of the economy. Health and well-being are thus in the core of developmental processes, and will be discussed in Chapter 7 which deals with population issues.

India is a democratic country where development efforts emerge from the political sphere and debate. When India as the first non-Western country chose democracy as its form of government, it did not merely adopt Western influences. Indian democracy and politics draw from local traditions and meanings. In this book, we do not merely examine politics as related to the development of political institutions and democracy in India. As anthropologists we have adopted a view of politics as a symbolically constructed sphere with local meanings and patterns. This anthropological understanding of politics enables an understanding of how culture and development efforts merge in practical politics, as discussed in Chapter 5.

We have been engaged in anthropological research on kinship, gender issues, politics, class and caste, population issues, and the appropriation of information technology in Indian society and culture for nearly twenty years. Sirpa Tenhunen has conducted field research in rural and urban West Bengal and Minna Säävälä in rural and urban Andhra Pradesh in southern India. In the following chapters, we offer the reader a tangible picture of mundane realities along with a more general picture of Indian society. We do not, however, present our fieldwork locations as typical villages but as examples portraying unique regional features that help the reader to fathom the multiplicity of actual everyday life in India. We have excluded detailed discussions on anthropological theory and analyses from the ethnographic descriptions we offer in this book in order to broaden the readership of the book. Those interested in more detailed anthropological theoretical debates and analyses are asked to turn to our monographs and journal articles.

In addition to our own empirical, field-based research, the wide-ranging description of the social, political, and economic situation in India derives from a close reading of research literature. For the sake of brevity and readability, we mention these sources when they refer to distinct analyses and challenged viewpoints, interpretations, or figures and leave out the sources on generally accepted historical and political facts and interpretations. While we discuss many disputed issues on which scholars have not reached a consensus, we have avoided far-reaching speculations and preferred more generally supported viewpoints. The aim of this introductory book is to provide a freshman in Indian studies with the basic understanding of key issues relating to development, politics, and culture in India. Academic controversies relating to different interpretations and intellectual frames of reference are kept in the background and reviewed only when they contribute to the general objective of this book.

## Contents

The following two chapters present information that facilitates the understanding of the subsequent chapters. In Chapter 2, we examine the country's long history of globalization; this offers a panorama of the multiplicity of Indian traditions and societies and the effects of colonialism. The third chapter offers a view of the diversity in India by describing regional differences and the spectrum of languages and religions, while to conclude the chapter we explore the factors that contribute to the coalescence of Indian diversity.

The fourth chapter examines changes in caste and kinship, which fundamentally affect politics, markets, and human choice as a whole throughout India. We describe how caste and kinship are made to work in a village as well as examine changes occurring in India as a whole and the role that caste and kinship play in work culture, consumer behavior, business, and cross-cultural communication.

After the first chapters which describe the most fundamental and general issues pertaining to all features of social and political life in India, we turn to the realities of politics. The fifth and sixth chapters concentrate on India's domestic, foreign, and trade policies. What kind of objectives do the main political parties have and where are they leading India in terms of trade and foreign policies? The fifth chapter describes the main stages in India's recent political history, concentrating specifically on the changes that occurred after the 1991 economic reforms. In Chapter 5, we also relate modern India's political history with the specificities of India's political culture. The sixth chapter deals with the emergence of political alternatives, such as fundamentalist movements and women's activism.

Within the next two decades India will have the world's largest national population. The seventh chapter examines population growth and its consequences particularly from the viewpoint of women's and girls' health and status. We discuss whether and how the government has been able to ensure reproductive rights while providing birth-control facilities and health care. We also examine the causes behind the rapid decline in the average number of children per woman and the consequences of the trend, particularly in the southern part of the subcontinent. This chapter also discusses demographic projections, taking into account the growing prevalence of sex-selective abortions in some areas.

The eighth chapter deals with the immense gap between the haves and have-nots in India while exploring poverty-related problems. Analysis is provided of the ongoing debate concerning developments in the proportion of people living in poverty, its relation to the period of economic liberalization, and the simultaneous process of polarizing income differences. Education and educational reforms are discussed as key factors in India's development and the pivotal social and political role of the middle classes is analyzed.

The ninth chapter examines growth in the different branches of the Indian economy. How do agriculture, industries, communication and IT businesses and outsourcing interact and contribute to the economic growth? This chapter also examines the impact of India's huge culture production industry in relation to development and cultural change.

New technologies offer developing countries a chance to speed up their development by leapfrogging to the latest technology. The tenth chapter deals with the introduction of new technologies, especially information technology, to India. Do these new technologies help to reduce poverty or do they increase disparities? How has India emerged as the world's fastest growing mobile-phone market, and how is mobile technology influencing its culture and society?

The eleventh chapter examines India's environmental questions. India's water supplies are meager in relation to the population, and climate change is likely to complicate the problem. The air in urban areas is highly polluted and so are the main rivers of India. Do environmental pollution and the shortage of water and energy threaten the welfare and the economy of the country? Is human development in India stalled by the ecological limitations and environmental degradation?

This book is a result of a long-lasting academic cooperation between the authors. Each author has been responsible for her own chapters. Sirpa Tenhunen wrote Chapters 2, 4, 5, 6, 9, 10 and 11 of the book as well as most of Chapter 3, with the exception of the section on religion, which was written by Minna Säävälä, who also wrote Chapters 7 and 8. This introduction and the concluding chapter were collaborative efforts.

# Chapter 2

# YOUNG NATION, OLD CIVILIZATION

India's emerging global position is not determined by its history; nevertheless, history makes India's breathtaking multiplicity as well as many of its present-day developmental challenges understandable. India's economic growth has accelerated thanks to the liberalization of the centrally controlled and planned economy which the government launched in 1991. India's economic policies, in turn, are inseparable from its history.

## 2.1 The Long History of Indian Globalization

Bustling trade relations across borders is not a new phenomenon on the Indian subcontinent. Up to India's independence in 1947, the subcontinent was not divided by national borders—areas which today consist of India, Pakistan, Sri Lanka, Nepal, and Bangladesh share a millennia-long history of interaction. If globalization is understood as a movement and supply of goods, services and knowledge across borders, the Indian subcontinent is one of the earliest globalized economies in the world (Kumar and Sethi 2005, 1). As early as 4000 BC, India already boasted a remarkable production of handicrafts, and Indian merchants were trading across political borders. The tales of India's fabulous riches attracted not only traders, but also foreign conquerors like Alexander the Great. There was already growth in trade between China and India in the fifteenth century after the Chinese had invented the compass to facilitate their seafaring quests. However, as historians have elaborated (Ray and Alpers 2007), the nature of these early maritime networks was culturally distinct and differed crucially from contemporary global networks.

Archaeologists discovered an astonishing Indus River civilization with carefully planned urban structures, irrigation, and sewage systems in 1922 (Bose and Jalal 1998, 14). This urban culture, which had developed around the delta of the Indus River in 2600–2000 BC extended its trading networks to Afghanistan, Persia, Egypt and Mesopotamia. The earliest literary sources of Indian civilization are the Veda religious writings compiled in Sanskrit by the Aryans who most likely arrived in India from the direction of the present Iran (1500–800 BC).

The continent's trade relations flourished during the Maurya dynasty (322–185 BC), which was the first empire to cover a large portion of the Indian subcontinent. The Maurya Empire had a highly developed taxation system and administration, and even state-owned businesses including mines, shipbuilding, and armaments industries, which were of considerable importance to the state (Wolpert 1989, 6). The most famous of the Maurya dynasty rulers was Ashoka (273–232 BC), who began his rule as military conqueror but later converted to Buddhism, adopting non-violence as his guideline. Ashoka strove to ground his rule on the principles of mutual tolerance and respect, conveying his philosophy to his subjects by engraving them on stone pillars in the form of edicts. During the Gupta dynasty (320–520 AD) arts and sciences flourished and trade routes spread to the Arabian Sea, Rome and other Mediterranean destinations, and Southeast Asia.

Expansion of trade also brought about the spread of Indian culture, such as the diffusion of Buddhism to Southeast Asia. Many principles of modern mathematics—zero, rules for multiplying and dividing fractions, square roots, cube roots, the minus sign, the value of the pi and principles of trigonometry— were invented in India to serve the bustling trade (Kumar and Sethi 2005, 43). An iron pillar near the Qutub Minar mosque in Delhi, made in the fifth century AD, exemplifies the high standards of chemistry and metallurgy in ancient India: to this day the pillar has not rusted.

Development and trade relations in northern India underwent a decline during the fifth century, whereas the southern kingdoms continued flourishing. Several conquerors, the most influential of whom were the Muslim invaders from Afghanistan, Turkey, and Persia, overran northern India. The first Muslim expeditions to India took place in the seventh century AD, while the era of Muslim kingdoms in India started in the sixteenth century and ended with the rise of British rule. The power of South Asian rulers was not based on a centralized monarchy, but rather on the rulers' fluctuating relationships with local authorities, so changes in rulers were experienced as periods of centralization and decentralization of governance in the Middle Ages (Bose and Jalal 1998).

Architectural monuments such as the stupas and pillars of the Maurya Empire (322–185 BC) in Delhi, Gujarat, Orissa, and Uttar Pradesh stand witness to past kingdoms. The ruins of the famous university of Nalanda, a Buddhist monastery in Bihar, and the sculptures of Ajanta, Ellora, Sanchi, and Sarnath are chronicles of the Gupta Empire (320–520 AD). The Taj Mahal and many historical buildings dominating the Delhi scenery are reminiscent of the Mughal Empire.

The rural areas of ancient India were also part and parcel of the vast network of trade relations which made medieval India a multicultural entity containing four major world religions: Hinduism, Buddhism, Islam, and Christianity. Hinduism and Islam, in particular, merged to produce syncretistic traits and forms. Christianity began exercising its influence in India in 52 AD when one of the disciples of Jesus Christ, Thomas, is said to have arrived in Chennai (formerly Madras).

## 2.2 The Colonial Burden

European journeys of exploration started a new phase in the history of India's globalization. India began to impact on European ways of life through trading. Thanks to cotton imports, Europeans could afford to possess more garments, which in turn improved the hygiene standards of the era. Tea and sugar from India became inseparable parts of everyday lives in many European countries. The Dutch were the first to discover Indian saltpeter, an ingredient of gunpowder. When the British discovered this Dutch secret, they reinforced their military might with legislation, which ordained that every ship returning from India to Britain should carry saltpeter in its cargo (Kumar and Seth 2005, 8).

When Europeans arrived in India the hold of the Muslim Central Government had already weakened, and India was ruled by several local Hindu and Muslim rulers. Nevertheless, trade and small-scale industries flourished. British commercial capitalism changed towards the end of the eighteenth century into imperialism when Great Britain commenced conquering territories and acquiring tax collection rights. The imposition of taxes, first in Bengal and later across the entire country, helped to lay the foundations of Britain's homeland industrialization projects. The aggressive and expansionistic policies of the British led to the subjugation of local rulers and forced other colonial powers to quit India—Portugal, Holland, France and Denmark had established colonies in India which they lost over the decades. British supremacy was enabled by Britain's powerful navy and military forces. Meanwhile, the British government pressured the East India Company to direct its commerce to benefit Great Britain. Indian manufactured goods such as textiles were burdened with such high import duties that their export to Great Britain ceased, while exports grew in raw materials such as indigo, jute, cotton and opium.

The assumption of power by the British improved the status of the Hindu elite in relation to the Muslim elite. The British administration offered new opportunities for elite Hindus who realized the benefits of obtaining a Western education. New urban salaried job opportunities led to the birth of a new kind of class structure among the locals.

The permanent settlement system which the British introduced in 1793 in most parts of India changed irrevocably the prevailing social system and ownership rights. Under Muslim rule, taxes were negotiated between the leaseholder (*zamindar*) and the farmer as a part of the harvest so that if the harvest was bad, the farmers could pay lower taxes. The British, however, regarded this land rule system as backward and prone to corruption.

To clarify landownership and to increase the efficiency of tax collecting, the British gave the *zamindars* ownership rights to the land they occupied and started to collect taxes irrespective of the yield of the harvests (Moorhouse 1983, 66). Since the farmers had to pay their taxes in cash instead of in produce, they had to resort to growing of new kinds of cash crops for the market such as the cotton, jute, indigo and opium regarded as desirable trade commodities by the British. When the harvests were bad, farmers had to take out loans to pay their taxes. Land became a marketable commodity and thus the object of speculation and investment; it not only changed hands according to the laws of the market, but the emergence of a system of sub-tenancy increased the farmers' tax burden.

As the hold of East India Company tightened on India, famines started to afflict the country. Almost a third of the population of the region perished in the great Bengal famine of 1770, which was followed by another disastrous famine in northern India in 1783. During the Second World War, in the 1943–4 Bengal famine, 3.8 million people died. Although there was enough grain in the stores to feed the people, the prices set by the British were too high for the majority of Indians (Bose and Jalal 1998, 54, 157).

Historians have demonstrated how the contest that culminated in independence was not initiated by the nationalistic movement of the educated classes, but was preceded and grounded in various mutinies and resistance in different parts of India from the beginning of the British rule. In 1857, several forces combined in the so-called Sepoy Mutiny, which was named after Indian soldiers, *sepoys*, who served in the British army. The soldiers mutinied, accusing the British of demeaning their religious practices by using pigs' or cows' fat for maintaining their weapons. The movement was joined by landowners, handicraft workers, laborers, and even members of the Delhi police. Indians attacked the British, who were generally few in numbers, in diverse locations across the country. To subdue the rebellion the British had to fight to recapture those areas village by village (Bose and Jalal 1998, 88–96).

After the mutiny was repressed, the Crown took over the governance of India from the East India Company which was then dissolved in 1858. Great Britain increased the percentage of British incumbents in the Indian army, developing it into a mercenary force with which to defend British interests in different parts of the world up to the Second World War. Queen Victoria became the empress of India in 1877, and the British authorities in India built Calcutta (now Kolkata) as their capital to reflect Britain's glory. It was in Calcutta that Hindu culture first came into close contact with Western culture.

## 2.3 Nationalistic Movement

The British blamed Hindu culture for many of the social problems they perceived in the country, especially child marriages and *sati*, the burning of recently widowed women—among some high caste groups in certain regions of India, a widow was considered able to purify her own and her family's sins by committing suicide on her husband's funeral pyre. Western influences stirred new interest in local traditions among Hindus. They started to cherish local languages and customs, basing arguments for methods of eradicating social problems on traditional Hindu sources.

Resistance against the British rule continued in many parts of India. Furthermore, the Western-educated Indian upper classes started to criticize the British rulers in the spirit of the French Revolution. British policies were increasingly seen as an unjust exploitation of the Indian masses and even some English people joined the ranks of the Indian nationalists (Moorehouse 1983, 81). The Swadeshi (indigenous) movement to boycott British products emerged during the early part of the twentieth century.

The British tried to break the resistance in Bengal by partitioning the state into two administrative territories in the early 1900s. The division, however, only intensified the anti-British movement. Unlike in the Sepoy Mutiny, the factions fighting for different reasons and in different localities joined forces. Mahatma Gandhi, who had studied law in Britain, organized an all-India non-violent protest against British rule, drawing arguments for his actions both from Hinduism and Christian ethics. The fight for independence was not, however, completely non-violent. Many groups taking part in the struggle took up arms against the British.

Towards the end of the Second World War, the British government was forced to admit that it no longer had the necessary resources to rule rebellious and strike-prone India. In July 1947, the British Parliament passed a controversial law, the Indian Independence Act, by which this economically and culturally conglomerated entity was partitioned into two states, the Hindu majority India and the Muslim majority Pakistan. Ten million refugees were forced to leave their homes to escape violence. Indian Muslims moved to Pakistan and the Hindus in Pakistan moved to India. Hundreds of thousands lost their lives in the riots that accompanied the independence process (Bose and Jalal 1998). Bilateral relations between India and Pakistan have continued to be strained, as exemplified by recurring armed conflicts and the arms race between the countries—both possess nuclear weapons (see Chapter 5).

Many inherent disparities which the British brought about during the time of the Raj have continued in independent India. The Indian government has often been more successful in safeguarding elite interests than in rooting out poverty. Ashis Nandy (1983) has argued that colonialism meant in addition to concrete rule by the British an insidious conquest of minds which did not cease when the foreign invaders left. The British viewed themselves as civilizers and the Indians as barbarians to be civilized. This colonial ideology caused an identity crisis among Western-educated Indians, which many solved by emphasizing their Indianness while simultaneously searching for British virtues in their own culture. Today Hindu nationalists seek to propagate a view of history in which the Indian subcontinent has always belonged to Hindus (see Chapter 6).

One indication of the desire to do away with colonial symbols has been the changing of the English names of many Indian metropoles to local language versions: Bombay to Mumbai, Calcutta to Kolkata, Madras into Chennai, and Bangalore into Bengaluru. Like many post-colonial researchers, Nandy emphasizes that freeing oneself from colonialism and its concomitant phenomena such as racism requires a thorough analysis of the colonial past instead of forgetting or ignoring it. Post-colonial scholars have uncovered concealed colonialist structures both in literature and research. Such discoveries include the view of ancient India as an immutable bearer of uniform traditions. Another example is the perception of women in developing countries as helpless victims of their culture and society without acknowledging those women's own endeavors to change their position or appreciating the diversity of their objectives.

## 2.4 Conclusion

The modern Indian state was built on South Asia's multifaceted millennia-long history. Regional ethnic diversity has its origins in the great number of its historical kingdoms which evolved in interaction with other civilizations and continents. One central task of the Indian government has been to try to foster unity by coordinating and managing the regional diversity. The colonial period strengthened elitist tendencies in the administration and the neglect of the welfare and education of the lower classes. Colonial policies also weakened the subcontinent's economy by destroying indigenous industries. The divisive politics of the British contributed to the ethnic conflicts between the Hindus and Muslims and the growth of caste-based politics. The partitioning of an economically and culturally conglomerated entity into two states, the Hindu majority India and the Muslim majority Pakistan, still places strain on regional cooperation in the subcontinent. The building of the modern Indian nation has required the management of these issues in the midst of Indian history being constantly reinterpreted as the nation seeks to reinvent itself.

# Chapter 3

# UNITY IN DIVERSITY

## 3.1 Regional Differences

India's 28 states and seven union territories are not only different culturally and linguistically, but also socially and economically. The British colonialists did not base their governmental units in India on local ethnic and linguistic identities. Consequently, one of the first tasks of the Indian Parliament was to deal with ethnic tensions. India's first prime minister, Jawaharlal Nehru, opposed, or at least wanted to postpone, the forming of linguistic states until India was stronger, in order to help build unity. Nehru, however, was forced to give in to popular will, as language groups one by one demanded their own states. The strongest of the movements was by the Telugu speakers, which resulted in the inauguration of the state of Andhra Pradesh in 1953. As Nehru had feared, the creation of Andhra Pradesh led to more such movements and demands by other linguistic groups (Guha 2007).

Geographically, the subcontinent has three major horizontal zones: the northern mountain belt, its neighboring Indo-Gagnetic alluvial plains, and the southern peninsula. The Himalayan Mountains have effectively protected the subcontinent throughout the centuries. Mountain glaciers formed India's river system, which has enabled agriculture and civilizations to flourish in the northern regions of the subcontinent, whereas south India has had to depend on rain for its water. Historically, north and south have represented two distinct cultural and linguistic regions (Wolpert 1989, 8). The hills of the Vindhya Range in central India has been the geographical dividing line between north and south India, as it slowed down some of the influences coming from Central and Western Asia to the Indian subcontinent.

Economic reforms of the 1990s enhanced the authority of the states, thus reinforcing their chances of development. Since richer states have generally attracted more investments than the poorer ones, interstate differences have increased during recent decades, although even poorer states have witnessed economic growth. A few coastal regions emerged as trading centers in ancient

**Figure 3.1.**

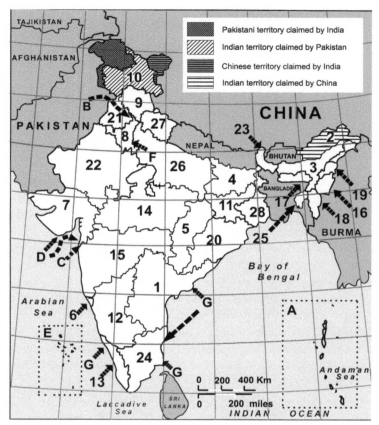

1. Andhra Pradesh 2. Arunachal Pradesh 3. Assam 4. Bihar 5. Chhattisgarh 6. Goa 7. Gujarat
8. Haryana 9. Himachal Pradesh 10. Jammu and Kashmir 11. Jharkhand 12. Karnataka
13. Kerala 14. Madhya Pradesh 15. Maharashtra 16. Manipur 17. Meghalaya 18. Mizoram
19. Nagaland 20. Orissa 21. Punjab 22. Rajasthan 23. Sikkim 24. Tamil Nadu 25. Tripura
26. Uttar Pradesh 27. Uttarakhand 28. West Bengal

**Union territories:** A. Andaman and Nicobar Islands B. Chandigarh C. Dadra and Nagar Haveli
D. Daman and Diu E. Lakshadweep F. National Capital Territory of Delhi G. Pondicherry

and medieval times, while the British colonial rule directed investments mainly towards the few coastal harbor cities; Mumbai and Kolkata, for example, still represent some of the biggest concentrations of wealth in India. Southern and western parts of India have tended to be either economically better off or socially more developed than northern and eastern regions.

India's interstate differences have to do with poor governance and ineffective policies at the state level as well as with the discrepancies in access to private and public investments between states. Since the Central Government still makes core economic decisions about allocations to different sectors of the economy, regional disparities continue to reflect the Central Government's policies. In the 1970s, large landholders in Punjab and Haryana benefited most from the Central Government's farming subsidies for new agricultural methods. Incentives directed at information technology by the Central Government have resulted in growth in Karnataka, Andhra Pradesh and Tamil Nadu, which has successfully promoted the ICT sector. The present Congress-led Central Government has strengthened inclusive growth among small farmers and the poor generally through high import tariffs on agricultural products, keeping the prices of domestic agricultural products relatively high, and increasing direct support to families below the poverty line.

Voters in India tend to increasingly vote for those candidates to state assemblies who can deliver growth and services. States in turn are able to induce growth through offering incentives for businesses and industries and by improving social welfare and education. Some of the poorer states have been able to make considerable progress at times, although their growth patterns have shown greater volatility in comparison to richer states.

**Chart 3.1.** Proportion of people below poverty line 2009–10 and total population in major Indian states in 2011

|  | % | Population, millions |
|---|---|---|
| **North** | | |
| Chhattisgarh | 49 | 26 |
| Haryana | 20 | 25 |
| Himachal Pradesh | 10 | 7 |
| Jammu and Kashmir | 9 | 13 |
| Madhya Pradesh | 37 | 73 |
| Punjab | 16 | 28 |
| Rajasthan | 25 | 69 |
| Uttar Pradesh | 38 | 200 |
| Uttarakhand | 18 | 10 |
| **East** | | |
| Bihar | 54 | 104 |
| Jharkhand | 39 | 33 |
| Odisha | 37 | 42 |
| West Bengal | 27 | 91 |

*(Continued)*

**Chart 3.1.** Continued

| West | | |
|---|---|---|
| Goa | 9 | 1 |
| Gujarat | 23 | 60 |
| Maharashtra | 25 | 112 |
| **Northeast** | | |
| Assam | 38 | 31 |
| **South** | | |
| Andhra Pradesh | 21 | 85 |
| Karnataka | 24 | 61 |
| Kerala | 12 | 33 |
| Tamil Nadu | 17 | 72 |
| All India | 30 | 1,200 |

Sources: Planning Commission (2012) and Census of India (2011).

### 3.1.1 The wealthiest

India's high-income states (assessed by per capita GNP) are the northwestern states of Punjab, Haryana, Gujarat and Maharashtra, and Tamil Nadu in the south. Punjab and Haryana benefited most from the Green Revolution as they were well suited for the improved crops that were being developed in the 1970s. The growth of Punjab and Haryana has, however, been sluggish during recent decades because of the misuse and overuse of fertilizers which, together with irrigation, have impoverished the soil and lowered the water tables (Debroy and Bhandari 2006). In addition to agriculture, Punjab and Haryana have developed a wide variety of industries: electronics, car manufacture, IT, medical equipment, electronics, pharmaceuticals, textiles and machinery (Manian 2007).

Gujarat, Maharashtra, Karnataka and Tamil Nadu received a lion's share of foreign investment in 1990s. These same coastal states also have a long history of wealth creation as trading centers (Purfield 2006; Sachs 2002). Since the reforms, Maharashtra, the country's financial center, has emerged as the center of the automotive industries, and its service sector has grown fast. Maharashtra is also home to the textile, food processing and leather industries, as well as floriculture (Manian 2007).

Gujarat has emerged as one of the fastest-growing agricultural producers thanks to the electrification of its countryside and building of successful large-scale irrigation systems. Gujarat's industries are IT, pharmaceuticals, biotechnology, jewelry, textiles and tourism (Manian 2007). Since the reforms, Tamil Nadu has established itself as the center of electronic industries, as well as other IT services and automotive industries. Tamil Nadu also has pharmaceuticals, textiles, leather, chemical, petrochemical and mineral-based industries (Manian 2007).

### 3.1.2 Middle-income states

The middle-income states are Kerala, Karnataka and Andhra Pradesh in the south, and West Bengal in the eastern part of India. Karnataka and Andhra Pradesh have prospered due to the growth in service and IT but their agricultural growth has been hampered by water shortages. Karnataka has India's largest bio-cluster and floriculture production. Karnataka and Andhra Pradesh are also home to textile industries, while Andhra Pradesh has pharmaceuticals (Manian 2007).

Kerala and West Bengal, the only states which have been governed by a coalition of left-wing parties led by the Communist Party of India-Marxist (CPI-M), have attained economic growth largely thanks to the land reforms. West Bengal has jute, car manufacture, pharmaceuticals, chemicals, aluminum and ceramics industries. Kerala's industries are marine products, textiles, spices, minerals, software, biotechnology, rubber and tourism (Manian 2007).

Kerala has emerged as a leading state in India in terms of health, education and gender equality (Purfield 2006; Sachs 2002). Despite the outstanding results in health and education, Kerala has not been among the top states economically because it began encouraging private investment later than the richer states. Instead of developing commerce at home, many Keralites have used their social and educational assets to migrate to work, mainly in Gulf countries—Kerala's remittances from migrants are three times higher than the support it receives from the Central Government. As communist-ruled states, both Kerala and West Bengal have had a history of labor unrest, but for decades both have emulated the example set by the Chinese encouraging the growth of new industries and businesses (Sachs 2002).

### 3.1.3 The poorest states

The poorest zone comprises Orissa, Chhattisgarh and Jharkhand, and the so-called BIMARU states. BIMARU is an acronym demographer Ashish Bose coined in 1985 by taking the first letter of four northern Indian states: Bihar, Madhya Pradesh, Rajasthan and Uttar Pradesh. The word *bimaru* means "sick" in Hindi, and is used to refer to the four states as a bloc. Chhattisgarh and Jharkhand were separated from Madhya Pradesh and Bihar in 2000. This group of the poorest states performed the worst on social indicators decades ago, and continues to lag behind national standards.

The eastern state of Orissa has traditionally been one of India's poorest states although its soil is well-suited for agriculture and it has the most productive mines in India. Orissa's industries include pharmaceuticals, aluminum, gems and jewelry, petrochemicals and car manufacture (Manian 2007). Orissa has 90 percent of India's chrome ore and nickel reserves, 70 percent of bauxite, and 24 percent of coal reserves (Sachs 2002). Mining industries in India have not been as lucrative as they could be due to state regulations on prices; major mining of ores continues to be regulated by the Central Government. Tourism is a significant source of income both in Rajasthan and Madhya Pradesh. In addition, Rajasthan has mineral-based industries, while Madhya Pradesh boasts biotechnology industries. Uttar Pradesh has horticulture, textiles, engineering goods and leather industries (Manian 2007).

## 3.2 Growth Patterns

The gap in income levels between rich and poor states per capita has widened over the past three decades. Rich states have grown over three times faster than poorer states. Haryana, Punjab and Maharashtra achieved the highest average annual growth rates during the 1970s. In the 1980s, Rajasthan, Haryana and Maharashtra were the top three performers with Gujarat and Tamil Nadu close behind. Over 1991–2 and 1994–5, the top performers were Maharashtra, Kerala and Gujarat, with West Bengal close behind. Thus, the group of high-performing states diversified in the 1980s and 1990s to include new states in addition to two states which have most constantly performed well, Gujarat and Maharashtra. The poorest states, as well as Kerala, have grown more slowly than the national average. From 1970 to 2000, the fast-growing states included the middle-income states Andhra Pradesh, West Bengal and Karnataka, as well as the two richest states, Gujarat and Maharashtra (Purfield 2006). Kerala, Tamil Nadu, Maharashtra and West Bengal have made the greatest strides towards reducing poverty (a 26–38 percent decrease during 1970–2000), followed by Madhya Pradesh, Orissa and Karnataka (decreasing 23–25 percent during 1970–2000). During the same period, Haryana, Rajasthan, Uttar Pradesh, Bihar and Punjab lowered their proportion of poor 13–18 percent (Purfield 2006). During 2005–10, some of the bigger states such as Bihar, Chhattisgarh and Uttar Pradesh showed only a marginal decline in their poverty ratio, particularly in rural areas; whereas the poverty ratio in Himachal Pradesh, Madhya Pradesh, Maharashtra, Orissa, Sikkim, Tamil Nadu, Karnataka and Uttarakhand declined by about 10 percent. In Assam, Meghalaya, Manipur, Mizoram and Nagaland poverty has increased (Planning Commission 2012).

The average figures of individual states hide vast heterogeneity in poverty. Poverty is very high in southern Bihar, southern Orissa, southwestern Madhya Pradesh and southern Uttar Pradesh; and high in Bihar, parts of Madhya Pradesh, inland Maharashtra, northern Tamil Nadu, eastern and central Uttar Pradesh, and parts of West Bengal. Pockets of low poverty can be found in the western coastal regions, all of Andhra Pradesh, Punjab, and parts of Madhya Pradesh and Rajasthan, which form the north–south belt affected by the Green Revolution (Sachs 2002).

Despite these accentuating differences, states are not separate entities; there is some economic spill-over from richer regions into poorer ones. For instance, Bihar's acceleration of growth since 2000 has been attributed to remittances from emigrants and the increase in agricultural productivity due to the increase of the unemployed migrating out of the state (*India Daily*, December 28, 2012). As a result, some richer states have in turn witnessed a birth of movements against immigrants. In Maharashtra, the Maharashtra Navnirman Sena (MNS) [Maharashtra Renaissance Army], founded in 2006, accused immigrant workers of spoiling Maharashtrian culture, which has instigated violence against them. After violent attacks in 2008, nearly 40,000 north Indian workers fled Maharashtra which led to an acute labor shortage affecting local industries. Violence against immigrant workers from Bihar has taken place also in Assam, a state rich in resources such as oil and tea gardens.

## 3.3 Social Development

Constitutionally, each state bears primary responsibility for providing elementary education. This has resulted in great regional disparities in literacy and learning levels due to the variation in educational policies. Kerala stands apart with more than 90 percent of its population literate, which is largely the result of mass campaigns and political action. States like Bihar, Rajasthan and Uttar Pradesh hover around 55 percent; while higher economic performers Karnataka and Andhra Pradesh have a literacy rate just above the national average. However, India is poised to achieve complete literacy by 2030 thanks to the Central Government's nationwide campaigns and policies, including a campaign to attain universal elementary education by 2010, Sarva Shiksha Abhyan, and a midday-meal scheme.

There is astounding regional diversity within India in terms of birth rates. In Andhra Pradesh, Kerala and Tamil Nadu the average number of children born per woman is below two. By contrast, in several northern Hindi-speaking states the fertility rate is still three to four children per woman (National Family Health Survey 2005–6). This figure in the high birth-rate areas is dropping,

**Chart 3.2.** States according to the percentage of children who are underweight

| Above 40% | 35–39% | Below 35% |
| --- | --- | --- |
| Uttar Pradesh | Assam | Andhra Pradesh |
| Bihar | Haryana | Goa |
| Chhattisgarh | Himachal Pradesh | Jammu & Kashmir |
| Gujarat | Maharashtra | Karnataka |
| Jharkhand | Rajasthan | Kerala |
| Madhya Pradesh | Uttarakhand | Punjab |
| Odisha | West Bengal | Tamil Nadu |

Source: National Family Health Survey 2005–6, http://www.nfhsindia.org/nutrition_report_for_website_18sep09.pdf

although not in the same scale as in the south. Chapter 8 will elaborate social development in India's different regions in more detail.

## 3.4 Rural–Urban Divide

Urbanization is often held to be the key to India's development since urban areas have traditionally been wealthier than rural areas. India's urbanization has, however, been slow compared to the rest of Asia. While rural–urban migration as a share of the total rural population was 6.5 percent in 1981, in 2001 it fell to 2.8 percent.

While only 28 percent of Indians live in urban areas, the total number of people living in urban areas has gone up substantially. By 2030, India is expected to have an urban population of 575 million, up from the present level of 286 million, with 41 percent living in cities and towns (UNDP 2009).

Much of India's urbanization is a result of the development of new cities and the growth of smaller metropolitan areas. There were 35 cities with populations greater than one million in 2001 and according to projections, there may be 68 such cities by 2020. The number of mega cities (above 5 million) is likely to increase to 10 by 2021 and 36 by 2051 (Kim et al. 2007).

The Central Government aims to divert migrants away from over-populated metropoles by creating jobs in second-tier cities, those with populations of between 1 and 5 million inhabitants. In 2007, the government invested US$29 billion towards improving these smaller cities' infrastructure. Since second-tier cities have lower labor costs than the bigger cities, they are expected to grow fast and gain importance both as engines of economic growth and as expanding consumer markets (Hodgson 2007).

Economic growth has not accelerated the decline in urban poverty rates. Urban poverty in India remains high, at over 25 percent (based on the National Sample Survey results and the Indian government's definition of poverty). A large number of states report poverty figures in urban areas much above those in rural areas. At the national level rural poverty is the higher of the two although the gap has been steadily decreasing over the last couple of decades. As the urban population in the country grows, so does the urban poverty (UNDP 2009).

The Indian Census collected data on slum populations of 50,000 or more for the first time in 2001 recording total slum population as 40 million, 14 percent of total urban population (Sivaramakrishnan et al. 2008). By definition, slums are poorly built, congested tenements in unhygienic environments usually lacking in proper sanitary and drinking water facilities. Slums are health hazards; nevertheless, they have also been argued to represent ecological urban lifestyles. Slums often have thriving economies which offer people both services and jobs close to their homes. Activists of the Dharavi slum, one of the largest slums in the world located in the heart of Mumbai, have successfully protected their rights to improve their living conditions although real-estate developers are lobbying for a huge relocation project (Engqvist 2008). However, slum improvement projects can fail tragically, such as in Indore, the commercial center of the state of Madhya Pradesh, where building of water closets in a major slum area ended up making the environment even dirtier than before as the sewage system had not been adequately planned or built (Verma 2003).

While the economic boom has turned many Indian cities into vibrant hubs that deliver dream growth rates, it has not benefitted the urban poor. Citizen groups of these global cities now campaign frequently for cleaner and more spacious neighborhoods devoid of hawkers and squatters, and courts deliver anti-poor rulings. As a result, the poor are increasingly pushed to the urban fringes. Rao (2010) found that the beautification of New Delhi through relocation projects has made the slum dwellers poorer. They now live in the fringes of Delhi, where they lack access to affordable markets and have to spend greater time and money to commute to work. The relocated residents of Delhi have not been given full ownership rights to their new dwelling sites so their status continues to be precarious even after the relocation.

### 3.5 Spectrum of Languages

There are around 1,000 languages spoken in India—an estimate because of the difficulties in drawing a line between a language and a dialect. There are more than ten main languages, the most common being (population proportion in parentheses) Bengali (8 percent), Telugu (7 percent), Marathi (7 percent) Tamili

(6 percent) Urdu (5 percent), Gujarati (4 percent), Malayalam (3 percent), Kannada (4 percent) and Oriya (3 percent). The official language of India is Hindi, which 41 percent of Indians speak as their mother tongue (Census 2001).

The other main languages are classified as national languages. Of the national languages, 13 belong to the Indo-European group (Assamese, Bengali, Gujarati, Hindi, Kashmiri, Konkani, Marathi, Nepali, Oriya, Punjabi, Sanskrit, Sindhi and Urdu); four belong to the south Indian group which are rooted in the ancient, Sanskrit-influenced Dravidian languages (Kannada, Malayalam, Tamili and Telugu); and one belongs to Sino-Tibetan group (Manipuri).

In spite of the many languages, most Indians speak only one. In 1972, it was estimated that bilinguals numbered only 13 percent of the population. British colonial rule made English the language of power and the elite, and it is still the most widely spoken language in the country; in south India, for example, Hindi is considered more alien than English (Spolsky 1978, 42). Although only 0.2 percent of the Indian population reported English as their mother tongue in the 2001 census, considerably more know it as a second or third language. According to the 1991 census, 11 percent of the Indian population reported English as a second or third language. India is the third-largest English-speaking country in the world on the basis of census figures on English speakers alone. India is also the third biggest English-language publisher after the United States and Great Britain.

Indian English speakers are mainly multilingual, using English especially in professional contexts (Hohenthal 2003). In rural India, knowledge of English is meager because of the low quality of English teaching, although it currently remains the main language of the best schools and universities. English also functions as a connecting language between the Central Government and the states, and as the language of the judiciary. There is great interest in English-language literature, theatre, cinema and music in India. Even though the arts and literature are also cherished in the local languages, many Indian writers, such as Salman Rushdie, Arundhati Roy and Vikram Seth have become world famous for their English novels. In addition to the local newspapers, India has an influential English-language press, and most of the scientific publishing done in India is in English.

## 3.6 Religious Strains

Religion in India is a highly controversial issue and any commentary on it tends to prompt both irritated and supportive reactions, depending on the political perspective of the listener. The subject is further complicated in the eyes of Western observers by the fact that Hinduism, the most commonly practiced faith in India, is more a social practice than a canonized and organized religion like Christianity and Islam. The Hindu religion lacks some of the features regarded as foundational for a religion by Christians: Hindus do not have any single holy text or book, although Mahatma Gandhi among others tried to promote the *Bhagavad Gita*, a poetic work and a Veda script, as the main holy text of the Hindus. The Hindus have not organized themselves into a uniform movement or church. They also do not recognize a common religious leader or leaders. Those who profess themselves to be Hindus have diverse religious beliefs, practices and dogmas of salvation. Despite the heterogeneity, Hindu beliefs and customs do have some fundamental unifying principles: most Hindus accept the sanctity of the Vedas and their lives are guided by the concept of dharma (moral law dependent on man's birth, gender and stage of life; right, duty or propriety).

Western media tend to refer to India as a Hindu society, forgetting that not all Indians are Hindus. In the 2001 census, the majority of Indians, about 80 percent, declared themselves to be Hindus; 13 percent declared themselves as Muslims. The latest census figures relating to the size of religious communities in 2011 have not yet been released by the Indian government, but it is highly probable that the proportion of Hindus in the population has dropped below 80 percent during the last decade and the proportion of Muslims has grown due to their higher birth rate. The spectrum of religious beliefs is more diversified than these simple figures let us believe. The largest religious minority, Muslims are divided into a number of group affiliations and divisions. The majority of them are Sunni, although there are also visible Shi'ite minority groups. The vast majority of the Indian Muslims are descendants of converts who were proselytized during the centuries of Muslim invasions from Western and Central Asia, although the very first Muslim communities in the subcontinent were formed in southern India as a result of interaction with Arab seafaring traders. According to Yoginder Singh Sikand (2004), along with the invasions, entire local caste groups and other populations underwent a gradual process of Islamization, during the course of which elements of the Islamic faith were incorporated into local cosmologies and ritual practice. Mass conversion to Islam was also rarely, if ever, a sudden event; generally it took the form of a gradual process of cultural change and consequently many of the converts retained several of their local, pre-Islamic beliefs and practices (Sikand 2004).

**Chart 3.3.** Indian population according to religious denomination in 2001

| | |
|---|---|
| Hindus | 80% |
| Muslims | 13% |
| Christians | 2% |
| Sikhs | 2% |
| Buddhists | 1% |
| Jains | 1% |
| Other | 1% |
| | 100% |

Source: Census of India (2001).

This gradual and group-based process of Islamization resulted in the present-day caste-like social structure which is also evident among Muslims in India. The major dividing line in the practice of Islam in India is, however, the difference between the "noble" *Ashraf* groups who find their ancestry in the ruling, intellectual or trading communities from Central and West Asia, and those who are described as *Ajlaf*, "inferior" or "low born"—the descendants of the local converts. The majority of Muslims in India practice an eclectic and devotional form of Islam in which the worship of Sufi saints and the paying respect to mausoleums, among other things, have been an integral part; the last decades have witnessed a growing pressure from Islamic religious leaders to give up such "low" practices and to turn to a more pure interpretation of Islam. This process has had several negative consequences, stemming from the growing tensions between religious communities as well as from global influences that are often transmitted by emigrants and their transnational networks (Sardar 2008).

Differences in social practice, rituals and religious convictions between low and high castes, as well as between regions, are considerable also among Hindus. A quarter of all Indians belong either to the Scheduled Castes (formerly Untouchables) or Scheduled Tribes, who were not fully recognized as Hindus until the early twentieth century. People who used to be called Untouchables, who nowadays often prefer to be called *dalits*, only achieved the legal right to enter Hindu temples in 1950 when discrimination against them was prohibited by the constitution. A little less than one-third of Indians belong to other lower castes, i.e. the category administratively labeled "Other Backward Classes" (see Chapter 2) and their religious and social conventions also differ significantly from those of the "forward" castes. Almost one-third of Indians can be classified as belonging to the forward castes. Because caste identity is not recorded in the Indian census operations, apart from Scheduled

Castes and Tribes, we do not have precise figures on the size of various caste groups. The figures derived from the censuses of the colonial era and other surveys are politically and socially controversial and debated because of the difficulties in classifying the multiplicity of groups amidst social changes. The proportions of different caste groups vary from region to region, while regional variation and sects add to the multiplicity of Hindu tradition.

The rise of Hindu fundamentalist groups since the latter part of 1980s has rendered Hinduism and its relationship to other religions a heated topic in the subcontinent. In contrast with the diverse forms and social practices of Hinduism, fundamentalist Hindu organizations emphasize its uniformity (see Chapter 6, which deals more specifically with Hindu fundamentalism). The fundamentalists view Hindu essence (*hindutva*) as surpassing mere religiousness and unifying all those who consider India their sacred motherland. According to the influential ideal presented by Damodar Savarkar (1923), all people belonging to religions conceived on Indian soil are "Hindus"—not only the followers of brahmanical Hinduism, but also the *dalits*, Buddhists, Sikhs, Jains and followers of local tribal religions. There is another faction who would like to designate Indian Muslims and Christians as essentially "Hindus" on the premise that the forefathers of those who converted to these religions during the past centuries were once "Hindus." However, Indian Muslims and Christians often feel that the fundamentalist view belittles their religious identity by nullifying and rendering it "un-Indian." Since Islam and Christianity did not originate in India, Hindu fundamentalists consider them an anathema to Indianness. Fundamentalists can accept the proponents of these religions provided only that they acknowledge the superiority of Hinduism. The question of who is Hindu, or what being a Hindu entails, arouses violent political passions in present-day India (see e.g. Hansen 1999; van der Veer 1994).

The division and mistrust between Hindus and Muslims has been the deepest and most fundamental religious feature of Indian social and political reality. The position of Muslims in India is a constant source of discontent for fundamentalist Hindus who feel that minorities have been favored since Independence. Outside the union territory of Lakshadweep islands, Kashmir is the only state where Muslims are in the majority. There are also significant Muslim populations in the northeastern states of Assam, Uttar Pradesh, Bihar, West Bengal and in the southern state of Kerala. Because relations between Hindus and Muslims are politically strained, there is much dispute about the number of Muslims in India. Both the fundamentalist Hindus and the Muslim leaders at times exaggerate the number of Muslims in the country—for opposing reasons. Hindu fundamentalists aim at cultivating a feeling of fear vis-à-vis the growing Muslim population, while Muslims want to be acknowledged as a numerous and thus an important section of the population and not merely an inconsequential minority. The Indian census is considered relatively accurate, however, so the actual number of Muslims is unlikely to differ radically from the 13 percent recorded in the census of 2001. On average, Muslims are poorer than Hindus; they are less educated and fewer occupy public office. A small portion of Indian Muslims are so-called Asraf-Muslims. They are highly esteemed and claim their ancestry from invaders who came to India from Western Asia. Although Indian Muslims feel as Indian as any Hindu and will express their binding loyalty to India, Hindu nationalists are suspicious of the genuineness of the minority's allegiance and are quick to view them as conspirators of hostile Pakistan.

Christians comprise the third-largest religious group in India, who constitute a little more than two percent of the population. Christians are more numerous in the small northeastern states, Goa and the southern state of Kerala. About two-thirds of Indian Christians are *dalits*. However, persons hailing from higher caste backgrounds usually hold the dominant positions in churches in both Catholic and a number of Protestant denominations. Like the Muslims, Christians have at times also faced opposition from fundamentalist Hindu groups. Some missionary stations and nunneries have been assaulted, particularly in Gujarat and Orissa.

The Sikhs are the fourth-largest religious group in India and they have a particularly important economic and political role in the agriculturally developed and affluent Punjab and in Delhi. Sikhism is a monotheistic faith born in the fifteenth century and is built on the teachings of a number of gurus. Many Sikhs practice their faith in a relatively syncretic manner so that they may visit Hindu temples in addition to their own places of worship, *gurdwaras*. Another important although very small minority faith group is the Parsis or Zoroastrians. They originally fled persecution from Persia to India in the tenth century, but have retained their own endogamous community thereafter. Parsis live particularly in Western India and have been influential in business circles since the colonial times.

Violent conflicts between practitioners of the Hindu religion on the one hand, and Muslims, Sikhs or Christians on the other, have been concentrated around particular politically sensitive areas, especially in Uttar Pradesh, Gujarat, Orissa and Mumbai and its surroundings. Although other religious groups apart from those mentioned above are relatively small, they have important social and cultural role in India and may be regionally central. Buddhism, as well as Jainism, was originally a protest movement against brahmanical Hinduism. Buddhism had its golden period in India during Emperor Ashoka's reign, but it has since shrunk into a marginal role in India. Some *dalits* have converted to Buddhism as a form of revolt against their subjugation in Hindu brahmanical thinking, following the example of their late leader B. R. Ambedkar.

As noted by Amartya Sen, a Nobel Laureate for Economics, it is problematic to describe India as a Hindu society. The country could just as well be called a peasant country, a country of unorganized labor, or a country of those who condemn religious persecution. The religion of the majority does not play a crucial role in all social issues even if religion has at times seized a central role in the public political arena. However, faith plays an important social role in India even among the better-off strata. Consumerism and the growing prosperity of the Indian middle classes have not paved the way to secularization or turned Indians away from religion. Religion plays an ever increasingly important role for Indian identities, including that of middle-class people (see for example Säävälä 2010a). Affluent Hindus arrange impressive rituals, go for pilgrimages and donate large sums of money for temple constructions (see Chapter 6). Many non-resident Indians donate a great deal to religious organizations and communities. For instance, the Vishwa Hindu Parishad (World Hindu Congress), an international fundamentalist Hindu organization, collects considerable funding from the United States and Great Britain. The Hindu religion is no longer only a regional feature of the South Asian subcontinent but a global force that has its own interests to guard among migrant Hindus all around the globe as well.

Religious practice is affected by the changes in the globalized entertainment and news industries. Cinema, television serials and the press are spreading the concept of a unified Hindu religion and rituals which leads to a certain homogenization of innumerable local and caste-specific practices (see e.g. Hancock 1999). Thus the Hindu religion is heading towards greater unification for political reasons and as a result of modern globalization. At the same time, instead of diminishing in importance, religion is emerging as a more crucial and visible factor of social cohesion in India.

## 3.7 Unifying Forces

India is split by many divisions, as the above discussion on regional, linguistic, social and religious differences demonstrates. Many predicted in the 1990s that India would disintegrate because of its diversity, just as the Soviet Union and Yugoslavia had done. At least 231 of the country's 608 districts were affected, with differing intensities, by various insurgent and terrorist movements in 2007 (*South Asia Intelligence Review* 2009). The question that thus arises is how India has been able to remain a single nation.

India is considered to have been traditionally held together by its tolerance of differences and multiplicity. The ancient rulers from Ashoka to Akbar developed forums of public dialogue where representatives of different religions could voice their views to each other (Sen 2005). Permissiveness has manifested itself as syncretism so that the symbols and rituals of different religions have often merged with each other. Indian civilization has been able to assimilate new influences without relinquishing its own specificity.

Caste, kinship and the brahmanical (high caste) values also contribute to Indian unity. For instance, marriage traditions have some similar features all over India. Most marriages are arranged and the marriage rituals, lasting several days, reflect the sacredness of the institution. Continuity of Indian civilization is, however, multifaceted. The Indian tradition embraces asceticism, spirituality and hierarchy, but also the arts of analyzing and debating as well as a long history of commerce, creation of wealth and consumption.

Indian identity has evolved through the country's interaction with the rest of the world. The word *Hindu* was first voiced by the Greeks and the Muslims, who used the word to denote the people living on the other side of the Indus River. One significant force unifying India is nationalism, which emerged during colonialism and culminated in independence in 1947. The railway network and the propagation of Hindi and the English language by the British have brought different parts of the country closer to each other.

There have been three major secessionist movements in independent India: in Nagaland since the 1950s, in Punjab in the 1980s, and in Kashmir in the 1990s (Guha 2007). These movements were based on ethnic and religious grounds, and the Indian state has sought to subdue them by forming new states and granting development funds. Punjab was divided into Haryana and Punjab in the 1960s. New states were also formed for tribal groups in the northeast (Nagaland in 1960s, Meghalaya, Himachal Pradesh, Tripura, Manipur and Arunachal Pradesh; Sikkim in the 1970s; and Mizoram in the 1980s), and in the year 2000 in northern and eastern parts of India (Chhattisgarh out of eastern Madhya Pradesh, Uttaranchal [since renamed Uttarakhand], out of Uttar Pradesh, and Jharkhand out of the southern districts of Bihar).

Government of India showed a green light to the formation of the state of Telangana out of Andhra Pradesh in December 2009. The defenders of the new state argue that Telangana region had been neglected by Andhra Pradesh, but strong opposition especially to Andhra Pradesh for giving up its capital Hyderabad to the new state made the government to postpone the decision until a consensus is reached. Planning the state of Telangana has led to more such movements: demands for new states now include separating Gorkhaland from West Bengal, Maru Pradesh from Rajasthan, Vidarbha from Maharashtra, and Harit Pradesh, Purvanchal and Bundelkhand from Uttar Pradesh (Gupta 2009b).

The reorganization of states has continued in modern India because it has proven a successful way of consolidating India's unity. Linguistic states have provided a legitimate avenue for regional identities without being in conflict with the broader Indian identity. Moreover, the breaking of populous states into smaller units has usually improved administration. Regional identities have therefore not excluded what Indians share culturally and historically.

## 3.8 Conclusion

The diversity manifested in the Indian subcontinent, be it religious, linguistic, cultural, social, political, geographical or economic, is breathtaking. It strains the functioning of the nation-state and presents a political challenge. However, the people of the subcontinent have a disposition to cope with diversity thanks to a millennia-long history of pluralism. Even if the coping strategies adopted have at times been dysfunctional and destructive, the reality of diversity may give India a great advantage in its search for a globally important role.

# Chapter 4

# CASTE AND KINSHIP:
# THE KEYS OF INTERACTION

The caste system is a social and cultural institution unique to Indian civilization. The principal of arranging social life according to inherited caste identities and the separation of castes through the avoidance of interaction has undergone many changes. Yet caste still crucially influences marriage, political organization and everyday interaction, especially in rural India.

Although the caste system has its origins in the Hindu world view, Christians and Muslims in India are also divided into caste-like factions which determine marriage. Of the total population, 8 percent—over 84 million people according to the 2001 census—are classified as *adivasis* and falling outside the purview of caste. *Adivasis* are mainly concentrated in the northeast and in the hilly areas of central India. The British labeled these culturally diverse groups as "tribals" imagining them to be similar to tribals in Africa, which in the 1930s were considered as isolated, primitive groups. *Adivasi* religious practices are, indeed, distinct from those of the Hindus, and their livelihoods have mainly consisted of subsistence agriculture or hunting and gathering.

*Adivasis* have experienced major changes in modern India as forest areas shrink. Some have reaped the benefits of education and experienced rising prosperity. Many, however, have been displaced from their homes by mining and forest industries and become involved in political conflicts and movements such as Maoists and the BJP. Shah (2010) argues that *adivasis* have, for centuries, been integrated with the broader society both economically and culturally. *Adivasis'* understandings of caste ideals in modern India remain largely unexplored, but Shah (2010) shows that Bhils in Rajasthan have been influenced by hierarchical caste ideals.

## 4.1 Caste Logic

The term caste derives from Portuguese traders who referred to the groups they met in India in the sixteenth century as castes (*casta*). The Indian Sanskrit term *varna dharma* says more about the character of the caste system than the

Anglo-Portuguese term, however. According to the religious thinking which emerged during the Veda epoch (1000–600 BC), the cosmic order (*varna dharma*) divides the world into four hierarchically organized categories or *varnas* based on purity.

Sanskrit religious texts narrate how the cosmic spirit sacrificed himself to the gods so that Brahmins (the highest caste) emerged from his mouth, Kshatryas (the warriors) from his arms, Vaisya (merchants) from his thighs and Shudra (laborers) from his feet (Stern 1993, 55). The origin myth delineates the characteristics of the castes. The Brahmins as the highest group are in charge of religious rules, speech and prayers; the Kshatriyas as the warrior caste maintain and conserve sacred order (*dharma*); while the Vaishyas as the merchant caste create prosperity. The Shudras, the lowest caste, serve the upper castes with their manual labor and are further divided into clean and unclean workers.

The strong emphasis on the principle of hierarchy has to do with the canonization of the brahmanical ideology expressed in the Sanskrit texts. The *varna* classification of the religious texts is theoretical in the sense that only the Brahmins are labeled by their *varna* title. Other castes are called by their local *jati* names—*jati* is a wide-spread local term for caste. Numerous *jati* groups' hierarchical standing is determined locally, but in relation to the *varna* hierarchy and its principles.

The origin of the caste system has been explained by the aspirations of invading Aryans to place themselves in a higher position in relation to the original native inhabitants although the theory about invading Aryans is a disputed one (Mendelsohn and Vicziany 2000, 7). The caste system is associated with a division of labor, but it differs from the European four estates in that the differences between the castes are based on concepts of ritual purity. The higher the caste, the purer it is held to be. The concepts of purity are not associated with hygiene but with the distance from biological processes like birth, death and refuse. For example, skinning animals, fishing, cleaning, cremation and laundering are examples of impure professions. Impurity is transmitted when a person touches one who is purer, or when the purer one enjoys food or drink prepared by someone who is considered ritually less pure.

Caste groups have been able to improve their position by imitating the higher-caste ways of life. Individuals, however, cannot change caste during their lifetime. Caste is something one is born into and, according to the caste ideology, a person who has fulfilled his duties in this life can be born into a higher caste in the next one. Many Untouchables or *dalits* have, however, attained a new position during their life time by converting to Christianity, Islam or Buddhism. Reform movements have also emerged from within Hinduism, such as the *bhakti* movements which started in the eighth century and emphasized human equality before God.

For anthropologist Louis Dumont (1970), India presents an ideal type of hierarchy which does not originate from political and economic power. Dumont sees Indian hierarchy as built on caste and purity concerns. Castes maintain distance because those lower in caste hierarchy are impure and can transmit impurity to those higher in hierarchy. The essence of Hindu ideology is, according to Dumont, hierarchy in contrast to the individualism of Western societies.

Early critics of Dumont, such as Das and Uberoi (1971), point out that hierarchy does not exclude equality concerns. People can perceive equality and be motivated by the quest for equality in hierarchical contexts, because within a hierarchy people are not only placed above or below each other but also at the same level. On the one hand, hierarchies do not necessarily exclude ideas of equality; on the other, despite their ideals of equality, Western people too can be aware of acting within hierarchies. Dumont acknowledges the presence of equality in hierarchy but argues that it represents a secondary phenomenon and is therefore irrelevant for the understanding of the dominant ideology; he focuses explicitly and consciously on dominant ideologies.

Critics argue that Dumont mistook the Brahmin view of caste as the general principle of caste system (Mencher 1975; Appadurai 1986; Srinivas 1989; Chatterjee 1993; Gupta 2000). Dumont had a formidable command of Sanskrit—it was with scholarship in this field that he launched his academic career. In addition to using primary data from his fieldwork and other ethnographies, Dumont also drew on these Vedic texts.

Researchers continue to differ in their opinions regarding whether the origin myth and the concomitant caste ideology represent only the views of the highest caste or whether they are also accepted by the low castes. Neither have they reached a consensus about the degree to which the low castes have accepted the axioms of purity which classify them as impure. Few scholars today try to dispute that caste is about purity but the emerging consensus is that it is not solely about purity. The resilience of caste in modern India has to do with the multiple meanings of caste. Low castes build their positive self-image on their shared myths about royal origins (Gupta 2000). Succesful *dalits* studied by Säävälä (2001b) emphasized auspiciousness in their ritual life instead of purity concerns.

## 4.2 Caste in a Village

The following description of social interaction in Janta, a densely populated village of 2,328 inhabitants in the Bankura district in the state of West Bengal, illustrates how caste is maintained and debated in present day rural India. The approach to Janta, where co-author Sirpa Tenhunen has been

**Figure 4.1.**

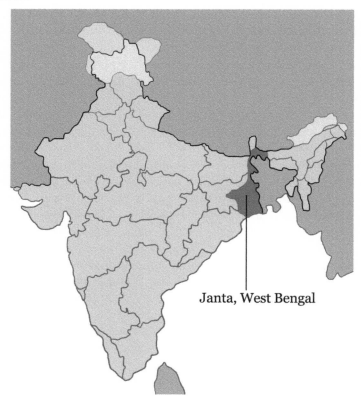

Janta, West Bengal

doing fieldwork since 1999 (see Tenhunen 2003, 2008a, 2008b, 2009), is a visually soothing trip along reddish dirt roads which snake across the shades of green of the lush paddy fields. The area is well-suited for cultivation thanks to its fertile soil and ample groundwater reservoirs. The main sources of livelihood are the cultivation of rice and vegetables. Of the village men, 62 percent are farmers who own the soil they till and 28 percent are landless workers.

The village comprises clusters of densely built mud houses and cement buildings, a few old temples and roofed meeting places. Housing materials are indicative of the village hierarchy: most of the upper-caste houses are concrete and most of the lower-caste dwellings are made of clay. The Tilis are the dominant caste and *jati* in Janta, both in terms of their numbers and landowning. The lowest caste, the Bagdis, constitute the second-biggest caste group. They earn their living as daily laborers in brick factories and on landowners' farms. Some castes continue their hereditary occupations (Tatis weaving, Kumars pottery, Napits barbering and Cutas carpentry), but with the exception of the carpenter caste, their hereditary occupations only supplement their income from farming.

There prevails a widespread agreement in the village that the gap between the high castes and low castes has narrowed. The upper castes note that the pride of the Tili caste has increased, and Tilis point out the same change within the lower castes. Land reforms introduced by the state government, along with new job opportunities, have lessened the landless laborers' dependency on the landowners. Thanks to inexpensive pump sets, which became available in the 1990s, even small-scale farmers have been able to afford irrigation technologies and are now able to cultivate more crops than before which has increased the need for labor.

Bagdis (the lowest caste) comment that there has been a remarkable improvement in their caste position and villagers' descriptions tend to hopefully exaggerate the changes:

> Nowadays it does not matter if there is touching, since it is possible to wash the pollution off. It is possible to go and eat in higher-caste houses without having to wash the metal utensils oneself. In earlier days, one had to sit in a separate place and wash one's own dishes. People's way of thinking has changed. Before, rich people did not care if poor people could not afford to eat and wear proper clothes. And now everybody has become the same. You eat and I also eat. Yes, they have realized that they need our labor and should not keep their distance. They are compelled to treat us better. (Bagdi man)

Yet, caste remains one of the villagers' primary identities. News from other villages is always told in relation to the caste identity of the people involved. Villagers know one another's caste identity, while strangers' caste identity is assessed on the basis of their dialect and behavior or is directly inquired, unlike in the cities where it is not considered an appropriate topic for conversation with strangers. Issues of pollution and physical contact are the key elements in how villagers perceive caste: "Here we have caste discrimination, *didi*. We do not touch the Bauris, we do not touch the Muslims. No Tili touches us," a Bagdi woman explained. Caste purity is chiefly maintained by caste endogamy and by avoiding touching or sitting at the same level as a lower-caste person, receiving cooked food from a lower caste, or touching the dishes from which a lower-caste person has eaten.

Upper-caste married women rarely venture outside their own neighborhood and village alone, although a Tili woman may travel alone to see a doctor or to visit her parental home if there is an emergency.

They usually leave the village—to go shopping, to see a movie in Vishnupur, or to visit their parents—with their husbands. Married women's movement outside the home is scrutinized, because of the potential threat it poses to the family honor. The higher the caste and class, the more restricted women's opportunities to move outside the house become. Women outside the home are not immediately suspected of marital infidelity; but it is understood as conveying a "wrong message," i.e. of carefreeness. Yet, most women do not live under constant surveillance and prohibitions. Family members usually share an understanding of the nuances of women's movements. Most women have the freedom to move about in their own caste neighborhood, and they can leave the village with their neighbors and in the presence of the family men.

In contrast to upper-caste women, the women of the low-caste, Bagdi neighborhoods move about relatively freely. They visit relatives and temples outside the village on their own and go to *jatras* (plays) and the cinema without needing permission from male family members. Unlike the upper-caste married women, low-caste women can work as laborers in the brick factories and in the paddy fields, transplanting, weeding and harvesting the paddy. They supplement their income from paid labor by fishing. Few Bagdi women continue the hereditary work of helping with deliveries at private homes and in hospitals. Other income generating activities, which have become less common due to the increase of other work opportunities for Bagdi women, include tending cattle, and collecting snails, dried twigs and manure. Bagdi women keep the money they earn for themselves and handle the household economy. Bagdi men usually hand their earnings over to the oldest woman of the household who is in charge of the shopping.

People of higher castes seldom visit lower-caste neighborhoods. Lower castes enter the higher-caste residential areas as laborers, to sell fish and vegetables or just to chat. When lower castes visit the higher castes, they usually stand or sit in the yard—they do not enter the house. Lower-caste laborers have their meals on the veranda as part of their payment, but they never enter higher-caste houses and higher castes do not accept food from lower-caste houses. They may take tea, but even this is considered an unusually liberal gesture. During my field research, Bagdis usually did not offer me tea, although many would later regret not having done so after I showed my reformist attitude by raising questions about Bagdi experiences and views of caste.

Villagers justify following the caste rules by saying that violating them would anger others, although it is also considered a sin to defile, i.e. cause impurity by touching, someone belonging to a higher caste. There is, however, interaction between the castes, because low caste people work in the landowners' fields and their payment often includes a meal from the employer's house. Despite the sweeping changes Bagdis describe, they still usually wash their utensils themselves to avoid contaminating their employer's family and are hesitant to enter a higher-caste house.

There are signs of decreasing caste discrimination, but the change does not seem as overwhelming as some Bagdis describe. Their exaggeration of the changes communicates their goals and their awareness of expanded opportunities, as well as a new sense of pride. There are no wealthy Bagdis in Janta, but the villagers know of low-caste people outside Janta who have became so influential that "even Brahmins take food in their house." They know that low ritual status does not prevent one from rising to the upper class. Their emphasis on being able to sit on the same level with others and not having to wash their utensils in higher-caste houses for the fear of polluting the host shows that these aspects of caste discrimination are among those that they experience as most humiliating.

Ideas of purity and pollution prevail in the village but they do so in a very different way compared to the *jajmani* system in the pre-British era, or to the post-British period, which lasted up to the implementation of the land ceiling laws after India's independence, when the low castes were dependent on the few large landowners of the dominant caste. Service relationships between castes have become secondary to market relationships, and no single large landowner can act as the highest authority in the village.

With the exception of the Tilis, the castes do not meet to discuss disputes as a community. The Tili committee (*samiti*) still announces rulings on disputes, but unlike the party and the *panchayat* (local governing unit), it cannot enforce its will on the villagers. Even the head of the Tili committee emphasized that the caste committee is separate from politics. The main tasks of the caste association are to give advice when families divide their property and to organize religious festivals. When I asked the villagers whether the Tili *samiti* ever discussed breaches of caste purity, I was told that the maintenance of caste purity is up to the individual households. Instead of a communal body supervising caste discrimination, caste practices are debated in various arenas. Moreover, opportunities for inter-caste socializing now start in the primary schools where children of all castes have their midday meal together (sponsored by the Central Government), and these opportunities have multiplied.

Many villagers are aware of the wrongfulness of caste discrimination and the arguments for the ending it, but tend to be more liberal in their speech than their behavior. Tili women criticize Bagdis for their impure habits, but they also admit that they follow caste rules for the sake of society. They say that in their hearts they know it is wrong. Most women have attended school and learned about anti-caste ideas promulgated by Hindu reformists such as Vivekananda. At school they have also met children from different caste groups and even made friends with them.

It is possible that the debates and the ambivalence regarding caste are creating space for change in dominant caste practices, such as caste endogamy in marriage (as has happened in urban India). The first inter-caste marriage took place in the village in 2002 between a Chasa caste girl and a Tili caste boy. Chasas are regarded as lower than Tilis, but perhaps because the distance is not very wide the union caused surprise but no major opposition in the village. There are still no marriages between the Scheduled castes and upper castes, and many are of the opinion that these unions would not be tolerated in the village.

Sanskritization, a term popularized by M. N. Srinivas which holds that lower castes may improve their position by adopting upper-caste practices, is one way of explaining the pattern of change in caste relations, particularly within the middle castes. This view has, however, been criticized for implying that the Brahmanical culture is a totalizing and monolithic entity capable of overwriting other traditions. Lower castes in Janta talk about imitating the upper strata of village society in terms of consumption, for instance eating and dressing so well that they are no longer recognized as low caste—thereby circumventing the purity criteria for social ascent by striving for a new identity through consumption. At the same time, they perceive their new affluence as contributing to the collective sense of pride in one's caste.

## 4.3 Changing Caste

Change in the caste system in Janta resembles what has happened in other parts of the country. Caste discrimination has lessened even if it has not disappeared. Caste discrimination has been more prevalent in the south than in the north, but the *dalits* of south India organized politically to improve their position earlier than those of the north. Although the prohibition of caste discrimination by the Constitution of India has not been fully effective, it has at least enabled appeal to the judiciary in cases of grave transgression.

New caste identities have evolved thanks to low castes being able to get an education and move to better jobs. Caste and class position appear interrelated in diverse ways. Rather than caste simply metamorphosing into class, few studies show how improvements in class identity may be accompanied by new pride and emphasis of one's caste identity (Tenhunen 2009; Ciotti 2006). The upward mobility within the caste system often has adverse impacts on women's position as women's mobility tends to be more restricted among the higher castes in comparison to low castes.

Caste discrimination is more concealed in urban areas compared to rural areas. Whereas villagers can openly admit that they observe caste rules, urban

Indians often tend to deny the importance of caste—and inter-caste marriages are indeed more common in the cities than in the countryside. However, class still matters in urban areas. Upper castes are overrepresented among the highly educated and underrepresented among the working class. High and low castes do not interact much except in superior–subordinate relationships. The servants, guards and gardeners of the middle and higher castes generally belong to the low castes.

Caste not only separates but unifies, creating networks which facilitate the establishment and maintenance of trade and business arrangements. For example, the Marwaris, who originate in Rajasthan, are India's most prominent business caste; they dominated business in India even during colonial times and their networks have since spread around the world. Brahmins have traditionally held government jobs, but in the recent decades they have shifted to new academic professions, especially in information technology, because caste quotas allocate government jobs to low castes and *dalits*. Caste networks have helped Brahmins to conquer the IT field and thus have excluded other castes from joining in great numbers.

Indians were formally categorized into caste groups during the British colonial rule, which served to solidify the caste-based distinctions and categories. The classifications also facilitated the rise of low-caste activism, and Untouchables started to fight for their rights, demanding to be identified as *dalits* instead of Untouchables, during the British regime. The Marathi language term *dalit* (broken) was first introduced by Jotiba Phule (a Marathi social reformer who was influential in Maharashtra in the nineteenth century) to illustrate the plight of the untouchables. The term *dalit* is used to shift attention away from ideals of purity to emphasize instead how *dalits* have been actively crushed by the holders of power (Government of Madhya Pradesh 2002). *Dalit* leader Ambedkar (1891–1956) also used the term, but it became widely accepted in the 1970s when the Dalit Panthers, (a pro-*dalit* movement concentrated in Tamil Nadu) adopted it. Although the term has not entirely replaced the names of the local *jati* groups, it is used more commonly in the west and south than in the east and north of India.

## 4.4 The Politicization of Caste

Caste identities linger on, partly thanks to the world's largest experiment in allocating quotas for the marginalized groups. Almost half of the jobs in Central Government and seats of education in India have been reserved by quota for *dalits*, tribals and low castes, and many states have even larger quotas (Varshney 2000). In the 1950s, 22.5 percent of governmental jobs and seats of education were reserved for the Scheduled castes (*dalits*) and tribals. The Janata Government appointed a Mandal Commission to study the position of the other socially and educationally backward groups and it recommended that these should also be included in the quotas and that the quotas should be increased to 49.5 percent. In 1990, the government, led by Congress Party leader V. P. Singh, decided to implement the recommendations, thereby strengthening the Hindu nationalistic party, BJP, which opposed the new quotas (see Chapter 6 for more on the BJP). In 2006, the government proposed that the quota of "Other Backward Classes" should be extended also to the private sector and to India's most esteemed seats of learning (among others, the Indian Institute of Technology, the Indian Institute of Management and the All India Institute of Medical Sciences). Acceptance of the new quotas by the Supreme Court in 2008 reserved half of the academic seats of these institutions for the lower castes.

Quotas have brought new opportunities to the *dalits*, but they have also polarized society to higher and lower castes, thus strengthening caste distinctions. The idea behind quotas is to raise the status of entire groups as more members rise socially thanks to better education and job opportunities. As in the United States, quotas have, indeed, had positive effects, although there has been a tendency for upper class *dalits* to start building new identities which separate them from their caste group (see for instance Ciotti 2006 on the fragmentation of Chamar identities). Ever since the establishment of quotas, a heated debate has prevailed on whether the so-called "creamy layer," those *dalits* and Other Backward Classes who are well-to-do and have reached higher social positions, should be excluded from quotas. The proponents of their inclusion argue that social capital is important for the quota job receivers to do well in their jobs and claim that giving quota jobs to people unable to perform them adequately would not help in creating positive identities. The Supreme Court, however, decided in 2008 to keep the top layer out, ruling that families earning more than Rs 250,000 per year will not be eligible for quotas.

Even though the majority of *dalits* still live in poverty, legislation and the quotas have succeeded in reducing social imbalances. Prohibitions on *dalits* moving in public spaces or fetching water from public wells have become rarer and can be penalized. The quotas have also prepared the ground for *dalits* to enter politics, by helping to create elite *dalits* who have organized *dalits* politically. The Bahujan Samaj Party established in 1984 by the *dalits* is the fourth largest in India after the Congress Party, the BJP and the Communist Party. Other parties have tried to maintain their constituency by nominating more *dalit* and low-caste candidates. Jaffrelot (2006) argues that power in India is gradually being transferred from the upper-caste elites to various subaltern groups. He explains the relative ease of the process by its incrementality: in most regions upper castes still dominate due to their better education and social standing.

Delhi was ruled by a coalition formed mainly by *dalits* during 1989–91 and 1996–8, and a *dalit* (Balayogi G. M. C. Baja) acted as Speaker of the Parliament prior to Manmohan Singh's first government. Parliament also elected a *dalit*, K. R. Narayanan, as president of India in 1997. The offices of the Speaker of the Parliament and that of president are significant if ceremonial posts.

An important landmark was reached when a *dalit* woman, Mayawati Kumari, was elected as chief minister of India's most populous state, Uttar Pradesh. Mayawati, a former teacher, was motivated to enter politics because of her own experiences of discrimination, and she became famous for her provocative speeches. As chief minister she has named state institutions after *dalit* leaders and initiated programs to help *dalits*. After Mayawati's short tenure as chief minister, her party's support doubled. She was re-elected chief minister of Uttar Pradesh for the fourth time in 2007, and was expected to rule longer this time because her coalition now had a clear majority. Mayawati's government consisted of an unorthodox coalition of *dalits* and Brahmins united by their desire to oppose the Samajwadi Party led by Mulayam Singh Yadav, a low-caste politician. It has, however, been problematic to attempt to deliver benefits for both the high castes and *dalits* at the same time. In 2012, Mayawati Kumar lost the state election to Samajwadi party led by Mulayam Singh Yadav's son, Akhilesh Yadav.

Low-caste politicians represent powerfully large OBC caste groups and have added new color to Indian politics. Yadav's caste[1] has emerged as one of the first beneficiaries of the quotas because they are more numerous and relatively more educated than other urban OBCs (Jaffrelot 2006, 384) For instance, Laloo Prasad Yadav, a former chief minister of Bihar and the railway minister in the Central Government, has benefited directly from the quotas—they presented him with a chance to get a university education despite his father's poverty. Yadav has consciously built an image that distinguishes him from higher-caste politicians. To the horror of upper-class Indians, he speaks a lower-class dialect and behaves in low-class ways—like spitting in front of television cameras. He dresses in peasant clothes and tours diligently in rural Bihar. Laloo Prasad Yadav's style has made him a target of upper-class criticism, but had brought him the votes of the low-caste majority. As minister for railways, he succeeded in increasing the profitability of the railways without cutting jobs or increasing fares and his achievements

---

1  Yadavs are classified as OBCs (Other Backward Classes) and they are referred to as low castes in research literature (see for example Jaffrelot 2006), but they are also sometimes classified as the middle castes.

have brought him invitations to lecture on his administrative strategies in American Ivy League universities.

## 4.5 Caste, Family and Marriage

Caste discrimination is forbidden in India by constitution, but caste identities will linger on as long as Indians marry within their own caste group. Since caste is maintained by endogamy (marrying within one's own group), kinship constitutes an important building block of caste. In a survey by the New Delhi–based Center for the Study of Developing Societies, 74 percent of Indians called inter-caste marriages unacceptable. Same nationwide survey found that 59 percent of young urban men and women agree that parents should decide their children's spouses (Centre for the Study of Developing Societies 2007). In most parts of India, descent is patrilineal (recognized through the male line) and dwelling arrangements are patrilocal (the married couple lives with the husband's parents). But there are also many communities where descent and dwelling arrangements differ from these patrilineal and patrilocal models, especially in southern India and in the northeast.

The most notable exception is the Nayars (group of sub-castes) of Kerala who have traditionally been matrilineal (descent recognized through the female line). Although women did not govern the household, the system accorded them greater freedom and choice than what was possible in patrilineal communities. Matrilineal features have weakened and given way to an increasing emphasis on patrilineality in Kerala, but Jeffrey (2010) argues that matrilineality paved the way for high literacy in Kerala. Patrilineality and especially patrilocality in northern and western India, in turn, can contribute to gender inequality. Although women are not totally cut off from their natal families, the move to husband's house and village largely isolates women from their natal families because women's mobility is usually restricted. Patrilineal descent encourages patrilineal inheritance so that women rarely claim their share of their parental property in most parts of India.

One feature of the Indian kinship is the joint family, which may include several generations and brothers with their families living together. Although not everybody lives in a joint household, it serves as a cultural ideal, connecting separately living nuclear families comprised of parents and their children. Many live in nuclear families because they cannot afford the space demanded by a joint family. Joint families usually split into nuclear units when the father of the cohabiting sons dies—or even earlier due, for example, to disagreements about household economy.

For Hindus, marriage is a sacred institution which entails much more than an agreement between two individuals. Wedding rituals which last several days involve all aspects of life: family relations, household affairs, economics and gift-giving, politics, ancestor worship and social structure. When a woman marries into a family of higher status, albeit within the same *jati*, it is considered to raise the status of the whole family. The marriage consists of two gifts: the gift of the virgin—with the father giving his daughter as a sacred gift to the groom's family—and the gift of the dowry which consists of material assets. Among the lower castes, the bride price, with the groom's family giving a dowry to the bride's family, used to be the prevalent custom, but low castes have increasingly imitated higher-caste practices of giving dowry to the groom's family. Historical research has only recently started to unveil the diversity of sexual and marital practices which have existed at the margins of earlier hegemonic formations in South Asia (Chatterjee 2004; Tiwari 2008).

Although arranged marriage has remained the principal form of marriage, the ways of arranging marriages have changed. Parents nowadays usually take into consideration their children's opinion when arranging their marriages and they may even allow the prospective couple to get acquainted before the wedding ceremony. Those who choose their own spouses may, in turn, confirm their union with their parents.

In the village of Janta, marriage practices have not changed, in the sense that most marriages are arranged and take place within castes (see Tenhunen 2008a). The gift of a virgin is the greatest and most auspicious gift a man can give, and this giving of a bride is accompanied by other gifts. The size of the dowry reflects the groom and the bride's parallel status, although the dowry's size is defined by many factors. Most women marry outside their native villages, and alliances are preferably sought from villages where a member of the extended kin can investigate the potential groom or bride. What has undergone drastic changes, however, is the brides themselves and the marriage gifts. Fifty years ago, the ideal bride was a child given to the groom's family along with a dowry of voluntary gifts of brass utensils and golden jewelry. Today the ideal bride is a high-school graduate, and the marriage arrangements always entail negotiations on the size of the dowry that the bride's side gives to the groom's side. The groom's side lists all the items on the basis of the negotiations, and the parties agree on the delivery schedule. A large part of the dowry is usually paid in installments after the marriage. The dowry is not accumulated just by the bride's family, but also by her extended kin and friends who are tied by a network of reciprocal obligations.

In present-day rural West Bengal, the highest dowry demands are made by large landowners and by government employees. Government employees are usually also large landowners because a substantial bribe is needed to acquire a government job. The highest strata of rural society can demand a dowry up to

Rs 150,000—an amount which puts them out of the reach of a working-class family. Laborer and marginal farmer families barely earn the Rs 3,000 a month that a family of four needs for basic expenses. For farmers, land is a crucial dowry measure. During the high point in dowry demands in 1999, I was told that a groom's parents could demand a dowry of Rs 20,000 per *bigha* (0.33 acre) of their land. Many small and middling landowners, especially families with more sons than daughters, have been able to increase their landholdings through marriages: land is often purchased with dowry payments or given as part of a dowry.

Elderly villagers explained that the onset of excessive dowry demands was caused by people becoming wealthier and wanting to secure wealthier families for their daughters. Indeed, since India's independence, the intensification of agriculture and land reforms has led to new types of economic differentiation in rural India. Cash and property first became part of the dowry when land became a marketable commodity during the British colonial rule.

## 4.6 The Dowry Problem

Dowry-giving continues all over India despite its concomitant aberrations and the fact that it was prohibited by law in 1961. Parents become indebted and have to sell land or other assets, or are forced to use their savings to pay the dowry. Growing dowry demands have also led to dowry killings, whereby a husband or some other member of the husband's natal family murders the wife so that the husband can remarry in order to receive a new dowry. Dowry murders are not a part of everyday life, however, but represent a rare type of crime and are considered heinous acts; if a woman dies soon after her wedding, the law insists that the case be examined as a possible dowry murder. Despite the law, dowry crimes are not easy to prove and can remain unpunished. Demands to abolish dowry-giving are as old as the practice itself, and the villagers do not hesitate to admit that giving money at marriages is a great social problem.

There are many reasons for the continuation of dowry-giving despite its aberrations and the burden it places on girls' parents. A dowry indicates a natal family's appreciation of a girl as well as her status in the conjugal village, and parents are ready to make economic sacrifices to see their daughters married into good houses. Moreover, the money given at marriages circulates. The bride-givers may run into debt, but the bride-takers become wealthier. Not only men are at the receiving end, as women consider a dowry to be their share of parental assets left behind when they join their husband's household. Many small farms are only viable thanks to the wealth that the wife brought to the house in the form of land or cash that was used to buy land.

Women's increasing education and new career options have made a woman's profession a criterion of marriage arrangements. In rural West

Bengal, even wealthy families do not necessarily demand dowry if the bride is well educated, of fair complexion or has a permanent job. Low-income families in particular find a woman's own earnings desirable, and they lower the dowry demands accordingly. However, highly educated wealthy families may still expect even a university-educated wife not to work outside the home after marriage, but to dedicate herself to the care of the home and family (Fuller and Narasimhan 2007; Donner 2008).

## 4.7 The Future of the Dowry

Dowry-giving has demographic implications. The ratio of women in the population is low in India: in the 2001 census there were 933 women per 1,000 men, and the ratio of female children in the age group of 0–6 years in 1991–2001 had gone down from 945 to 927 per 1,000 male children. Researchers explain the imbalance on the basis of poorer nutrition and health care for girls than for boys, as well as the higher rate of abortion of female fetuses. Wealthy urban Indians in particular influence the sex ratio by detecting the sex of their unborn child using ultrasounds and aborting female fetuses, even though it is illegal in India (Chapter 7 deals more specifically with the sex ratio distortion). In addition to dowry issues, parents' concern for their old age security influences preferences for boys: parents want a male heir because it is considered a son's duty to take care of aged parents.

There are also significantly fewer girls than boys in Janta, which may indicate neglect of female children rather than evidence of villagers detecting the sex of unborn children with ultrasound, of which I did not find any evidence. The villagers are well aware of demographic pressures and many believe that dowry demands will decrease because of the distortion of the sex ratio. Men holding permanent jobs can still demand and get large dowries whereas small-scale farmers, the landless and the unemployed have to be satisfied with less. The unbalanced gender ratio may be doing more to alleviate the giving of dowry than its prohibition by law—as noted above, dowry-giving was prohibited in India in 1961 to no perceptible effect. The dowry system offers a means to maneuver in a new class society, and what may be required to end it is the diminishing of the sharp differences between the standards of living of different classes.

## 4.8 Changes in Marriage Practices

Rising dowry demands have led to alternative marriage practices (Tenhunen 2009, 2008a). Marriages in Janta are often arranged suddenly in order to bring down the cost of feeding the extended kin who will attend a large traditional wedding party. These shortcut marriages are arranged at either the bride or groom's home, or in a temple, which lowers the cost even further. Shortcut marriages are often, but not always, love marriages. Indians themselves distinguish between two kinds of marriage—the arranged marriage and the love marriage. While marital love is considered an essential outcome even of arranged marriages, they are considered to differ from love marriages insofar as they support kinship and caste hierarchies without posing a threat to the husband's strong ties with his parents and brothers.

It is certainly the villagers' perception that love marriages have become more common during recent years, although debates on and disputes over love relationships are no novelty in Bengal. The difference between the past village generations and the new generation of unmarried boys and girls is that young people now proudly talk about their relationships, whereas no one appeared eager to speak about the love affairs of the past. Most of the men and women with whom I talked in Janta said they would accept it if their children wanted to choose their spouses themselves, provided that the union took place within the caste. In reality, tolerance of love marriages is neither instant nor easily come by and it is felt that love marriages should be met with disapproval, at least initially. Yet many family members and bystanders lean silent support to these lovers, and love letters are passed along by trusted people, sisters, brothers, and friends. When the couple's guardians discover the relationship, they often beat the errant girl or boy in an effort to persuade them to end the relationship. The girls and boys triumphantly told me how they had suffered the beatings without agreeing to marry anyone but the one they had chosen. The couples invariably succeed in running away and having their marriage registered, whereupon the parents usually agree to finalize the marriage, negotiating the time of the marriage ceremony and settling the dowry. The latter is generally considerably less than would have been paid to the groom's family if the marriage had been arranged. The differences between the two types of marriage are revealed in the marriage ceremonies. Arranged marriages require traditional marriage rituals in the homes of both the bride and the groom, whereas the ceremonies for love marriages can either be an instant ceremony in a nearby temple, or a complete marriage ritual in both the bride and the groom's parents' homes.

The general answer given to the question why guardians do not usually approve of love marriages is that they had wanted to marry their daughters and sisters off to better families. Yet, with dowry demands continuously increasing, it is doubtful whether a marriage to a more prosperous house is always possible. Another explanation offered for their disapproval is that love marriages upset the family hierarchy, for instance when a younger brother or sister intends marrying before older siblings. The main objection, however, is generally tacit and stems from the desire to protect family honor. No father or older brother is willing to allow his daughter or sister to meet a boy before marriage, especially unsupervised. If such a boy is then not willing to marry his girlfriend, arranging the compromised girl's marriage to someone else might prove complicated and require a larger dowry.

In Janta, the acceptance of love marriages is facilitated by the fact that they support caste endogamy and resemble arranged marriages, insofar as the parents or guardians of the couples usually get to negotiate the dowry and set the marriage date. Nevertheless, love marriages may induce changes and those which are the particular focus of village speculation are variation in the relationships with the in-laws, rather than the possible difference that such a marriage could affect in the marital relationship. Perhaps the marital relationship is considered equally unpredictable in both types of marriages. On the one hand, love marriages are known to lead to divorces; on the other, arranged marriages are entered into with the expectation that they will lead to a loving relationship between spouses.

Most love marriages occur between people from the same village; however, many married women considered it absurd to be able to see one's parents' house from one's in-laws' house. The proper relationship between the houses would, according to these women, require distance. They feel that distance contributes to the woman's adjustment, because problems and conflicts that should be settled within the confines of a single house cannot extend to any other house. Distance also sustains the meanings of kinship, thus upholding honor between the houses. Even if in-laws have come to accept a love marriage, if their son-in-law lives next door, his visits do not become such momentous events as they would if he were to visit from further away. And if there is no proper meaning assigned to in-laws, this could lead to their not fulfilling their obligations. Women stated that the benefit of an arranged marriage is that the parents who arranged the marriage feel an obligation to see to their daughter's well-being even after the marriage. Love marriages are therefore experienced as a change in the alliance patterns and in the integration of families into kinship networks.

In urban India, love marriages more easily find approval than in the countryside, but even in the cities arranged marriages remain the dominant form (see for instance Donner 2008; Fuller and Narasimhan 2007). Parents usually look for a spouse for their children within their own surroundings and networks, but they may also place marriage advertisements in newspapers and on the Internet. The advertisements list the spouse seekers' caste, views on inter-caste marriage, education, salary and the color of complexion. Growing incomes influence dowry demands to the extent that urban dowries may even include cars. However, not everyone pays inordinate dowries. The size of the dowry depends on family status, negotiations and the desire to give or demand large dowries. The law prohibiting dowries helps bride-givers insofar as it offers the bride's family the possibility of reporting inordinate extortion of dowry to the police.

A study by Aura (2006) shows that divorces are becoming more public and less frowned on than before, although divorces are seldom reported officially. Divorces are considered highly disruptive for entire kin groups, and consequently, dissolution of marriages is not commonly reinforced in the court of law in India. A divorce severs the union of two spouses, but it also disrupts the unity of two family groups as well as social hierarchy. Divorced women have even formed their own organizations to help each other in building new lives, meanwhile trying to persuade society to see the woman's viewpoint in marriage arrangements and family life. The poor treatment of Hindu wives and exorbitant dowry demands have also encouraged the development of a new phenomenon: educated women opting for a career instead of marriage, although singlehood is still rare in India (see Chapter 7).

## 4.9 Family, Caste and Interaction

The influence of family is not limited to parental decision making about their children's marriages. Indians feel great loyalty towards their family and kin. Parents are prepared to make great sacrifices on behalf of their children, and in return they expect to be looked after in their old age. The importance of the family shows in consumer behavior in that family members seldom decide alone how to use their earnings. A household's economy is often run by the eldest male member of the family or by the mother, to whom all the family members give their earnings. Research in West Bengal indicates that the former practice is followed more by high castes and the latter by low castes (Tenhunen 2003). Consumer goods are bought especially as wedding gifts, but also as gifts during annual celebrations.

Although few educated Indians emphasize the importance of caste, the cultural principles of the caste system affect their lives in many ways. Most Brahmins are generally vegetarians and do not consume alcohol. Even young middle-class women may carve a personal niche for themselves in their husband's families by taking on ascetic practices such as becoming vegetarians, as Donner's (2008) study from Kolkata illustrates.

The strictest vegetarians cannot accept vegetarian food cooked in the same kitchen where meat dishes are prepared. Thus, if an Indian invites a guest to have a meal with him, a refusal may easily be interpreted as the invitee's show of superiority—in a hierarchical culture a person of higher status is not supposed to dine with one of lower status. It is also deemed a demonstration of superiority on the part of the host if the guest is not offered hot food because sharing cooked food signals equality. Since impurity is mediated by touching, hugging and handshaking are not common forms of greetings in India. The traditional Indian way to greet is to join one's palms together at the chest level although many Indians are familiar with the Western handshake.

Family and caste hierarchies also influence work and business cultures. Family businesses are the most common forms of enterprise. Even the giant Indian enterprises, like Reliance Industries (a US$20 billion company, which the Ambani brothers divided between oil and telecommunication in 2006), Tata (automotive, chemical and steel industries) and Aditya Birla (now a multinational corporation) have originated from family companies.

An Indian worker does not so much seek a formal relationship with his employer but rather expects the employer to build a personal and emotive, patron–client relationship. The higher status individual enjoys his employees' loyalty and his willingness to serve and, in turn, protects and cares for his employees comprehensively. Indian culture includes a strong analytical tradition and Indians can be splendid conversationalists, but this does not help in developing open communication between different levels of hierarchy. Indian workers have been reported to follow directions which they know to be wrong because they do not want to argue with their superiors (Erikson 2003).

## 4.10 Conclusion

The meaning of kinship in India has not diminished over time, although new alternatives are emerging: more tolerant attitudes towards self-arranged marriages, divorces, singlehood and women's careers. Yet the arranged marriage is still the predominant form of marriage. The ideal is not a free individual, but someone who acknowledges his duties and is willing to make sacrifices for his or her family. As Indians become more affluent, they are ready to spend more on rituals, gifts, and especially dowry gifts. As summarized by Fuller and Narasimhan (2007), who studied the newly rich middle class in Chennai, the IT professionals do not view themselves as selfish materialists, but urban professionals whose well-paid work allows them to lead better lives with their family according to their own tradition.

Uberoi (2006) maintains that the ideological value of family in India has amplified as India has globalized. She suggests that the idea of the traditional family now represents a new, imagined community replacing other traditional identities and communities amid urbanization. In tune with the popular imagination, the media, especially television serials and cinema, celebrates family unity instead of elaborating the emerging alternatives.

The caste system is transforming: legislation has succeeded in weeding out the most blatant forms of discrimination, and the association between caste and profession has largely disappeared. The expectation to follow purity rules has become relaxed and interaction between castes has increased, especially thanks to the expanding education system. Although discrimination still exists, particularly in some parts of rural south India, former Untouchables are fighting for their rights and bring offences to the public. Rather than reflecting an imitation of Western lifestyles, growing commodity consumption has its roots in local social structures: lower castes are able to improve their position by striving for upper-class consumption patterns. Caste, however, is not disappearing. Caste quotas and caste-based political organizations sustain caste distinction and the polarization of society into low and high castes.

Furthermore, the importance and influence of caste and family are not limited to homes but also extend to the workplace. Caste acts as an important resource in connecting people. Not all relationships are hierarchical because caste and kinship hierarchies also entail equal positions. However, communication in hierarchical relationships requires special encouragement and attention if they are to succeed, because strong hierarchies tend to hamper communication between the top and the bottom of the organization.

# Chapter 5

# POLITICAL TRANSITIONS

One of the key dilemmas of governing modern India has been how to arrange and regulate the relationships between the Central Government and states. When India gained independence from Great Britain in 1947, it adopted British democratic parliamentarianism combined with Soviet-style planned economy, which strengthened the power of the Central Government. Economic reforms of the 1990s marked a shift towards decentralization as individual states were largely freed from the economic regulation of the Central Government. While policies by the Central Government have impacted local governance, India's political culture has been marked by a strong continuity of patron relationships between political leaders and their supporters which has, over the decades, manifested in various ways.

Unlike many former colonies, India has remained a democracy since attaining its independence. China and India, two of the world's fastest growing superpowers, differ insofar as China, unlike India, does not have electorally chosen decision makers at the central and local levels, nor does its constitution provide an independent judiciary or the protection of private property. India is ruled by a prime minister and a cabinet appointed by the prime minister. The government, based on the political party that gains the most electoral constituencies, stays in power to the end of the electoral term of five years, unless toppled by a vote of no confidence by the parliament before the scheduled election. The president's position is subordinate to the prime minister and thus mainly ceremonial. The Central Government decides on foreign policy, defense, communications, currency, company taxation and taxation of forms income other than that from agriculture, and the railways. The state governments are fully empowered to promulgate laws to regulate public order, public health care, local government, gambling, taxation of agricultural income and alcoholic beverages. The Central Government and the provincial governments share the authority to decide among other issues on criminal law, the ordination of labor unions, social security and education.

To the many newly independent former colonies, the Soviet Union represented a success story of how a predominantly agricultural country could transform itself into an industrialized state within one generation. In India, centrally controlled planning was seen as an effective way to allocate and use scarce resources. The new official machinery in charge of granting industrial licenses in India gained the name "Licence Raj," after the British colonial government which was called by a Hindi term, *raj* (rule).

During their colonial rule, the British transferred considerable wealth from India to Great Britain by turning India into a producer of raw materials. India became an export market for British goods, which ruined India's flourishing cottage industries. Newly independent India consciously isolated itself from the world trade and custom policies that benefited old colonial powers. Instead, India adopted an import substitution policy aimed at replacing imports by its own industrial production. As a result, India's share of world trade declined from 2.2 percent to 0.5 percent during 1948–80 (Srinivasan and Tendulkar 2003, 8).

The mixed economy of India consisted of a powerful public sector, state-owned businesses, private enterprises regulated by the state and an unofficial sector covering small enterprises exempted from governmental regulations. Multinational companies were allowed to operate in India provided that they conformed to state regulations. When the state tightened its hold of foreign companies at the end of the 1970s, multinationals, such as Coca-Cola and IBM, left the country. The Indian government declared that it would replace these with local production. Thumbs Up, a home-grown beverage brand, as well as several Indian software companies which would later grow into giant corporations, were formed to fill the market niche left by the multinationals.

The main objectives of the Indian planned economy were to reduce dependency on foreign capital and technology, and to create a foundation for indigenous industries. In practice, the planned economy led to inefficient production, low economic growth and widespread corruption (Kim 2006, 29). Earlier governments attempted to remedy the problems, but radical action was only undertaken as a result of the acute economic crisis of 1991. The state could no longer guarantee the payment of its debts, and the international banks lost faith in India's capability to meet its obligations. Simultaneously India's ally and trade partner, the Soviet Union, collapsed in 1990, and the Iraq War of the early 1990s hampered trade with the Middle East, raising India's oil bill to record heights.

## 5.1 The Economic Reforms

The crisis enabled the coalition government, formed by the Congress Party and its allies, to introduce sweeping changes. Licence Raj was terminated, and the rupee was devalued. The state's budget deficit was reduced by cutting expenditure and by privatizing state-owned companies running at a loss. At the same time, India lowered its custom duties and freed foreign investments from regulation (Kim 2006, 70). One of the principal architects of the reforms was the economist and finance minister, Manmohan Singh, who became the country's prime minister in 2004 and was re-elected in 2009.

Despite their radical appearance, reforms were realized without jeopardizing important interest groups. Farmers' resistance made the government back down from its decision to reduce agricultural subsidies by 40 percent; they were eventually cut by 10 percent (Azam and Pradhan 2005, 258). Indian civil servants' support for the reforms was ensured by preserving their number and salaries. The upper echelons of the public service, the Indian Administrative Service, were granted their highest pay rise for decades. State employees were able to retain their power as executors of the reforms, as the state governments adopted a new role of business facilitators. According to Das (2005), the new economy, invigorated by the reforms, has even given state employees new opportunities for illegal enrichments.

The terms of the loan which the World Bank provided required India to embark on a structural adjustment program. However, awareness of the need for the reforms was not new—similar policies had been advocated in India from the 1960s. The post-reform economic growth rate—on an average of 5–6 percent per year during the 1990s (about double the average from independence to 1990) and 7–8 percent per year since 2000—convinced even the opposition forces of the benefits of liberalization. Based on the National Sample Survey results and the Indian government's definition of poverty, during the years 1973–99 poverty in India decreased from 55 percent to 26 percent (Kumar and Sethi 2005, 34). However, as Chapter 7 illustrates, although these figures evidenced poverty mitigation, the earlier definitions of poverty grossly underestimated the number of the extreme poor. A new, higher poverty line was adopted in 2011, and according to this line, the proportion of Indians living below the poverty line decreased from 37 percent to 32 percent from 2004 to 2009 (*The Hindu*, April 21, 2011).

Following the reforms, India was the second fastest-growing economy after China for two decades. In addition to reforms, General Agreement on Tariffs and Trade (GATT) agreements and the establishment of the World Trade Organization (WTO) in 1994 also spurred the growth of India's trade and economy by reducing tariffs, even though Western countries still continue to protect their own interests against those of the developing countries, such as India. India's economic growth has prevailed even in the midst of the global recession. In 2008, the Indian economy grew by 9 percent and continued to grow by 7–8 percent during 2009–11. India's public deficit has not allowed India to put together as massive a stimulus package as China, but it has been better insulated from the global recession than China thanks to its greater dependence on domestic markets. Exports and imports account for approximately half of India's GDP whereas the comparable proportion for China is over 80 percent. Moreover, service exports which form a significant part of India's trade did not suffer as much of a decline as merchandise exports on which Chinese growth has greatly depended on. State regulation of finance has saved India from falling prey to the global banking crises. Large domestic savings and corporate-retained earnings are financing investment. While the global recession has hit urban consumption, rural consumption has remained stable (Roubini 2009; Thakurta 2009).

## 5.2 Electoral Shifts

India has been a democratic state since its independence, except for a period of 20 months when Indira Gandhi declared emergency to silence the opposition and to prevent investigations into her alleged election fraud in 1975. The nation protested vehemently, and the Congress Party lost the election after Indira Gandhi declared the emergency had ended. India's political history is not devoid of sudden shifts of power dictated by election results although the Congress Party has been ruling independent India for most of its history.

The first prime minister Jawaharlal Nehru (1889–1964), who hailed from a wealthy Kashmiri Brahman family and was educated at Oxford, was a prominent figure in the nationalistic movement. As a prime minister he concentrated power for the Congress Party, and the Nehru-Gandhi dynasty has represented a symbol of unity for the nation ever since. Despite the socialist leanings of Nehru, the Congress Party was dominated by elites: the upper-caste intelligentsia, business community and landowners. Consequently, no large-scale reforms were implemented, and the land reforms did not address the needs of the poor (Jaffrelot 2006, 492). After Nehru's death, his daughter Indira Gandhi[1] became the president of the Congress Party and prime minister of India (1917–1984). The Congress Party leaders who appointed Indira were counting on the Nehru family charisma to woo votes for the party, wrongly assuming that the newly elected young woman would allow senior male politicians to exert their influence through her (Frank 2002).

During Indira Gandhi's rule, the Congress Party's strategy of securing votes changed irreversibly which contributed to changes in Indian politics. Under the leadership of Jawaharlal Nehru, the Congress Party had developed an intricate

---

1 She was not related to Mahatma Gandhi, rather she took on her husband's (Feroze Gandhi's) surname.

network of patronage based on loyal elites. In order to strengthen her position, Indira Gandhi often bypassed the old elites and the formal structures of the party, creating a new parallel system of authority based on personal loyalties. New candidates were selected from among locally prominent and influential wealthy persons who could finance a winning campaign. Effective slogans revolving around single issues and lavish campaigning were used to ensure electoral victories. The new strategies for mobilization and political bargaining created instability within the Congress Party, turning political support into an increasingly fleeting and fluid phenomenon (Hansen 1999, 135).

During India's first two decades of independence, the Congress Party was in power in the Central Government as well as in most states. From 1967 to 1989 (except for the brief Bharatiya Janata party government period), the Congress ran the Central Government in New Delhi, while it shared power with its rivals in the states (Guha 2007). Since the 1990s, no single party has been able to get enough votes to form a government on its own, and the era of coalition politics has changed Indian federalism. Now the biggest governing party has to succumb to compromises with its coalition partners, and even smaller parties, each powerful in a single state, need to be cajoled into joining the coalition. At the same time, economic reforms have limited the power of the Central Government over the state economies.

In 1996, the Congress Party lost the parliamentary elections to the Hindu nationalist party, the Bharatiya Janata Party (BJP), forcing the Congress to re-evaluate its objectives and strategies. In 2004, the new president of the party, Sonya Gandhi, widow of Rajiv Gandhi (1944–1991), succeeded in leading the Congress Party back to victory. The BJP lost largely due to the rural electorate's disappointment with economic reforms as well as people's disdain for the religious conflicts propagated by the BJP. The Congress Party returned to power by promising to foster inclusive development.

Few had believed in Sonya Gandhi's chances against the BJP. She had long been a silent observer of politics as Rajiv Gandhi's Italian-born wife, who had moved to India after her marriage. The average Indian, however, hardly thinks of her as a foreigner but as a wife of the Nehru family. Sonya Gandhi speaks fluent Hindi, wears saris and has behaved like an ideal Indian daughter-in-law and widow. After the death of her husband, she withdrew from public life, reappearing only when she was needed to salvage the Congress Party—her extended family. Sonya Gandhi has been offered the post of prime minister of India twice, in 1991 and 2004. On both occasions, she has declined—the unselfish gesture has added to her popularity (Price 2000).

In 2004, Sonya Gandhi declined the offer of the post of prime minister because of vehement opposition by the Hindu fundamentalists who rallied around the issue of her being a foreigner; she appointed Manmohan Singh, an Oxford-trained economist belonging to the Sikh minority, as the prime minister. Singh has worked as an economist and a university professor, as well as a civil servant in India's Ministry of Finance and in the UN-affiliated UNCTAD. He was also the finance minister in the government which initiated economic reforms. In 2009, Manmohan Singh became the first prime minister since Jawaharlal Nehru in 1962 to be re-elected after completing a full five-year term.

Sonya Gandhi's son, Rahul, contributed critically to the Congress victory in 2009 by campaigning tirelessly. His youth helped to energize especially the young voters. The charisma of the Gandhi family is, however, no guarantee of a victory. The Congress Party lost in 1977 when led by Indira Gandhi, and in 1989 led by Rajiv Gandhi. Nevertheless, the Congress Party would not turn to the Gandhi dynasty repeatedly if it did not help to consolidate its support. The problem of the Nehru dynasty—or any nepotistic dynasty which are not uncommon in India's other political parties—is that family connections tend to block the rise of talented outsiders.

In 2004, the Congress was able to form a coalition government with the help of support from left-leaning parties. In 2009, the United Progressive Alliance (UPA) led by the Indian National Congress formed a government based on its strong showing in Andhra Pradesh, Rajasthan, Maharashtra, Tamil Nadu, Kerala, West Bengal and Uttar Pradesh. UPA won 260 seats, compared to 218 in 2004, and no longer required support from the Left in order to run the government. The four biggest parties in the elections of 2009 were the Congress (with 29 percent of the votes), BJP (with 19 percent), BSP—the Dalit Bahujan Samaj Party—(with 6 percent) and CPI-M—the Communist Party of India-Marxist—(with 5 percent) (Chapter 6 focuses on these political alternatives).

## 5.3 Foreign Policy

### 5.3.1 From non-alignment to power politics

The newly independent India disdained military power and promoted international cooperation under Jawaharlal Nehru's leadership. Nehru's disregard of the military not only reflected the Indian tradition of non-violence, which Mahatma Gandhi famously propagated during the independence struggle, but Nehru also suspected that a strong army could attempt a coup if assisted by foreign powers (Cohen 2001, 128, 132). India was forced to re-evaluate its foreign and military policies when Chinese troops marched across the border in 1961, after the two countries had failed to solve their border dispute through negotiations. India had wanted to ratify the border line drawn by Great Britain, but the Chinese disagreed. India's leaders did not expect China to embark on a military invasion, and the country was so unprepared for military conflict that Chinese troops marched further into Indian territory than they had threatened, although they later withdrew behind their proposed border.

The humiliating defeat forced India to strengthen its army in order to be able to fight on two fronts—against Pakistan and China. In 1971, India successfully helped East Pakistan gain independence from Pakistan and become a new sovereign country, Bangladesh. The victory boosted India's military self-esteem and prepared the ground for a new foreign policy—the Indira Doctrine. According to this, any country that did not acknowledge India's dominant position in South Asia was taken by Indira's India as acting against its interests.

India's foreign policy leaders considered the United States as having joined the enemy camp, because it wanted to restrict India's nuclear technology while at the same time allowing China to arm Pakistan with nuclear weapons. Indira Gandhi aimed to ward off the threat posed by the United States, China and Pakistan, and the years before her assassination in 1984 turned out to be militarily the most active in the history of independent India. She began extensive arms imports from the Soviet Union and initiated a missile development program. India's support of Sri Lanka's Tamil separatists eventually led to India's sending peacekeeping forces to Sri Lanka who withdrew from Sri Lanka in 1990 after suffering heavy losses.

In 1984, Indian forces seized Pakistani-occupied territories on the Siachen Glacier in Kashmir. This led to counterattacks by Pakistani forces, followed by war and a stalemate. Indira Gandhi gave her consent to Operation Bluestar, the assault on the Golden Temple, in 1984, during which Indian troops killed over 400 Sikh separatists. In revenge, Indira Gandhi's own bodyguard murdered her in her garden the same year. Rajiv Gandhi (1944–1991) followed his mother as the president of the Congress Party and the prime minister of India (1984–1989). A suicide bomber murdered Rajiv Gandhi in 1991 in protest against Indian peacekeeping forces fighting Tamil guerrillas in Sri Lanka.

### 5.3.2 The Kashmir crisis and the Cold War

During the early days of independence, India succeeded in getting aid both from the United States and the Soviet Union. Relations with the United States, however, cooled along with the Cold War: India felt that the United States had sided with Pakistan, and, conversely, the United States saw India as a Soviet ally. The multifaceted conflict between India and Pakistan became another part of the Cold War between the East and West.

When the British left India, India was partitioned into Muslim-majority Pakistan and Hindu-majority India. A great Muslim minority, however, remained in India, and Congress Party–led India has propagated itself as a multicultural and multi-religious entity to which both the Muslims and Hindus belong. However, Pakistan has perceived India as a threat from the very beginning—the breaking away of East Pakistan with the assistance of the Indian army to become Bangladesh intensified the situation even further. Many Pakistanis fear that fundamentalist Indian Hindus aim to gain dominance over the whole of South Asia (Cohen 1991, 203–4).

The problems brought about by the partition of India culminated in the dispute between the two countries over Kashmir, a geopolitically important region both to India and Pakistan populated by Buddhists, Muslims and Hindus. In the partition, Kashmir was divided between the two countries, with India taking areas where Muslims form the majority. Pakistan considers these areas to be rightfully its. Kashmiri Hindus in turn do not want to be ruled by Muslims.

Kashmir was of great significance in the relations between India and Pakistan during the wars in 1948 and in 1965. The Kashmir question was less important before Pakistan acquired nuclear weapons towards the end of 1980s. In spite of the international community's opposition, India too developed its nuclear technology and carried out a nuclear test in 1998, which was followed by a Pakistani nuclear test. The unsolved struggle and the decades of violence have encouraged a growing number of young Kashmiri Muslims to support Kashmiri autonomy. Pakistan has tried to weaken India's position in Kashmir by encouraging terrorism; as a result terrorists have launched several bomb attacks in different parts of India. The end of the Cold War did not solve the conflict between India and Pakistan, but it lessened its intensity. The new political reality was reflected by the United States' reaction to Pakistan's attack on India in 1999. Instead of condemning India's military action, the United States demanded that Pakistan withdraw behind the 1947 ceasefire line.

### 5.3.3 Asian integration and lingering conflicts

The collapse of the Soviet Union together with India's economic crises forced the Indian government to quickly launch a new course for its foreign policy. Relations between India and the Soviet Union had been so close that, according to Mohan (2005), the collapse of the Soviet Union presented India's foreign policy leadership its most traumatic experience. Whereas India had previously stressed shared ideological principles and acted as the representative of Third World nations in international forums, it now began to prioritize its own economic and commercial interests under the leadership of the Congress Party–led coalition government of Narasimha Rao (1921–2004; prime minister 1991–1996). India began to develop and strengthen its trade relations in all directions.

A ceasefire was reached in Kashmir in 2004. The following year witnessed the opening of the first bus service between India and Pakistan in 60 years through the military-occupied areas. To encourage trade, India initiated the construction of new supranational highway projects with Afghanistan, China, Thailand and Myanmar. The road connection between Bangladesh and India is being built as a part of the All Asia Highway network, which was already initiated in 1959. This modern Silk Road got an additional boost in 2004 when 23 Asian countries agreed on the routing of the highway network. The Soviet Union's collapse and China opening its trade across its western border have also advanced trade and traffic in Asia.

India's new foreign policy doctrine, "Look East," focused first on the growing markets of Southeast Asia. India established relationships with ASEAN—a free-trade organization of Southeast Asian nations—which invited India as its dialogue partner in 1995. India established a free-trade agreement with Thailand in 2003 and with Singapore in 2005 intending to make similar agreements with all the ASEAN countries. Concurrently, India's trade with Japan, South Korea and especially China has grown. Increasing trade relationships along with economic growth has increased India's importance internationally; however, despite India's attempts it has not been able to secure a permanent seat in the UN Security Council which China possesses.

The two Asian giants reopened trade across the 4,545-meter Nathu La pass in 2006. The countries have lowered custom duties on selected articles. In 2008, China emerged as India's top trade partner as India's exports to United States declined because of the recession. In just five years, trade between China and India has zoomed from $15 billion to $50 billion. Balance of trade has, however, been in China's favor, which explains why India has not actively pursued a free-trade agreement with China. The major items of export from India to China are ores, cotton yarn and fabric, organic and inorganic chemicals, precious stones and metals and machinery, while the major items imported from China to India are electrical machinery, organic chemicals, iron and steel, fertilizers and mineral fuel (Nayar 2009).

The increasing trade within Asia has led to the idea of an Asian Free Trade Area, and the existing trade agreements may represent its beginning. A significant step to end the continent's economic compartmentalization was taken when India and Pakistan opened their borders to trade in 2005, so that they no longer have to trade through a third country. The agreement of the South Asian Free Trade Area (2004, SAFTA) came into force in 2006 creating a free-trade area comprising seven states (Bangladesh, Bhutan, India, the Maldives Islands,

Nepal, Pakistan and Sri Lanka). The member states have agreed to reduce their custom duties gradually. Since 1985, the same countries along with Afghanistan have been members of the South Asian Association for Regional Cooperation (SAARC). The organization's impact has been limited due to its principle of requiring unanimity and keeping contentious issues off the agenda.

The hope is that increasing trade will reduce poverty, increase Asia's economic importance and ease political tensions in the region. According to a more pessimistic perspective, increasing prosperity may bring greater inequality and thereby increase internal conflicts; indeed, economic cooperation can be hampered by internal conflicts such as military coups in the region which ultimately destabilize foreign policies. The unsolved conflicts between Asia's superpowers also cast a shadow over Asian prospects for integration.

Even though the former enemies have started to trade with each other, India's borders with Pakistan and China continue to be under dispute, and the attacks by Kashmiri terrorists continue. Terrorist attacks such as the one in Mumbai in October 2008 make it politically difficult for India to develop closer ties with Pakistan, a situation that will remain fraught unless Pakistan makes decisive efforts to curtail groups such as Lashkar-e-Toiba (LeT), which was responsible for the attack (Andersen 2010).

Similarly, China has not approved of India's relationship with the exiled Tibetan leader, the Dalai Lama, who lives in India. When in 2009 the Dalai Lama visited the disputed broader region of India claimed by China, China announced its dissatisfaction. The Chinese claims on the disputed Arunachal Pradesh seem to have acquired a new stridency over the past two years, and China has not missed an opportunity to express its position that Arunachal is not recognized as part of India.

### 5.3.4 Look West

India's current relationship with Africa has been fuelled more by pragmatic concerns over resources and development than the rhetoric of historical and cultural links which dominated India's engagement with Africa during the Cold War. India has traded with Africa since the fourteenth century, and during European colonialism these links strengthened as both regions shared colonial masters. For instance, the British East Africa protectorate which comprised present-day Kenya and Uganda, was originally administered from Bombay (Mumbai). Many African countries have influential minorities whose ancestors came from India during the colonial times. Mahatma Gandhi's civil disobedience movement against British colonial rule began in South Africa, and independent India has supported independence movements in several African nations (Bajpaee 2008).

India now seeks to gain access to Africa's natural resources—particularly energy—in return for increased aid and low-cost solutions to battle poverty. India's trade and business relationships with Africa, which have grown since the early 1960s, have increased rapidly in recent years. Trade between the two regions increased tenfold during 1997–2007. India–Africa bilateral trade is projected to grow by over nine times from US$26 billion now to US$150 billion by 2012, according to an estimate by the Associated Chambers of Commerce and Industry of India.

In 2004, India entered into an economic, commercial and technical collaboration agreement with eight West African countries: Burkina Faso, Chad, New Guinea, Ghana, Guinea Bissau, Ivory Coast, Mali and Senegal. India has also launched the "Focus: Africa" program under the EXIM Policy 2002–7. The first phase of the program includes trade-promoting activities in Mauritius, Kenya and Ethiopia.

India has identified opportunities to increase its agricultural production through large-scale commercial farming in Africa. The state of Andhra Pradesh has signed a preliminary deal with Kenya and Uganda to send 500 farmers to cultivate land in the East African nations as entrepreneurs and landowners. Indian firms have also signed land deals in Ethiopia, Kenya and Madagascar to produce a range of food crops: rice, sugarcane, maize, pulses, oilseeds, tea and even vegetables.

India, Brazil and South Africa agreed upon mutual economic, commercial and political collaboration (IBSA) in 2004. So far IBSA has concentrated on collaboration in WTO negotiations. In 2003 and in 2004, India concluded agreements with MERCOSUR, a free-trade area of 217 million inhabitants, which comprises more than a half of the GNP of Latin America.

India's trade and foreign policies have focused on the South and Asia, because India sees more possibilities in the developing countries' growing markets than in the West where growth rates are more moderate. Moreover, the developed countries still protect their markets from developing countries' exports. India's focus on Asia and South–South relations does not, however, mean that India is shunning Western relations. One of India's most significant foreign policy changes has been the rapprochement with the United States which most notably took place during the Bush era (see Chapter 6). The Obama administration's strategic interest in South Asia has shifted from managing the rise of China, where India plays a major role, to defeating radicalism that is lodged in Afghanistan and Pakistan, where India's role is marginal. Consequently, Obama's administration has so far not actively developed new forms of cooperation with India (Andersen 2010). Prime Minister Singh's visit to the White House in 2009, however, conveyed the Obama administration's interests to activate building relationships with India and acknowledge India's role in the world economy and politics.

The European Union is still India's most important trade and investment partner. India and the European Union have held annual summits to conduct dialogue about trade relations and scientific, technological, environmental and energy issues since 2000. In 2004, India became a strategic partner of the European Union, and in 2007, the European Union and India started to negotiate a free-trade agreement. India is the greatest destination of British investments. Russia and India have not renewed their friendship and collaboration agreement (1971), although they continue their relationship along less ideological grounds.

## 5.4 Grassroots Politics

Both India's domestic and foreign policy are ultimately forged in small places. Unlike in Western democracies, in India the poor, the uneducated and the rural population vote more than the affluent, educated and urban (Yadav 1996, 1999). When India as the first non-Western country chose democracy as its form of government, it did not merely adopt Western influences. Indian democracy and politics draws from local traditions and meanings.

The villagers of Janta, West Bengal say that it is impossible to live in their community without the protection of the main parties. The power of the parties derives largely from their role as arbitrator in disputes: anyone who feels they have suffered an injustice can call a village meeting led by local political leaders during which a solution will be negotiated. The parties also have their elected representatives in the local decision-making bodies—*panchayats*—which have authority over the distribution of local public finances (Tenhunen 2009).

The villagers judge the parties not so much by their political programs as by their morals. The understanding of politics as morality is in line with the literal meaning of the Bengali term *rajniti* (politics), which is a compound word consisting of the words *raj* (king, ruler, state or government) and *niti* (morality, principle). The voters give the party their support and in return expect assistance when they face hardships. The party, for instance, assists small-scale farmers by distributing crop seeds. Party leaders act as conciliators in family conflicts, try to help gamblers and alcoholics recover from their addictions, mediate in divorce proceedings and concomitant property disputes, and help with the registration of property. Since the local public health centers do not have sufficient resources to treat patients with serious illnesses and the poor cannot afford private doctors, the indigent villagers' only hope is to request the party to arrange for special treatment of seriously ill patients.

The rural poor of West Bengal supported the Communist Party following 1977, because it was their only mainstay when adversity struck. However, helping the poor figures not only in the Left's programs; all the main political parties engage in social work among the poor in order to gain support. The CPI-M, the ruling party of West Bengal, succeeded in staying in power thanks to its abundant resources and power over state agencies which enabled it to help its supporters better than the opposition parties.

As the local leaders of the West Bengal Communist Party belonged to the upper classes of the region, political work resembled the patron–client relationships which prevailed before the land reforms, when the landless had to rely on the big landlords for work and protection. The difference is that the Communist Party and its leaders were considered to be more just and understanding than the great landowners of the past.

Followers of the same party form a kind of kinship community, calling each other by kinship terms such as sister and brother, aunt and uncle. Kinship provides the metaphor for the party and its activities so that kinship-based party membership is differentiated from other types of relatives. Kinship ties imply certain expectations of solidarity and serious disagreements about these solidarities can lead to the splitting of the joint family or termination of interaction among certain kin. Since party members are party brothers, conflicts are as inevitable as they are between blood-related brothers. As an informant stated, "Big parties, like large families, do not stay together." Brothers should not fight, but they do.

Although political relatives resemble other types of relatives in a moral sense, there are also crucial differences. Party membership is, after all, less arbitrary than kinship: one cannot select new blood relatives or relatives through marriage as one can change one's political affiliation. In Janta, the whole neighborhood changed its affiliation from the Communist Party to the BJP to protest a local Communist Party leader's action when the wealthy landowner stabbed his cousin over an inheritance quarrel. The perpetrator and the victim were not only kinsmen, but they also belonged to the same party. The opposition, BJP, perceived this conflict as an opportunity to enhance its support and organized a village meeting at which the whole neighborhood changed it's affiliation to the BJP.

When I mentioned in the village that the communist parties in Eastern Europe had faced resistance when they had tried to abolish religion, the villagers drew an analogy with the Left Front's attempts to deprive party members of their relationship with in-laws (*kutum*) who do not support the Left Front. The BJP activist in the village emphasized that his party, unlike the CPI-M, allows people to maintain their relationships even with relatives who support a different party. But when I asked the BJP supporter about his relationship with his brother, who is a CPI-M supporter, he replied that he had told his brother that they could be on good terms, but that if the brother got into trouble he could not be of help.

It is the overlap between party membership and kinship that allows parties to be efficient, but also makes politics a vulnerable and conflict-ridden business. National party organizations intervene and consolidate their power by expanding and aggravating local family disputes. Local politics in Janta is, by its cultural definition, burdened by conflicting loyalties and unforeseeable connections between the local and national. No wonder most villagers also characterize politics as trouble.

What inevitably makes this system based on bonds of local patronage fragile is the party's inability to extend scarce benefits to all equally. Small and marginal farmers losing their livelihoods because of land acquisitions or pricing policies of agricultural produce served to help the opposition to grow. On the one hand, growing economic disparities raise people's expectations of the party. On the other hand, in Janta it was those needing less patronage, the newly prosperous entrepreneurs, who led the revolt against the CPI-M. After the opposition won the state election in 2011 elections, villagers of Janta have turned to the new ruling party for support.

Populist mobilization through clientelistic networks characterizes Indian politics in general. The close connections between politics, patronage and kinship manifest in national politics as relationships enhanced by corruption and dynastical transfers of power; another similarity lies in the practice of parties gaining supporters by providing their electorate with aid packages.

## 5.5 Public Deficit

The necessity for political parties to gain support through populist mobilization by promising aid packages contributes to one of India's most pressing political and economic problems: public deficit. Reducing the public deficit has proved difficult in India, in spite of the fact that all the main parties support economic reforms. India's fiscal deficit and government debt are among the greatest of the developing markets. India's state deficit has persisted at around 10 percent of the GDP, and the share of the state debt of the GDP has varied between 70 and 80 percent (Rawkins 2006).

The biggest reason for the deficit is the paucity of states and Central Government's income from taxation. The greatest part of tax revenues are collected from businesses as sales tax, company taxes and customs duties. In spite of economic growth, only 1 percent of Indians pay income tax, and the share of tax revenue of the Central Government's income has fallen to 14 percent of the GDP while expenses such as salaries, pensions, subsidies as well as interests on loans have risen (Rawkins 2006). The Central Government's biggest expenditures are loans (25 percent of the outlay), defense (15 percent) and various subsidies (9 percent).

The deficit hinders India's ability to invest in improvements in infrastructure, health care and education. India is faced with the difficult task of reducing the deficit and cutting the vicious circle of poverty by developing basic education, social security and public health care, all at the same time. The emerging solution is to improve the efficiency of governance and cut subsidies which do not benefit the poorest.

Indian states are also suffering from budget deficits, and the emergence of local parties has not improved the situation. It is easier to get voters by promising new subsidies than by threatening with budget cuts. For example, the state government of Uttar Pradesh had committed itself to balancing the economy, but the deficit kept growing when former chief minister Mulayam Singh Yadav directed subsidies to farmers who were to a large extent from his own caste; he was succeeded into office by *dalit* leader Mayawati, who channeled funds to the *dalits* (Pai 2005).

Even chief minister of Andhra Pradesh Chandrababu Naidu, who was dedicated to reforming the state economy, guaranteed his re-election in 1999 by initiating several subsidy programs before the election—the most controversial of which was the additional gas subsidy for households already able to purchase gas at a subsidized rate. In the 2004 elections, he did not resort to such aid packages and lost the election to a coalition formed by the Congress and the Left, who had criticized the Naidu government for supporting big enterprises and the elite at the expense of the poor and the rural population (Suri 2005).

## 5.6 The Burden of Corruption

Although the end of the license economy has reduced government officials' opportunities to demand bribes, corruption-prone reciprocal service relationships are still dominant in business, politics and administration at many levels. According to a Transparency International's estimate, a single truck pays nearly Rs 80,000 annually as bribes at toll plazas and other checkpoints (Balwantray, Vidya and Masjid 2006). Even households below the poverty line have to pay bribes to avail themselves of basic public services such as hospital, education and water to which they are entitled as a right.

Sondhi (2000) has estimated that the reduction of corruption in India to a Nordic level could raise investments by 12 percent and the national product by 1.5 percent annually. Appointment to even the lowest rank of government job in the countryside requires the greasing of palms. Corruption eliminates qualified but indigent candidates, thus reducing social mobility. Corruption reduces tax revenues and works as an additional tax on investments, thus diminishing investors' earnings. Expectations of pay-offs tempt government officials to support those investments which entail lucrative bribes instead of education and health care. Corruption curtails investments because unlawful income is generally used for private consumption instead of legal investments and economy. Furthermore, it is detrimental to the infrastructure. For example, in Delhi, losses in electricity distribution have been estimated to consume up to 50 percent of the production, out of which 30 percent is attributed to the theft and connivance by electricity board employees. One of the directors of the Delhi Electricity Company was apprehended after having unlawfully accumulated Rs 140 million.

Businesses can persuade the government to change legislation through bribes, and ensure government orders and permits by the same means. Criminal organizations get involved in politics in order to find legitimacy and security as well as to expand their activities and to get a share of government finances and projects. It has become so common for members of parliament, chief ministers or top officials to get caught accepting bribes that they may even get re-elected after having been convicted for bribery. Criminal organizations have moved from bribing politicians to entering politics themselves. Out of 4,092 parliamentary representatives in India, 700 had a criminal record in 2005—a figure that includes members of both the Central Government and state governments (Radhakrishna et al. 2005, 153). Politicians' criminal records are, however, no longer kept secret but are publicly debated; politicians and other influential persons like movie stars have even been sentenced during past years.

It is difficult to weed out corruption especially from the upper echelons of police and government; nevertheless, the fight against graft goes on. The Right to Information Act was passed in 2005 at the initiative of civic organizations. This law safeguards the rights of ordinary citizens to get information on public services and faults in the system; it is better than earlier legislation as it makes almost all official decisions public and has a set a maximum period within which the officials have to comply with the applicant's request for information. It is now more difficult for officials to demand bribes for providing information, because they can be sued easily, and civic organizations and private citizens have taken advantage of the new law to uncover the misuse of public funds and other misdemeanors.

A few Indian companies like Tata, Wipro and Infosys take a zero tolerance stand on the acceptance of bribes. According to the Forbes ranking, India managed to move out of the truly corrupt group in 2007 (Andelman, 2007). Transparency International ranked India 82nd in 2008 in terms of integrity. Globalization may reduce corruption as the growing weight of multinational companies in the economy strengthens business practices that do not build on corruption, although even the multinationals can secure their marketing positions with the help of consulting firms which resort to bribery. Nonetheless, the emerging administrative culture may increase the likelihood of being caught and convicted of bribery in today's India.

Large-scale corruption scams have been uncovered in the media regularly over the past years. Among the biggest was the 2G spectrum scandal which involved officials undercharging mobile telephony companies for 2G licenses for personal gain, which was estimated to have cost Indian government US$33 billion in 2009. This and many other scams contributed to a growth of a civil movement against corruption in India led by Gandhian social activist Anna Hazare whose role had previously been instrumental in the creation of the Right to Information Act. Hazare agitated for passing of a strong anti-corruption Lokpal (ombudsman) bill in the Indian Parliament. The Indian government has partly agreed to his terms after Hazare's hunger strikes in New Delhi became the center of media attention and the campaign escalated into a mass movement supported by the middle classes. Despite the campaigns to end corruption, corrupt practices are often interpreted as signs of power, which newly elected representatives of lower castes are keen to adopt, as Witsoe (2011) argues.

## 5.7 Conclusion

Political power has shifted from the Congress Party to coalition governments, and economic reforms have transferred power away from officials to the actual functionaries in the economy and to political decision makers. The greatest stumbling block of coalitions is their inability to reduce the public deficit, which has had a huge financial burden on loan management and endangers investments in infrastructure, education and health care. Indian democracy and politics draw on local traditions and meanings so that unforeseeable connections between the local and national have been facilitated by both civil activism and corrupt practices. Corruption prone politics increasingly undermines the political legitimacy of the ruling coalitions both at central and state levels. The rise of the anti-corruption movement strengthens political volatility—and the possibilities for changes in the administrative culture.

In its foreign policy, India emphasizes economic interests instead of ideological objectives, but India's role in Asia's economic integration as well as the South–South collaboration keep alive Nehru's vision of the Third World bearing a global influence through cooperation. Nonetheless, while economic growth has strengthened India's international importance, strained relationships with China and Pakistan continue to hamper the prospects of Asia's cooperation and India's quest for leadership role in South Asia.

# Chapter 6

# POLITICAL ALTERNATIVES

Critics argue that economic reforms have harmed Indian democracy by subjugating the political domain to global economic forces. Reforms have, however, also decentralized power by increasing the power of provincial states. The liberalization of television broadcasting has facilitated expression of opinion and the airing of conflicts. In addition to the many local parties which have increased their influence in parliament and the Central Government, there are alternatives to the Congress Party as the pan-India party such as the Left and Hindu Nationalist Party (BJP). Women's entry into politics has also contributed to the pluralism. One significant source of changes, the low-caste political movements, was discussed in Chapter 4.

## 6.1 The Influence of the Left

The Left had a crucial impact on the pace of India's reforms during 2004–9 when it controlled the balance of power in parliament. The flow of foreign investments into India has grown since liberalization, but the Left prevented the entry of foreign companies into the Indian retail market. Supporters of investment restrictions argue that they secure the livelihood of small-scale local entrepreneurs, whereas opponents maintain that the entry of foreign companies into the retail trade would create new jobs, offer lower prices, and improve the quality and the selection of goods.

Many perceive the sale of government-owned companies as an opportunity for the state to acquire funds for building up the infrastructure and improving education and health care. The Left, however, prevented the sale of profitable government businesses and those companies that control India's natural resources. Furthermore, the Left's prohibition on the full convertibility of the rupee is supported by many economists who argue that full convertibility would lead to the exodus of capital from India.

Another major dispute has revolved over a labor law which prevents an enterprise employing over 100 workers to fire any of them without permission from the local labor court. The law seeks to protect employees from arbitrary treatment, but its opponents, point out that it causes employers to limit the number of staff thereby protecting the interests of organized labor at the expense of the unemployed and unorganized labor.

The Congress Party's victory in the elections of 2009 freed it from compliance with the Left's demands. After its victory, the Congress-led government has continued with moderate reforms, but it has so far not embarked on radical reforms such as overhauling labor laws, allowing drastically more direct foreign investment in insurance, telecom and retail or divesting itself of assets in state-owned companies. It has not made it easier to dismiss workers nor has it launched privatization or financial sector changes which could interfere with state-run insurance firms and banks—measures which could all damage Congress's popularity. Instead of radical liberalization, the party has continued to focus on helping the *aam admi* (common man), who fills the main voting bank. The government is likely to liberalize fields where reforms can increase jobs but restrict foreign access to those domains of the economy where such a move would lead to job loss. Controlled liberalization serves the party's interest in retaining popularity but it also reflects growing disillusionment with the merits of radical liberalization in the midst of global financial turmoil.

The Congress-led government has fought rising inflation rates by raising interest rates which in turn has been a main factor in curtailing India's growth rates. Lower-than-expected economic growth in 2011—6.9 percent in the last quarter—has created expectations for new reforms. In 2012, the government opened the stock market to individual foreign investors to attract more foreign investment. In 2011, the government tried to open up retail sector to foreign investors but was forced to shelve these plans due to widespread protests.

### 6.1.1 The Left and US relations

The relationship between India and the United States emerged as the biggest controversy between the Congress coalition and the Left front. For many Leftist politicians, the US still represents military and economic imperialism as it presses for freer entry into the Indian market, especially in the retail and agricultural sector. Yet, it has been reluctant to lower its own agricultural subsidies, which prevent Indian farmers from being able to produce goods at competitive prices for the world market.

Nevertheless, the United States and India's shared interests have become accentuated since the end of the Cold War and particularly after the September 11 terrorist attacks of 2001. The two greatest democracies of the world have become major targets of Islamic terrorism. During the Cold War, India accused the United States of supporting the same terrorist groups in Pakistan that were also fighting in Afghanistan against the Soviet occupation. Since the

2001 terrorist offensives, the United States has demanded that Pakistan end terrorist activities in its territory.

In addition to their shared interest in curbing Islamic terrorism, the United States and India are both interested in cooperation to counterbalance China's emerging dominance in world politics. In 2006, the United States and India signed a nuclear agreement by which the United States allows India access to civilian nuclear technology, while India agrees to allow the US greater scrutiny of its nuclear program. Critics of the agreement have argued that this agreement allows the United States to limit India's development of nuclear technology by blackmailing India through the threat of closing the flow of nuclear technology whenever deemed politically advantageous. Supporters of the treaty maintain that the Indian energy sector has suffered already from nuclear technology boycotts and that India needs American technology and expertise to upgrade its nuclear power plants and build more of them in order to secure sufficient energy for its growing economy. A study by the McKinsey & Cohen Consultancy has estimated that India needs to triple its power-generation capacity by 2017 in order for the economy to expand at 8 percent a year (Leahy 2008). The Left withdrew its support from the government because of the signing of the treaty, but the Congress-led governing coalition survived the vote of confidence in 2008.

### 6.1.2 Impasse of the Left in West Bengal

Although the multinational companies and the United States represent the enemy for many Leftist politicians, the Communist Party is not opposed to economic reforms. In fact, some of the most prominent protagonists of the reforms are communist leaders such as Buddhadeb Bhattacharjee, the chief minister of West Bengal during 2000–11. West Bengal is the only state in India where the Communist Party (CPI-M) ruled continuously for decades (1977–2011).

Unlike its neighboring states to the east, West Bengal is not among the poorest states of India, although it has not fared as well as other parts of India in terms of infrastructure or providing education and health care. The greatest achievements of communist rule in West Bengal have been the maintenance of communal harmony and land reform. In West Bengal, the plots of land distributed to the landless are too small to sustain entire families throughout the year; nevertheless, they have provided landless laborers with additional means of livelihood.

Before communist rule, West Bengal was one of the most industrialized areas in India and the universities of West Bengal, particularly of Kolkata, were among the best in the country. Labor unions which were formed in

India during British rule have been especially powerful in West Bengal. Strikes became such a common phenomena in Communist-led West Bengal in the 1980s that industries gradually closed most of their units there. The majority of West Bengal's labor force, consequently, has had to find employment in the unofficial sector and small-scale industries which are not bound to obey labor laws due to their size.

Educational standards in West Bengal fell, particularly in higher education, because teachers were hired more on the basis of their party affiliation than on merit. The Communist Party terminated the teaching of English in primary schools in 1983, arguing that it is more important to reinforce children's knowledge of their mother tongue than to teach them English at an early stage. The objective was also to make education more accessible to the poor. As a result, generations of public school students have found it difficult to qualify for well-paid jobs in fields such as the rapidly growing outsourcing sector which require a good command of the English language. Public schools have to bear with teachers' frequent absenteeism and poor standards of teaching, which has led to a mushrooming of private institutions and thus a paucity of students in public primary schools. Even the poor want to send their children to private schools, but they cannot afford to pay the school fees and, as a result, the education of poor children often remains sporadic.

The Writers' Building, a British-built coliseum containing the government offices of West Bengal in Kolkata, conceals in its labyrinthine halls dusty stacks of official documents. The officials themselves trickle in around mid-morning or even later, and the corridors are filled with clerical workers, many of whom sleep, read newspapers or talk in their mobile phones for the major portion of the working hours. The decision makers fully understand the need to improve the government's efficiency, but reducing the number of government jobs is a delicate matter—government jobs are regarded as permanent and the bureaucracy still wields disproportionate power over the political decision makers.

Many Communist Party reforms which aimed at bringing about equality have, in fact, worked towards strengthening the affluent classes within the party. By turning academic appointments into political issues, the party eliminated potential critique. By terminating teaching English in the primary schools, it has strengthened the private schools and improved the status of those able to send their children to them.

The Communists reintroduced English-language teaching at the primary schools in 2000. Former chief minister Buddhadeb Bhattacharjee also admitted that academic positions should be filled based on academic merit. The West Bengali Communists acknowledged as early as the 1990s the inevitability of economic reforms and started to emulate the economic strategy of the Chinese

Communist Party by welcoming new businesses and industries. Subsequently, this densely populated state has become one of the most lucrative investment destinations in India thanks to its large markets and geographic position: the harbors of West Bengal are India's gateways to Southeast Asia.

The state government has boosted the development of new industries by creating special economic zones (SEZs), for which it acquires land on the basis of the Land Acquisition Act, which was passed during the colonial regime and gives the state a right to redeem land for public purposes. Finding vacant land in the most densely populated state of India is difficult, and compulsory acquisitions have not helped although farmers' land has not been taken without a reimbursement. In 2007, West Bengal was forced to reverse its plans of setting up a chemical hub in Nandigram because of the farmers' resistance. The proposed special economic zone would have consisted of irrigated land and the farmers who lived and worked in the more than 30 villages that would have been affected by the plans were not willing to trade their livelihood for a monetary compensation they considered too meager. Although the state had promised to respect the villagers' opinions, it sent a police force to subdue farmers when they put up a resistance. The police fired at the villagers, killing 14 and injuring many. The news of the incident spread quickly through the 24-hour TV channels which the state's population had ample time to watch, as they could not leave their houses because of the ensuing riots and the general strike announced by the opposition. Almost overnight the chief minister's image was transformed from that of a heroic leader to a villain whose effigies were burned on the streets.

The newly established opposition movement, the Bhoomi Ucched Pratirodh Committee, chased Communist Party supporters away from the villages of the affected areas. When the Communist Party attempted to secure their supporters' return to their homes the area transformed into a war zone, with Communist Party cadres against the forces of the opposition. In addition to the main opposition parties—the Congress, Trinamul Congress (a party led by Mamata Banerjee, a former Congress Party politician), and BJP—the Bhoomi Ucched Pratirodh has received support from the Maoists who took advantage of the opportunity provided by the land dispute to broaden their base in West Bengal. The battle in Nandigram became brutal and bloody in the virtual absence of any state mechanisms. The guerrilla war culminated in chief minister Buddhadeb Bhattacharjee sending party cadres to take over the villages by force. After the take over, the Central Government sent its own police forces to keep peace in the region.

The disputes over land led the Tata Motors to relocate its Nano car factory from West Bengal to Gujarat in 2008. These protests arose out of the real worries and crises caused by the farmers' loss of livelihood and healthy environment. Farming in present-day rural West Bengal is far from lucrative for small and marginal farmers and they do realize the value of new jobs provided that they are created, so that they stand to benefit more than they lose. Far from resisting industrialization as a whole, they opposed the Communist Party's methods of implementing its plans. The conflicts spurred by land acquisitions have been ferocious not only in West Bengal but they are spread all over India (see Chapter 9).

West Bengal's reputation as a promising investment destination has suffered but new plans to build industries in different parts of West Bengal have been introduced. The Communist Party educated people using television commercials and the slogan "Agriculture is our foundation and industries our future." The campaigns, however, did not prevent the ruling CPI-M from suffering its greatest electoral defeat in decades. The West Bengal state assembly election in 2011 marked the defeat for the longest-serving democratically elected communist government in the world.

## 6.2 Hindu Fundamentalism

Despite its position of power in parliament, the Left was not willing to try to overthrow the government until 2008 because the Left and the Congress coalition shared an interest in preventing the rise of Hindu fundamentalists to power. The BJP's victory in the 1996 parliamentary elections came as a surprise, because the party's ideology of an India united by Hinduism had, till then, generally appealed only to the upper-caste minority. The BJP was established in 1979 to continue the work of the former fundamentalist Hindu party Jana Sangh, but its roots go back to the colonial era. Rather than representing traditional Hinduism, Hindu nationalism represents a new interpretation of Hindu tradition which is based on Western influences (Jaffrelot 1999). The Hindu culture has, over the centuries, embraced newcomers as part of local hierarchies instead of ostracizing them. During the colonial era, foreign influences were, however, regarded as a threat, which was counterbalanced by reformulating Hindu ideals to match Western values.

The reaction of Hindu reformers to British colonialism and Christian missionaries was to reinvent the past golden age of Hinduism thereby providing the Hindu elite with a way of embracing Western ideals and at the same time retaining the essence of Hinduism. The social evils inherent in Hindu society, such as child marriages and *sati* (widow burning), were explained as products of the degeneration of Hinduism and alien influences: it was presumed that they did not exist before the arrival of the Muslim conquerors, in the golden age of Hinduism. When the Hindu reformers adopted the idea of the nation, based on a shared ethnic identity from nineteenth-century German nationalism, fundamentalist Hinduism was born. Western influences are also evident in the fact that, according to Hindu extremists, people who have converted to other religions can and should be reconverted to Hinduism—traditionally it has not been possible to convert to Hinduism.

The most influential form of nationalism in India, however, has not been Hindu fundamentalism but that propagated by the Congress Party, which argues that India as a nation includes all the religious and ethnic groups that inhabited former British India. Post-partition violence and the murder of Mahatma Gandhi by a fundamentalist Hindu caused the Congress Party to oppose vehemently the rise of Hindu nationalism. It is, therefore, no coincidence that the rise of the BJP is linked to the economic reforms and the concomitant decline of the dominance of the Congress Party. As Hansen (1999) argues, efficient political organization was not the sole reason for the rise of the BJP. The success of the BJP was also enabled by changes in Indian politics and society. During the 1980s, Indian economy and media took first limited steps in liberalization, which, according to Hansen (1999), generated a feeling of misplacement in India. At the time, India's economic growth and living standards appeared low when considered internationally. Exposure to global media flows, therefore, deepened the view of India as sliding downward in the global hierarchy of the nations. By emphasizing the superiority of the Hindu way of life, BJP helped tackle the feelings of inferiority. BJP appealed especially to old elites and middle class who felt threatened by the new entry of low classes to the political elite thanks to caste quotas and the low-caste political mobilization.

The BJP was founded to continue the work of the Jana Sangh party, which had become politically marginalized due to its extremism, and to pursue a more moderate program than followed by the Jana Sangh. The BJP, however, did not concentrate merely on socio-economic reforms but started to woo the voters with objectives linked to key symbols of Hinduism. Most significant of these has been the demand to construct a Hindu temple on the site of a mosque located in Ayodhya.

The Babri Mosque was built in 1528 in Ayodhya, Uttar Pradesh, on the supposed birth place of Rama, a Hindu god and an incarnation of the god Vishnu. The nationwide campaign to build a Hindu temple on the site of the Babri Mosque culminated in infuriated Hindu fundamentalists demolishing the mosque in 1992. Violent confrontations between Hindus and Muslims followed all over India, resulting in the deaths of thousands of people. Since the demolition of the mosque thousands of Hindus have travelled to Ayodhya to pressure the government to build a Hindu temple on the site. A new wave of Ayodhya-related violence occurred when a train carrying Hindu demonstrators caught fire in Godhra in 2002. Although it could not be proved that the fire had been lit intentionally, fundamentalist Hindus blamed Muslims and attacked them.

After the demolition of the Babri Mosque, Gujarat, a stronghold of the BJP, was the worst hit: 20 out of its 25 districts were affected. For the first time, rural areas were also widely hit by riots and crops were destroyed. Fundamentalist Hindus attacked Muslim homes, burning houses, raping women and killing entire families. 200,000 Muslims had to flee from their homes in Gujarat. According to the official estimate, the death toll was 600 while unofficially it was put at 2,500 (Mahadevia 2005). About 1,150 hotels and restaurants were destroyed and 270 mosques demolished. The Chamber of Commerce of Gujarat estimated that the violence cost the state Rs 25 billion. Investigations into the riots have revealed them to be carefully organized by fundamentalist bodies. Although the police and the state administration did not actually participate in the riots, they did nothing to stop them either; whereas those states where the police were ordered to prevent violence were saved from unrest (Mahadevia 2005, 312–13). Since the riots, Gujarat has become a divided state in which Muslims can freely move about only in their restricted areas and have to pay more than Hindus for land and other commodities.

The demolition of the Babri Mosque was not merely a victory for Hindu fundamentalist forces; the riots gave the electorate a graphic example of to what Hindu fundamentalism can lead. Furthermore, the demolition of the Babri Mosque eliminated the movement's central aim and after the Ayodhya riots, the BJP turned its attention from religious issues to socio-economic questions, utilizing the disappointment of different groups with Congress Party rule and offering them a channel to voice their grievances.

To appeal to the upper castes, the BJP promised to oppose the quotas allotted to the lower castes. To the entrepreneurs they vowed to create a more business-friendly economic policy, meanwhile assuring aid for those who had suffered as a result of the economic reforms. The BJP even succeeded in wooing voters from the lower castes by arranging aid programs in poor neighborhoods. Women's support was sought by demanding a uniform civil law, which would improve women's inheritance rights. Women have been allotted a prominent role in the party as preservers of Hindu tradition and morality following the Hindu nationalist elite's solution to the women question. During the colonial era, the nationalists left the preservation of Hindu tradition to women, arguing that men could embrace Western ideas in the public sphere, while women should cherish Hindu traditions in the homes (Basu 1996).

Civil organizations play a significant role in building up support for the BJP. The largest of them is the Rastriya Swayamsevak Sangh (RSS), a voluntary national organization with 1.3 million members. The organization was established in 1925 to defend Hindus during religious riots and to build

Hindu India; its members receive military training and wear uniforms, and it has a wide network of cooperation with organizations comprised of students, workers, women and devout Hindus.

Despite its current comparative moderation and focus on social and economic issues, the BJP still contains an influential fundamentalist faction, which does not shun the use of coercion and violence. The BJP government continued with economic reforms but their achievements have been overshadowed by the frequent attacks on minorities and by the culmination of the conflict between India and Pakistan in the short Kargil War. The party has attempted to censure newspapers and researchers. It has even fired academics for ideological reasons, especially attacking historians who have criticized Hindu fundamentalist interpretations of history which, for instance, deny the theory of Indo-Aryan migration to India.

In BJP rhetoric, national policies have been reinterpreted so that national security references the threat from Pakistan, immigration policy references Muslim immigration and the uniform civil code is that which is directed against Muslims. While the Muslim intelligentsia in India is becoming increasingly critical about Islamist fundamentalism, it has also become more commonplace among middle-class Hindus to blame the Muslim minority for various problems in India such as population growth and national security issues (Basu 1998).

It has been easier for the BJP to shower diverse and even conflicting promises on the electorate from the opposition benches—promises it has often been unable to honor—than to rule a state. The BJP's campaign "India Shining" ended in a defeat in the 2004 parliamentary elections; and since BJP representatives have been revealed to have been involved in corruption scandals, it is no longer able to present itself as a morally superior party. BJP's loss in the 2009 elections reflects a host of problems stalling its growth. BJP has its strongholds such as Gujarat and Rajasthan, but it is not popular in big states like West Bengal, Andhra Pradesh, Tamil Nadu or Kerala. Many allies have left BJP due to fears of losing the Muslim vote. Even BJP activists confess today that confusion prevails about the party's core ideology and the meaning of *hindutva*, as well as its overall political agenda. Rising economic prosperity among the middle and upper classes may corrode BJP's ability to appeal to feelings of betrayal and displacement. However, the BJP is still the country's single largest opposition party and in a strong position to rise to power and form a future government.

BJP government would be likely to continue with economic reforms even more radically than the Congress Party because it does not represent the Nehru-Gandhi dynastic bureaucracy. In Gujarat, for example, the authoritarian use of power by the BJP has actually facilitated economic reforms. Mahadevia

(2005) polemically remarks that the union of liberal economic policy and fundamentalist Hinduism is based on the fact that both share such traits as selfishness and greed.

The BJP has ruled Gujarat, one of India's fastest growing economies, almost continuously since 1995. In 2008, Narendra Modi led the party again to victory despite his regime having been responsible for instigating violence in the community. Modi's popularity is the result of a combination of a carefully created public image and the good economic performance of the state. In addition to making good use of the Internet and mobile technology in campaigning, Modi turned his supporters into walking advertisements by giving them Modi masks to wear.

The BJP's rise to power is likely to pose a security threat, as the areas where the party has been in power have witnessed more religious conflicts than others. The biggest confrontations have occurred between the Hindus and Muslims, but missionaries and converts to Christianity have also been attacked. The BJP's return to power would increase the likelihood of riots and isolate minorities. Violence against Muslims would, in turn, increase the likelihood of Muslim extremist terrorist attacks in India.

The bomb attacks in Mumbai in 1993, in which 257 people were killed and 1,400 injured, were executed by Islamic terrorists in revenge for Ayodhya-related violence towards the Muslims. The bomb attacks in Mumbai in 2006 took place in areas and on trains used by affluent Gujarati Hindus, and as such they are suspected of being Islamic fundamentalist revenge for the Gujarat riots after the train fire. The violence that the BJP propagates against minorities can weaken the general security of the region and thereby hamper economic growth. Its return to power would also hinder Asia's economic integration by straining relations between India and Pakistan.

Gunmen killing nearly 200 people and injuring hundreds in a series of coordinated attacks on the main tourist and business area of India's financial capital Mumbai in 2008 did not contribute to the popularity of the BJP, despite its criticism of the Congress government for its soft stance on terrorism and failing to prevent the attacks. Voters did not react by showing preference to the hardliners of BJP over the Congress Party in great numbers in the general election of 2009.

## 6.3 Maoist Rebellion in the Countryside

The protest of the poorest rural areas is gradually being canalized towards another fundamentalist movement, namely the Maoists, who do not belong to the Left coalition in parliament. The same Maoist movement has gained power in Nepal, and the role of the movement in overthrowing the king of

Nepal has also strengthened the confidence of the movement in India. The Maoist movement in India is, however, territorially more limited than in Nepal. The movement does not carry weight in domestic politics because the Indian Maoists shun participation in democratic institutions. Instead, their aim is to topple the system.

Also known in India as Naxalites, after the region in West Bengal where the movement was initiated in 1967, Indian Maoists began by organizing rebellions of landless workers in West Bengal, Bihar and Andhra Pradesh. From there, the movement has spread to the mineral-rich states of Orissa, Chhattisgarh and Jharkhand. It is estimated that there are 20,000 armed Maoist guerrillas in India. By 2009, the Naxalite movement was present in 20 states, and it aims to bring the whole country under its control (Yardley 2009). The movement has gained dominance over one-fifth of the forested area of the country—the government has assigned a special administrative status to the forests in order to ensure the land rights of the tribal communities.

The Maoist movement defends tribals and their livelihoods by demanding higher prices for the products they collect from forests. In many areas the movement has also set up schools, health clinics, seed banks for farmers and initiated irrigation projects (Navlakha 2006). The militaristic movement finances its activities by taxing the population in the areas where they rule. It supplies local supporters with a collection of arsenal from First World War carbines to Chinese Kalashnikovs and rockets. The Naxalites have their own well-developed espionage organization and courts of law in the areas they dominate (Bowring 2006). They have found supporters especially in the regions neglected by the government. The Naxalite commander of Chhattisgarh has declared that the movement wants to guarantee the citizens their rights, although, ironically, the Naxalite attacks also contribute to governmental neglect: Naxalites have attacked development projects, industries, power plants, police stations and even schools, and have killed government officials, police, missionaries, tourists and teachers (Bowring 2006). The Naxalites have killed more than 900 Indian security officers in the last four years (Yardley 2009).

The Government of India has been arming some residents of Chhattisgarh with firearms and bows and arrows to fight against the Naxalites, which has turned the area into a war zone. More than 50,000 people have had to leave their homes because of the fighting. The government has concentrated its military action in the Chhattisgarh region because of its rich ore deposits, as it sees the utilization of natural resources as a prerequisite for economic growth. The Naxalites oppose the entry of the big corporations, arguing that the companies take away natural resources, leaving the local people with nothing

(Ramesh 2006). Approximately half the population supports the Naxalites in the tribal areas, either voluntarily or by coercion. People living in the guerrilla-infested areas also constantly report the terrors perpetrated both by the police and the Indian army which destroys homes and moves residents to camps, which are considered by the army to be safe havens, but are perceived as prison camps by their inhabitants (Ramesh 2006).

The growth of the Naxalite movement is linked to economic reforms because the Naxalites gain supporters from people whose livelihood is threatened by mining companies and industries. The breadth of its support is an indication of the extent of gross marginalization present in India today. So far, the Maoist movement represents a minority even in rural India, but the growth of the movement will depend largely on how efficiently the Indian state is able to foster inclusive growth. Prime Minister Singh has admitted to the exclusion of tribals from the benefits of industrialization. At the same time, the Central Government has chosen to concentrate its efforts on force not concrete development efforts, sending 70,000 paramilitary forces to hunt down the guerrillas (Yardley 2009).

## 6.4 Women's Activism

Another ongoing revolution in India gets less publicity than that afforded to the Maoists. Women's participation and share in both local and national politics has increased since 1993 when women were allocated quotas in local governing organs, *panchayats*. At the turn of the millennium, when the number of female chief ministers was at its peak, two-thirds of India was governed by a female provincial chief minister. After the 2009 elections, the number of women members in parliament crossed the 10 percent threshold for the first time in Indian history. In 2009, the Central Government increased women's quotas in local governing organs from 33 percent to 50 percent. In 2010, the upper house of India's parliament approved a bill to reserve a third of all seats in the lower house of the national parliament and state assemblies for women.

Dynastic transfer of power is one gateway for women into politics. The most prominent examples are India's first prime minister's daughter, Indira Gandhi, who became the country's first female prime minister, and Rajiv Gandhi's widow, Sonya Gandhi, who is the president of the Congress Party. Inheriting power does not necessarily constitute the female leader as only a representative of the men in her family, although there are also examples of such cases. Most famous of these is the illiterate Rabri Devi, who on several occasions acted as the chief minister of Bihar on behalf of her husband, when he was imprisoned for corruption.

Most of the present-day female leaders in India are elected to political leadership after they have already made a significant career in party organizations. For example, Sheila Dixit had a long career in the party and various women's organizations before she was elected the chief minister of Delhi. She led the Congress Party to election victory by emphasizing environmental issues, and during her rule she has focused on eradicating Delhi's pollution problems.

A former teacher, Mayawati Kumari is a professional politician who was elected as a chief minister in 1995 as India's youngest politician and the first *dalit* to hold the office. Mayawati Kumari has been in charge of the most populated state in India, Uttar Pradesh, for short periods and she returned as the chief minister during 2007–12.

Vasundhara Raje, a princess in a Rajasthani maharaja family, led the BJP to its greatest victory in the Rajasthan state elections in 2003 and was appointed as the chief minister. Vasundhara Raje learnt about politics from her mother, who was elected member of parliament after she was widowed. Before her election as chief minister, Vasundhara Raje had made a long political career as member of parliament herself, and as a minister in the BJP-led government. Vasundhara Raje, who has studied social sciences, ensured her party's phenomenal success by assigning a record number of female candidates who were chosen after a careful analysis of the electorate. Instead of her party's fundamentalist Hindu objectives, she concentrated her election campaign on developmental issues like bringing relief to the drought-stricken state and improving women's and *dalits'* position.

The erstwhile film star Jayalalithaa Jayaram, who was re-elected chief minister of Tamil Nadu in 2011, was helped into politics through her association with former chief minister of Tamil Nadu M. G. Ramachandan who also had been a popular film star before his political career—and they have co-starred in several films together. In spite of her controversial reputation, Jayalalithaa Jayaram has many administrative merits. Tamil Nadu, which has been governed by Jayalalithaa Jayaram on and off since 1989, is one of India's foremost centers of information technology and India's automotive industry; it was also able to resettle tsunami victims sooner than any other tsunami-struck state.

Jayalalithaa Jayaram is adored by her fans, but her personality cult also evokes opposition. At the peak of her power, her huge statues dominated the Chennai skyline, and Chennai buses carried her name. She has been accused of accepting bribes on several occasions. According to the BBC, police confiscated 24 kilograms of diamond-studded gold ornaments, over 10,000 saris and 750 pairs of shoes from her when she was arrested (BBC News, March 30, 2009). She made it into the Guinness Book of Records with the extravagant wedding party she arranged for her adopted son.

Uma Bharti, who was chief minister of Madhya Pradesh during 2003–4, is one of the most controversial and charismatic right-wing leaders in India. She belongs to a Lodh community, which is listed under "Other Backward Castes" (OBC) in Madhya Pradesh and comes from poor origins. She has taken her vows as a nun and dresses in the orange-colored garments of one. She openly supports fundamentalist Hindu aims such as banning cow slaughter and building the Ayodhya temple on the site of the demolished mosque. Bharti has been important for the BJP because she can appeal emotionally to the rural and urban poor in order to gain their support. She was expelled from the party in 2005 because of her conflict with party leaders over an appointment but returned to the BJP in 2011.

Mamata Banerjee rose to become one of the most powerful female leaders in India by defeating the Communist Party in West Bengal in both the parliamentary elections in 2009 and West Bengal state elections in 2011. Mamata Banerjee has a law degree and she comes from a poor neighborhood in Kolkata, where she joined the Congress party in the 1970s, rising fast into a prominent position in the party. She founded a new party, the All India Trinamul Congress, in 1997 to protest the Congress Party's deals with the ruling Communist Party in West Bengal. Mamata Banerjee's lively style and appeals to her supporters' moral sensibilities helped her to become the principal opposition force in West Bengal. She has taken full advantage of the ruling Communist Party's highly unpopular land acquisition policies as well as their authoritarian style of governing.

Although some of the abovementioned women leaders have a family background in politics, they do not function in politics as proxies for their families. Research on the political participation of rural women has also shown that although the family often influences and even supports the woman's decision to enter politics, this does not necessarily mean that she is merely a figurehead carrying out the wishes of the men in her family (Datta 2000). All the female political leaders emphasize the woman's perspective, although there is a wide range of difference in their views. Uma Bharti fosters the traditional Hindu fundamentalist concept of womanhood, while the other female leaders consciously fight for changes and improvement in women's position. They have all taken advantage of the meaning of womanhood in Hindu culture when building their political image. Since womanhood symbolizes tradition and moral purity for many Indians, women politicians have benefited from voters' disappointment in corrupt male politicians.

Indian women came forward and became visible in public activities for the first time when they joined the nationalistic movement. The movement had propagated the idea of women as the treasurers of the traditional

Hindu way of life at home as men adopted features of Western culture in the public arena. Consequently, women were encouraged to take part in politics, not for the purpose of changing their position but to uphold and maintain the core of Hinduism reinvented by nationalists. Forbes (1999) cites an illustrative example of women's role in the Independence movement: when a husband heard his wife had taken part in a demonstration, he congratulated her but at the same time rebuked her for not having asked for his permission first. The nationalist resolution of the women question still burdens the political participation of Indian women and most political organizations still have a women's wing which places more emphasis on preserving Hindu traditions than on women's own aims or developing possibilities for change. However, the spectrum of women's organizations in contemporary India is diverse and includes large-scale, determined work to improve women's position.

Female leaders in provincial governments represent only a fraction of the political activities of modern-day Indian women. Women's quotas were introduced to local administration in 1993. There are female leaders in 175 district *panchayats*, 2,000 women act as leaders in regional *panchayats* and 85,000 in village *panchayats*. In Kerala, Karnataka, Andhra Pradesh, Tamil Nadu and Madhya Pradesh, there have been more women in the local administration than the 33 percent prescribed by the law in 1993. There are also many all-women *panchayats* in India (Datta 2000).

In the village of Janta in West Bengal, women's entry into politics and *panchayats* happened without much opposition. As described earlier (see Chapter 5), politics is not understood as a separate sphere from the home and family but as a part of kinship and the domestic sphere. Consequently, raising women's concerns is not considered a major departure from the traditional concept of politics. But since the women's world is considered to be separate from that of men, women still do not participate in traditional, unofficial village meetings except as bystanders and listeners (Tenhunen 2003, 2009).

Women have organized themselves into women's committees under the Communist Party CPI-M in most parts of West Bengal. These committees resemble traditional village meetings insofar as the women settle village disputes and may impose fines as their sentences. Their latest activity centers on a micro-finance program based on women's self-help groups, in which women in addition to saving money advise and help each other in solving the problems of daily life. The savings are lent by turns to members for undertaking productive activities such as buying cattle. Women's committees defend women in family conflicts and foster awareness among women regarding women's rights, work which they call *jagaron*—awakening in Bengali.

The separate sphere excludes women from some of the decision making, but at the same time it promotes women's collaboration. As one of the Janta's first female *panchayat* members proclaims:

> We were six or seven women, always talking about our work. We never spoke much to men. Why should we be depending on men? We women try to raise funds for women. If I raised my opinion alone in the *panchayat,* nobody listened to me. So I talked to other female members and we surrounded the *panchayat* office in order to get funds for women. I demanded money for people who had lost their houses in floods, who had no clothes for the winter or whose roofs were leaking. I helped those who could not afford to educate their children or whose husbands had deserted them. After finishing secondary school, I thought I would like to do something. I was thinking of my sisters, my own life, the general welfare and that women should be able to move forward.

In the last few decades, the life of women in the countryside has changed but not radically, and gendered division of labor persists. The majority of marriages are arranged, and the dowry system prevails. However, women's education has improved considerably and nowadays practically all girls are sent to primary schools.

The few village women who have succeeded in educating themselves and securing government jobs present an encouraging example to others. The women are aware of the need for change, but they feel that in practice women's rights are best served not by radical action but by reforming the family and kinship. Janta's first woman representative describes the difficulties in bringing about these changes:

> We want to increase women's awareness. We tell them that they need not tolerate bad treatment. We explain to them that something can be done. Women are in no way less valuable than men. There are many rules in our communities to regulate the behavior of women. If women break these rules, men might get angry. They may even beat their women or maltreat them. I tell the women they should behave well as far as possible. They should try to accommodate. If your husband does something wrong, try to speak to him and guide him to do the right thing. Many women do this and they are better off than before.

In the past few decades, women's decision making in family affairs such as marriage arrangements has increased, and violence against women in the village has lessened. Participation in politics has widened women's sphere of activities—now they can legitimately educate themselves, attend meetings and even work outside their homes, which earlier was impossible particularly among the upper castes. Women in need of assistance from the *panchayat* find it easier to approach female representatives with their concerns.

Thanks to women's quotas in local governing organs, the same type of women's silent revolution is going on elsewhere in rural India, too. This movement is silent because, unlike the Maoist guerrillas' militant attacks, rural women seldom make the headlines in the press and also because the ongoing changes are not radical. However, even the silent reforms in family life are significant to women, and the small improvements may culminate in bigger changes in the future. Many women who did not receive the benefits of these new freedoms in their own lives are concentrating on guaranteeing a better childhood, education and a carefully arranged marriage for their own daughters.

## 6.5 Conclusion

Even though all the main political parties are unanimous about the need for economic reforms, Indian politics is not devoid of alternatives. The Congress Party now rules as part of a coalition and, unlike during its earlier rule, it has faced stiff electoral competition from such parties as the BSP and BJP which have grown into pan-Indian parties. This new political situation has contributed to the Congress Party's emphasis on the inclusive growth.

Parliamentary elections of 2009 revealed both the Left Front and the BJP as weakened. Both are faced with the challenge to renew themselves and create a positive agenda that appeals to voters in an era in which lower castes prefer to ascertain their rights within their own parties instead of through the patronage offered by upper-caste-dominated parties. New economic opportunities are likely to reduce feelings of displacement among the middle and upper classes, so strong economic growth could reduce the appeal of the BJP among the upper classes.

India's emerging political pluralism has strengthened its democracy. Although it has been criticized for its greater restrictions on entrepreneurship, foreign trade and investments compared to China, Indian democracy has brought stability both to India's economy and to its foreign policy, strengthening its ability to face crises peacefully. In comparison, while the Chinese government is also interested in diminishing inequalities, the lack of democracy makes it more difficult for the Chinese government to listen to its citizens and to forestall brewing problems.

# Chapter 7

# POPULATION GIANT

India is a country of large numbers. United Nations Department of Economic and Social Affairs, Population Division (2011) has estimated that after 2028 there will be more people living in India than in China—making India the most populated country in the world. In the census of 2011, the total population was 1.2 billion, meaning that more than every sixth person in the world was an Indian. Population growth has become slower in the last few decades (currently at 1.64 percent annually), but when we are dealing with large numbers like these, the annual increase is huge—about 17 million people per year. The good news in the 2011 census was that in the decade from 2001 to 2011 there was a lower net addition in population than the previous decade. A similar situation but in a smaller scale is shared in all the nations of South Asia, except in Sri Lanka which reached lower level of fertility long ago and where population growth has stabilized. The shared basic principles of patrilineal kinship and colonial legacies explain the similarity of demographic and reproductive health challenges in South Asian, particularly in the northern parts of the subcontinent.

Is population growth a cause for developmental problems in India or is it more accurate to conceptualize it as a consequence of inability of Indian society to develop? In the UN Population Conference of 1974, the Indian representative formulated the socialist-influenced basic principle of population policy: "Development is the best contraceptive." The originator of this slogan, Dr. Karan Singh, later felt he had been misunderstood and added, "Contraception is the best development." These two sentences embody the reproductive health and population policy dilemma of many developing countries today, as well as the two approaches to the population question. On the one hand, it is a demographic given that improvements in welfare, the decrease of abject poverty and rises in the level of education almost automatically lead to lower fertility and thus social and economic development is followed by lower fertility levels and controlled population growth. On the other hand, the developing countries just cannot sit and wait for economic progress and increased equality to restrain population growth, because a rapid rise in population in itself is an obstacle to social, and arguably also economic, development that devours a nation's public resources. In a changing socio-economic milieu, those who keep on having many children, tend to lose out as their strategies no longer produce beneficial effects for them at an individual or household level. Reproductive health needs particular attention for global, national and local policy-makers to be able to respond swiftly to the widely emerging interest to limit the number of children in families in developing societies.

Even though policy-makers have an interest in the number of children women give birth to, political bodies should direct their interest more to people's needs than to macro-level phenomena. Childbearing is an intimate, important choice for an individual and a family, and any outside manipulation here is questionable. The sixteenth article of Proclamation of Teheran of the United Nations 1968 International Conference on Human Rights states, "Parents have a basic human right to determine freely and responsibly the number and the spacing of their children." In reproductive health and rights policies, the common interests of society and the human right to self-determination should be articulated simultaneously.

Given the sheer size of the Indian national population and the population prospects, how can society ensure economic and social progress and confidence in a better future? Constantly swelling numbers inevitably bring with them growing demands for food, water, education and health services, in addition to the need for raw materials, energy and the ecological burden. In the following, we examine the Indian attempts to control its population situation and describe the advances and setbacks in the sphere of reproductive health.

The demographic situation in India is only intelligible in the context of gender relations and the inequity between men and women, young and old; consequently, gender is of crucial importance when we examine the demographic present and future of India. Addressing reproductive health issues and the gender bias within them has direct bearing on families' ability to thrive and to get out of poverty, and thus on overall developmental goals. Following the capabilities perspective on development (see Chapter 1), we consider how reproductive rights and people's opportunities to make conscious choices concerning procreation are ensured or ruled out in Indian society.

## 7.1 Indian Population Will Increase for Decades

Despite the slowing rate of annual increase, the population is expected to continue to grow for decades. The United Nations presents three different scenarios for population growth. Even the lowest, less-probable scenario would mean a population of 1.47 billion in 2045 (see Fig. 7.1). Whatever the increase, it is quite probable that the Indian population will grow *at least* by 300 million from the present population figures and most probably by around half a billion. The causes of this future population growth will be examined below.

**Figure 7.1.** Three population projections for India

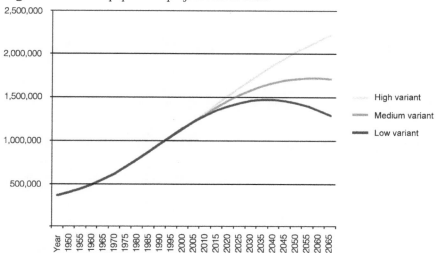

Source: United Nations Department of Economic and Social Affairs, Population Division (2011).

Along with the attention paid to the huge national population, it is important to recognize the vast geographical size of the Indian nation. In the 2011 census, the population density was 382 persons per square kilometer, which is higher than in Belgium. Neighboring Bangladesh suffers a much more extreme situation—three times as many people per square kilometer live there compared to India. The population is distributed relatively unevenly so that coastal areas and the great fertile plains surrounding river valleys manifest high population density while the Deccan Plateau in the middle of the subcontinent and hilly or mountainous regions are rather sparsely populated (see Fig 7.2). Unlike in many other Third World countries, in India the great majority still live in rural areas. More than two in three Indians live in villages, while only less than one in three in urban settings. This reduces the local concentration of people even in the most densely populated states. For example in Kerala, which is among the most densely populated states with a population of 33 million in 2011, no megacities exist. The majority of the population lives is contiguous large villages or small or medium-sized towns.

Population growth will continue in India in the future through the combined effect of the above-replacement level of births, declining death rate and lack of massive emigration. Although people still live much shorter lives than in affluent societies, the average life expectancy has risen in the last few decades due to improved health care, sanitation and nutrition. A child born in India in 2011 has a life expectancy of 67 years, whereas in 1955 it was barely

**Figure 7.2.** India's population density visualized in an annual composite of night-time lights from 2003; the most densely populated areas are around Kolkata, in the southern state of Kerala and in the areas around Mumbai and Delhi

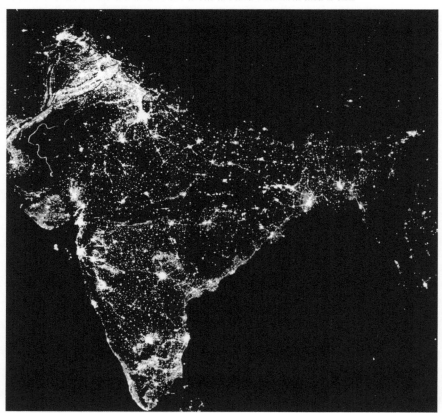

Source: Courtesy of NOAA/NESDIS/National Geophysical Data Center.

39 years. As people live longer lives and fewer children die, an ever-larger mass of people are living simultaneously, thus swelling the population. Longer life expectancy is an outcome of increased well-being and health, and thus is desirable irrespective of its influence on population growth.

Migration, both emigration and immigration, is another factor that has an influence on national populations. Indians left the subcontinent in great numbers in earlier centuries and they now form one of the largest ethnic minority groups outside of South Asia. Indian diasporas have a long history, beginning with the great influence of ancient Hindu civilizations in Southeast Asia and merchants settling in East Africa and the Arabian peninsula, continuing in the colonial times in the form of indentured contract workers transferred from the subcontinent to the Caribbean, Mauritius, Fiji, and East and South Africa, among other areas. These emigrant groups have retained much of their Indian ethnic identities throughout the centuries. More recently, people from the subcontinent have left for the colonial metropolis, as well as to other European countries, the United States and Australia, as well as to the Gulf area, mainly as labor migrants, students or following family members. People of Indian origin are among the largest migrant populations in the world; in 2005, the Indian government estimated that the community of Indian migrants and their descendants numbered approximately 25 million (Naujoks 2009). However, emigration from the country has not been extensive enough to have had any significant effect on its population growth. Immigration to India exists, particularly from the neighboring Bangladesh and Nepal, but the numbers are insignificant in terms of population growth.

The most important factor behind the continuously swelling population in India is an in-built mechanism deriving from the structure of the population. Even if the women of India were from now on to give birth to only two children on average, thereby only reproducing their own generation, the population would inevitably continue to grow for the next 50 years. This is because in addition to the rise in life expectancy, the proportion of women of childbearing age in the population is so large. Only 20 percent of the current population growth is caused by the desire to have more than two children, whereas 20 percent is accounted for by unwanted pregnancies and 60 percent by the large number of women of fertile age (Visaria 2002). This means that even if the nation managed to provide appropriate contraceptive methods that averted the unplanned 20 percent of births, and could convince everyone to decrease their preferences to two children, the population would still grow considerably. As long as people are not pressured or forced to decrease family size to one child, the projected 60 percent of the current growth will continue. A one-child policy in the manner of China is hardly an alternative for democratic India as it would be considered monstrous by most people, thus India's only option is to learn to cope with its growing population and to do its best to deliver to its citizens the means to control their reproduction according to their own determinations. Coercive fertility control was trialed for a period of a few years in 1970s, but the results were very discouraging both from the democratic and the demographic perspective (see below).

Attention to the population numbers alone is considered by many critical thinkers, particularly feminist scholars and activists both in India and abroad, damaging and imprudent. Since the 1994 UN Population and Development Conference in Cairo, it has become widely accepted that governments should turn their attention from population policy to the sexual and reproductive health and rights (SRHR) policies. Instead of paying attention to the sheer numbers and figuring out how to control people, governments should consider how to ensure that people are able to make decisions concerning procreation and sexuality and have accessible and acceptable means for carrying out their own procreative will. Reproductive rights derive from basic human rights to self-determination. The most important acknowledgement in the global Cairo consensus was that women's empowerment and gender equity are essential prerequisites for development and for solving the population problem. In India as elsewhere, the attention paid by some demographers, administrators and politicians on numbers and population control has been generally been incommensurable with the activists' and concerned scholars' perspective on rights of women and generally of the disadvantaged. Although probably no scholar fails to recognize the undesirability of the current population growth, these two perspectives lead to rather different policy recommendations and practical solutions. The last decade has witnessed a recurring international interest in family planning and contraception; it has been recognized that family planning needs more attention and should not be treated simply as one among many reproductive health prerogatives.

## 7.2 The Potential Advantage and Burden of Population Growth

The population scenario in India is not altogether somber and without some developmental advantages. In India, the ratio of working age population to children and the aged—i.e. the dependency ratio—will remain favorable for economic growth for a long time to come and this may prove to be an asset in global economic competition if the government manages to improve the population's educational level. In 2020, the average Indian will be much younger—29 years old—than the average Chinese or American (37 years), European (45) or Japanese (48) (Chandrasekhar, Ghosh and Roychowdhury 2006). The dependency ratio in India is currently 0.6 and according to the population projection by the Planning Commission (Office of the Registrar General 2006), it will remain around this level until at least 2026. Of the total population, 63 percent are of the working age (15 to 59 years of age).

The fast decline in fertility has created a "demographic window of opportunity" which will improve the dependency ratio for at least 40 years. This may result in a positive situation for the economy, to raise savings and encourage investment when a relatively smaller part of the national income needs to be put aside for children's education, old age and health care. Also women are able to join the labor force in larger numbers when they are less tied down with pregnancy, childbirth and sole responsibility for childcare in a patriarchal society. The estimates show that nearly one-third of the economic boom of the last decades in East Asia can be attributed to the benefit of the demographic dividend (James 2008); the same effect was seen in the Euro-American societies when the post-war baby boom generation reached working age.

Can India repeat the process witnessed in other East Asian societies? Researchers do not share a singular view on the situation. For C. P. Chandrasekhar, Jayati Ghosh and Anamitra Roychowdhury (2006), positive outcome is far from self-evident. They state that if the policy environment does to improve the employability and health of the population, no positive effect will be reaped from this "demographic window of opportunity." They end with the blunt conclusion that "[i]f the economy does not generate adequate employment of a sufficiently attractive nature, the demographics could deliver not a dividend but anarchy" (2006, 5,061). However, some researchers are far more positive. K. S. James's (2008) analysis leads to the conclusion that the boom in the working age group population will have a powerful positive impact on economic growth, irrespective of low educational achievements, poor health conditions or a slackened pace of employment creation.

Despite the disagreement among academicians concerning the economic benefits of the demographic dividend, it appears as safe to say that in order to reap the full benefits of the emerging situation, the educational, health and employment sectors need serious public attention. Even without additional investments in these sectors, the youthful population bulge is bound to create at least some positive effects for the Indian economy. The weakening of the dependency ratio will start to become topical in India little by little only after 2025 (Dyson 2004). In this respect, India is in a better position than China which has reaped the economic benefits of the demographic dividend.

Irrespective of whether the stable Indian population will be over or under 1.5 billion around 2050, one of the most crucial concerns facing India's future is the sufficiency of food (see Chapter 9 on productivity of agriculture). Although India reached self-sufficiency in food grain production largely thanks to the Green Revolution which has boosted the productivity since the 1970s, during the last decade food grain production has grown annually slower than the population (Office of the Registrar General 2011b). A recent projection of future food grains demand and supply came to the conclusion that the domestic supply of rice and pulses will not be able to cover the demand of the growing population in India and the gap is bound to grow from 2012 onwards (Vishwakarma 2012). According to this projection, the sufficiency of wheat production in turn has better prospects. This would suggest that India will need to import rice in near future.

The productivity of agriculture in India would have to grow much faster than it has done in recent decades if India wants to retain its self-sufficiency in food grains. The most critical issue in boosting productivity, particularly in water-intensive rice cultivation, is the availability of water. Water resources cannot increase on the same scale as population, so water resources must be utilized efficiently and innovatively (see Chapter 11). As global food production, particularly rice production, is expected to be severely affected by global warming in years to come, and the world market price of food grains has become unstable, the future of food sufficiency to the growing population in India is bound to raise serious concerns. Even if the Indian national economy experiences a fast growth that will make importing food grains a less threatening reality, the global food grain market will be heavily influenced by the growing demand that Indian consumers will create. Adding to the picture are the potentially changing dietary patterns that are bound to raise meat consumption even in India, despite the high prestige granted to vegetarianism. The unpredictability of the future of the global food market becomes even more evident.

The fact that population growth is greatest in the economically poor and socially deprived parts of the country aggravates regional tensions within the nation. It also encourages domestic migration, particularly from the northern plains towards economically vibrant centers such as Greater Mumbai. In Maharashtra, this has led to rise of local political movements and eruptions of violence against labor migrants from the north. Such regionalization and ethnicization of politics may be one concomitant of the demographically and economically imbalanced regional development in the country.

## 7.3 No Single Explanation behind High or Declining Total Fertility

How did India end up with its huge present-day national population? Have politicians, administrators and citizens lacked consciousness of the situation or willingness to do anything about it? In order to influence the population situation, some understanding of the underlying factors behind population growth is necessary. Extensive demographic research has been carried out in India; however, no widely shared consensus exists on the causes of high fertility in some areas of the country or the fertility decline in some others.

The tradition of having many children has been rationalized in various ways and has been constitutive to a kin-based society such as found in rural India (see e.g. Jeffery, Jeffery and Lyon 1989). Child mortality has been perennial and it has been thought better to have numerous children to secure the survival of at least some offspring. Children are needed as a workforce at home, in the fields, in family business or as wage labor. Having many children has brought esteem and influence in village communities to their fathers, mothers and whole families. Children, particularly sons, are the only security for old age or when illness, widowhood or other misfortune hits. Despite these rationalizations which have not altogether lost their relevance, the number of children has decreased considerably, beginning with educated, affluent town dwellers and lately also among indigent rural families and farmers in many parts of the country.

From a classical demographic perspective, India has entered the process of demographic transition relatively late, due to slow decline in child mortality which has reflected slow economic and social development. In the classical demographic transition model (see e.g. Caldwell et al. 2006), a pre-industrial population first experiences a decline in child mortality, then has a period of very fast population growth as fertility still remains at a high level, and finally fertility declines when society is fully industrialized and society enters a period of slow population growth. Many demographers believe that the process of fertility decline is basically inevitable and largely irreversible after the decline in child mortality has started. Although this "traditional" form of demographic transition theory has been widely criticized, many researchers still firmly believe that economic development is the key to population transition, because without it decline in child mortality is difficult to realize. There are nevertheless also many critical voices, and the case of India and its widely varying regional population models poses an interesting case.

The main factor affecting demographic transition is fertility: the average number of children to which women give birth. Despite the traditional expectation of giving birth to several children,[1] particularly sons, average number of children that Indian women give birth to has lately declined considerably. The probable number of births per Indian woman in her reproductive life span (total fertility rate, TFR) varies greatly by region, and is generally lower in the south and west than in the north. According to the census figures released in 2011, the total fertility rate in India is 2.6 children per woman (Office of the Registrar General 2011). In the southern states, the total fertility rate is quite low; for example, in Andhra Pradesh and Kerala it is 1.8 children which is as low as, say, Finland in Europe (International Institute for Population Sciences and Macro International 2007). The other south Indian states, Karnataka and Tamil Nadu, have similarly low fertility rates across all socio-economic groups, and the situation in the western states of Maharashtra and Gujarat is close behind, approaching net reproduction rate of 2.1 children per woman.

The north Indian Hindi-speaking states (Bihar, Madhya Pradesh, Rajasthan and Uttar Pradesh) represent the other end of the spectrum with markedly higher fertility figures: women tend to have around 3 to 4 births on average. Other areas fall somewhere in between the extremes of the "Hindi belt" and

---

1 "May you be a mother of a hundred sons" is a common form of well-wishing to a newly married wife.

the southern states, although even in the northern Hindi Belt fertility has declined, albeit much more slowly in rural than in urban areas. The "Hindi belt" is the most populous region of India and thus plays an important role in determining the demographic future of the country. The population of the most populous state Uttar Pradesh is nearly 200 million, more than in Brazil.

The explanations of the regional differences in fertility have long attracted the interest of demographers and other social scientists. Economic theories fail to account for the differences, as economic parameters in regions do not incontrovertibly differ according to total fertility levels. The wealthiest state, Punjab, has a fairly low total fertility level in Indian terms, while the southern states that are doing best in terms of fertility rates have had only average performance in economic terms. If we look at the socio-economic differences in fertility within states, it is evident that the poor in Tamil Nadu have lower total fertility than the better off in Bihar. Social and economic fertility differentials have diminished and in south India have almost disappeared. There even the less educated, landless laborers mostly opt for only two children.

Some researchers (e.g. Dyson and Moore 1983) hypothesize that the differences in childbearing between regions are linked to women's relatively better social and economic position in the south and generally better social welfare, educational levels and more equitable economic development. South Indian Hindu women have traditionally been economically active in the labor force, which has been thought to relatively strengthen their influence in family negotiations. Women have an important role in rice cultivation in southern and eastern India; whereas in the north, in those areas where wheat is the predominant staple grown, especially higher- and middle-caste women generally do not work in the fields as day laborers, nor do they till their family's own soil. Marriages between cousins and other affines and within the same village are allowed and even encouraged among the Hindus in the south, unlike in the north, where the young Hindu bride begins her married life in the husband's home among strangers, far away from her natal village. In the southern states, women's literacy is much more prevalent than in the northern states and women's movements outside their homes and families are less overtly restricted by the demands of *parda* (literally veiling, referring to the need to control interaction with unrelated males). This is visible in the fact that southern Hindu women mostly do not cover their head in public unlike in the north. Women's educational level is among the most frequently mentioned factors that tend to co-vary with regional fertility levels. However, some demographic research has also challenged this rather common sense explanation and brought up some other aspects, such as the diffusion of the small family norm (see Guilmoto and Irudaya Rajan 2005), and new temporal orientations toward the future and social and political reform, even among those living in poverty (Säävälä 2001a).

All in all, it is practically impossible to point out any one definitive factor behind differences in fertility decline; the process is engendered by different factors in different contexts (see Säävälä 2010b).

Fieldwork conducted by Minna Säävälä in the southern state of Andhra Pradesh in mid-1990s indicated that reproductive aspirations and practices had already radically changed from the traditional Indian model (Säävälä 2001a) (see Fig. 7.3). A steep decline in fertility in a rural setting was based on both economic and socio-cultural, even political changes. Villagers had become aware of the adverse effect of land fragmentation when agricultural land is divided among several sons, generation after generation; having as many sons as possible was no longer considered desirable for a landowning family. As well, both the educated and the illiterate had come to realize the huge importance of schooling in present-day India and they considered it essential to do their best to provide their offspring with some education. For a family of many children, securing education was difficult because it is costly in practice, even in government schools that are basically gratis. Furthermore, children had started to create many other kinds of expenditures for the household: the cost of health care, dressing them neatly, giving them good nutrition. Even the poorest of the poor in Gopalapalli, the fieldwork *panchayat* (local administrative area), realized that their children should not have to reprise their parents' miserable living conditions; that they had the right to a better life. This transformation in the horizon of expectations and aspirations is a political phenomenon in a hierarchical caste society, and it explains the reduction in the number of offspring better than rational and economic cost and benefit calculations that demographic theories tend to offer. If and when an effective, accessible and acceptable contraceptive method is available—such as female sterilization—the women of Gopalapalli, like elsewhere in India, are usually eager to adopt it.

The power balance between sexes and generations has its own effect on the practice of family planning. Everywhere in India the older generation and the males have a legitimate authority to rule over young married women in questions of childbearing. Mothers-in-law are commonly the powerful figures who rule in the household or family. The young daughter-in-law is expected to give birth to the offspring soon after marriage and to secure the male heirs of the kin group. It is also in the interest of the young woman to prove herself in childbearing because failure to give birth to a son would lead to her marginalization within the family and later, to old age insecurity. After marriage the young couple usually lives at least a few years with the husband's parents, often sharing the household with other patrilineal relatives as well. In principle, the new wife has to subject herself to the will of her mother-in-law,

**Figure 7.3.** Gopalapalli, the fieldwork area of Minna Säävälä in Southern India

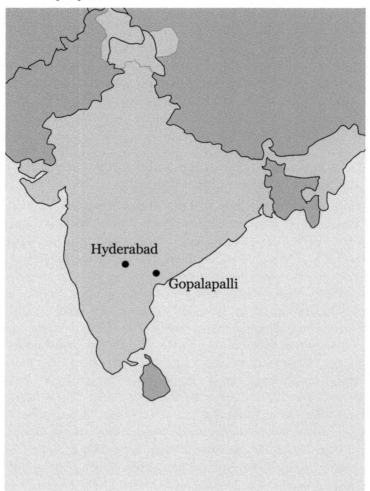

especially in the early stages of the marriage when important reproductive decisions are made.

Nevertheless reality does not correspond neatly to the ideal picture of how family relations are thought to be arranged. In spite of the legitimacy of the elders' and males' domination, in south Indian Gopalapalli young brides at times took the matter of contraception into their own hands, as many of them wanted to have fewer children than their mothers-in-law expected. In the study area, some rural men wanted to have more children than their wives, but the majority of them shared their wife's ideas on a smaller family.

The predominant method of contraception available in India is female sterilization, a practically irrevocable operation. According to the National Family Health Survey of 2005–6, more than half of Indian women in their 30s and 40s are sterilized (International Institute for Population Sciences and Macro International 2007). Young women in Gopalapalli see this irreversibility as mostly positive, even though it has some inherent dangers: if some of their children should die they will be unable to replace them, plus the operation itself has medical risks as it is often carried out in clinics that offer substandard hygiene and equipment. Nonetheless, when young wives in south India visit their parents, they may choose the occasion to have a sterilization operation—sometimes even without the knowledge of their mother-in-law, yet with the support and care of their own mothers. Once a woman is sterilized, the operation is virtually impossible to undo, whatever the mother-in-law or anyone else may say. In some Gopalapalli families, this independence of decision making has precipitated serious quarrels, sometimes even resulting in the banishment of the young woman to her natal home. This latter state of affairs is usually temporary, however; the sterilized woman is the mother of children in the affinal home and sooner or later she will be reconciled with her in-laws.

The situation for Gopalapalli young daughters-in-law shows how south Indian women have a rather different decision-making power than in some other parts of the country. In south India, kin structures take the mother's side more into account than elsewhere in India. A married couple with children tends to move to live on their own and separate from the older generation and/or husband's siblings earlier in the south than in north India. A study on male involvement in reproductive health issues in the starkly patrilineal and patrilocal setting of Madhya Pradesh in central India, for example, shows that there women still yield to the power of the mother-in-law in decisions concerning female sterilization. However, even there, the couple tended to have more say in their decisions on using temporary contraception like pills or condoms (Char 2011).

The case of Gopalapalli shows that, in the south, women have an interest in family planning if acceptable services are available; the kin structures give them opportunities to act according to their own wishes. As the health services in Gopalapalli function relatively reliably for India, this has enabled the women of the village to opt for fewer children than most of their northern sisters. The pattern of women's fertility in India (also evident in Gopalapalli) is very different from that in many other countries: women marry early and begin childbearing immediately so that a third of 19-year-olds in India have already either given birth or are pregnant; children are born in relatively quick succession and women then have themselves sterilized at an early age.

The effective reproductive span (difference between mean age at marriage and sterilization) is only 6.4 years (Sample Registration System 2007).

## 7.4 National Population Policy and Reproductive Health Services

The predominance of female sterilization as a contraceptive method has its own rationale and demographic history in India. Population growth and family planning have been politically critical and sensitive subjects in India since the 1950s. Elites have been concerned about population expansion for decades; among letters to the editor in the English-Indian press one can regularly find acidic comments on population issues and sometimes demands for coercive solutions. Many middle-class people actually openly express their respect for the initiative of China's Communist Party dictatorship to regulate childbirths with enforced legislation.

The darkest moments of Indian population control were seen towards the end of the 1970s under the state of emergency declared by prime minister Indira Gandhi. Democratic rights were curtailed, the press was censored and Mrs. Gandhi's political opponents were imprisoned. Sterilization campaigns directed at Indian men were also introduced at the same time, whereby men were enticed along to sterilization camps and municipal officials were given sterilization quotas which had to be met in each administrative area. There were reports of men being bribed to undergo sterilization with the promise of a transistor radio, without their proper knowledge of the effect of the operation. Both old and young were sterilized to fulfill the quotas; some were even sterilized twice. Unarguably, the realization of the program was, at worst, a violation of human rights; at best, politically questionable. The campaign soon aroused protest and the disapproval it incurred was an important factor in Mrs. Gandhi's electoral loss in the free elections she called after ending the emergency. Since then, no politician has been prepared to actively target men's reproductive capacities again, despite the medical fact that male sterilization is a less risky and demanding operation than female sterilization.

At the moment, male sterilization is a marginal method of contraception, and the use of condoms remains likewise relatively unpopular despite the government's attempts to popularize their use in order to prevent the spread of HIV. In recent years, the government's family planning program has endeavored to market non-scalpel vasectomy, with poor results. Controlling population growth remained a top priority after the emergency, however, and during the 1980s government family planning services were directed towards promoting female sterilizations, which the majority of Indians find to be a culturally acceptable contraceptive method—although Muslims have a more reserved attitude to the procedure. Furthermore, female sterilization was considered an administratively attractive method of contraception to advance because it could be closely monitored. As a legacy of the state of emergency, the principal instruments of government policies to control population growth were "targets": each administrative unit was allotted explicit numerical targets for female sterilization and the adoption of intra-uterine contraceptive devices (IUDs), condoms or oral contraceptive pills. Every month local health workers had to persuade a stipulated number of women to undergo sterilization, otherwise they and their superiors would suffer cuts in income and other penalties. In order to facilitate persuasion, women undergoing sterilization were paid a small amount of cash as compensation for the loss of daily earnings due to the operation and a subsequent period of recovery.

A turning point in the implementation of these kinds of population control policies in India came with the UN Population and Development Conference of 1994 in Cairo: during this crucial meeting a worldwide consensus was reached concerning the basic principles which should govern population policies and reproductive health and rights. People's needs and the right to self-determination were declared to be paramount principles everywhere, with population control and administrative objectives rendered secondary. The system of sterilization targets was obviously contrary to this approach: it was bureaucratic and based not on people's needs but on the aspirations of the Indian government and consequently the target approach came to an end in 1996. In the spirit of the Cairo conference resolutions, the Central Government renounced its annual targets of sterilizations and distribution of temporary contraceptives which, since the 1960s, had guided and motivated the persuasive efforts of local health workers and aroused the international and national disapproval of activists and scholars. Fulfilling the targets did not, in practice, work well administratively either: it could lead to falsification of statistics and bribery, because the main aim was to show on paper that the administration had been "efficient." Meanwhile, costly contraceptives like IUDs could simply be thrown away rather than put to their proper purpose, in order that stocks could be seen to conform to what appeared in the statistics.

Following the Central Government's new policy, the state governments—which are relatively autonomous in their implementation and formulation of family health policies—gradually stopped demanding the fulfillment of regional, method-specific targets which caused a decline in the Couple Protection Rate,[2] as there was no longer any need to tamper with the statistics. However, although the targets were officially relinquished by the Central

---

2   Couple Protection Rate is the proportion of married couples who use contraception.

Government in 1996, they still influence the practical work of officials in some states who may use them to direct the actions of health workers and doctors at the village level. Although the official National Population Policy of 2000 affirms the commitment of government towards voluntary and informed choice and consent of citizens while availing of reproductive health care services, and continuation of the target free approach in administering family planning services, this encouraging principle has not been fully realized by all states and districts. The most serious factor that undermines the commitment of the national and state governments to secure informed reproductive choice of couples is the sole reliance on female sterilization. In practice, health workers do not even offer any alternative contraceptive method. For example, in Andhra Pradesh, where female sterilization is so widespread that two-thirds of women in the reproductive age group are sterilized, only 14 percent of the sterilized women reported that they had been informed about other potential contraceptive methods by health worker (in International Institute for Population Sciences and Macro International 2008).

Besides the targets, the use of incentives as an instrument of population policy has also met with much criticism as it was suggested that cash compensations might entice indigent women to adopt sterilization or another form of contraception against their better interests. There is, however, no evidence that incentives have had a major influence on female decision making with regards contraception, and fieldwork in an area of very high sterilization prevalence indicated that monetary compensation was a marginal factor in choosing the operation, even among women living in material deprivation (Säävälä 2001a). The operation makes physical labor impossible for a number of days if not weeks and the monetary compensation was not even enough to feed the family during the recovery period. In some states, for example in Kerala and Tamil Nadu, monetary compensation for sterilization or the insertion of an IUD has long since been discontinued. The current National Population Program presents various incentives and rewards whereby state governments and local administration are encouraged to try to redirect childbearing decisions towards the postponement of marriage, lengthening the interval between pregnancies and being satisfied with only daughters, although the practical realization of these schemes cannot be very successful until a ubiquitous civil registration of vital events (births, marriages and deaths) is established. One of India's most prominent demographers, the late Pravin Visaria estimated before his death in 2001 that it would take 15 to 20 years or more to attain the goal of 100 percent registration in the country. In 2008, two-thirds of births were registered, according to the Registrar General of India, and the national goal of reaching full registration by 2010 was not realized. A much smaller proportion of children receive a birth certificate, and this remains one of the important issues campaigned for by the UNICEF among others.

Female sterilization continues to be the number one contraceptive method in India. In rural areas, everyone knows who is sterilized and who is not, as it has become one of the socially shared turning points of the female lifecycle. Other means of family planning, referred to as "spacing methods," are used by relatively few, although the number is growing somewhat, particularly in some states and urban areas. Condoms are more popular in the cities than in the countryside, while oral contraceptives and the IUD are more common with the affluent and the educated. Temporary contraceptive methods are not supported by sufficient health care facilities and personnel in rural areas for clients to cope with the possible side effects and complications, which reduce their attraction. Traditional methods like abstinence, coitus interruptus and traditional herbal preparations are also known and still used in some areas.

Male sterilization experienced such a huge backlash in the 1970s that its use is practically non-existent at present. Negative attitudes towards male sterilization reflect a perceived danger to a man's virility and life and it is often confused with castration, losing one's manhood. Women feel that it is their duty to sacrifice themselves and their bodies for the welfare of the family, and men have been secondary in the implementation of the governmental family planning program. A rural 32-year-old man in Madhya Pradesh said to a researcher:

If I get it done, people will laugh at me and say, "Why are you doing the women's thing?" (Quoted in Char, Säävälä and Kulmala 2009)

The need to involve men in reproductive health issues has been recognized internationally and also in the Indian population policy. However, the actual grassroots health services have not been actively encouraging men to take responsibility in family planning and to carry their part of the burden.

The majority of women's sterilizations are done in small health centers under the public health system. The standards of the health services vary throughout the country. In some places, they work relatively efficiently and the quality of care is satisfactory; in others, services are practically non-existent or operations unhygienic and sloppily conducted, leading to common complications such as infections and failed sterilizations. It is evident that the health care system has not been able to respond to people's need for family planning; the desired number of children is lower than the actual number of children born to people, showing the prevalence of unwanted pregnancies. Also pregnancies that occur too soon after the birth of the previous child are common, proving the unmet need for temporary contraceptive methods.

Longer birth intervals are desirable from the perspective of the mother's and the children's health and they also would slow the annual population increase.

## 7.5 From Population Control towards Family Welfare

India's official demographic policies affect the life of every citizen because these regulate the availability of reproductive health services—not only contraception, but also pre- and post-natal care, safe delivery, treatment of sexually transmitted diseases, menstrual and other gynecological problems, vaccinations and infertility treatment. Besides services directly related to reproduction, population policies relate to larger strategies that affect, for example, expenditure utilized for girls' education and even such issues as conditions set for those who aspire to political assignments and governmental jobs.

Even though coercion was used in India to attempt to control the growth of population for a short while towards the end of the 1970s, the current situation is much brighter with regard to human rights than in China, where couples are limited having one child in urban areas. The Chinese policy is possible only in totalitarianism, whereas India is a democratic country where elected representatives have to face media coverage and political responsibility for their decisions, at least in principle. Therefore it is not possible to control the great majority with regulations that are seen as blatantly unjust. Even with all its faults, since the end of 1990s the national population policy of India has aspired to take into consideration not only the common good but also the reproductive rights of individuals.

Even though India's population policies nowadays clearly excise all coercive measures to limit childbirths, many states enacted laws in the beginning of this millennium which run counter to these principles. In India, the population policy is under the Central Government, while family policies, health and other welfare services fall to the state governments. In practice, the state governments do not necessarily follow guidelines laid down by the Central Government. Despite the national rejection of coercive population policies, some states that have large populations (Madhya Pradesh and Rajasthan, for example) have enacted laws that politically penalize couples having more than two children. Their rights to stand as candidates for local elections or apply for public jobs have been forfeited. If a third child is born to a person acting as a democratic representative in the local *panchayat* (municipal council), she or he has to vacate his or her seat.

Reproductive health services and concomitant policies define in a very tangible way living conditions for all Indian women and men. At the extreme end, the maintenance or neglect of reproductive health services is reflected in maternal mortality: does every woman preparing for delivery also have to prepare for potential loss of life? Or can she rely confidently on the availability of adequate resources if problems arise during childbirth? Maternal mortality at present is estimated at 254 deaths per 100,000 childbirths, or roughly one death per 400 deliveries (Sample Registration System 2009), although much higher estimates have also been presented. Regions vary greatly: maternal mortality rates are much higher in the Hindi-speaking north and northeast Indian states.

As family health services have concentrated on limiting births, especially through female sterilization, many other essential services have been left undeveloped. Maternal mortality is a clear reflector of women's position in society; the figures tend to be high in places where less value is placed on women's lives and this remains one of the most significant barriers to reducing maternal mortality throughout the country. The Central Government is paying special attention to this issue as it is one of the UN Millennium Development Goals to reduce by three-quarters maternal mortality between 1990 and 2015. Since 2005, a program called Janani Suraksha Yojana has been attracting women to give birth in public institutions. The program is a conditional cash transferral scheme that offers a woman from below a poverty-level household, as well as the local health worker who enrolls her to do so, considerable monetary incentives if she gives birth to first and/or second children in a health institution. There is preliminary evidence that this program has managed to considerably raise the proportion of deliveries attended by qualified medical personnel, at least in the states of Uttar Pradesh and Bihar (Khan 2012).

The governmental project to bring institutionalized delivery services to poor women is helping to reduce the risks of childbirth. Providing contraception, particularly temporary contraceptive methods to young married and unmarried women in order to cover unmet need for contraception in India would help to reduce maternal mortality considerably. WHO has estimated that fulfilling the unmet need for contraception would globally lower maternal mortality by one-third (Gupta 2012). Most important, however, would be an attitudinal change in gender relations: women's true worth needs to be recognized so that they are protected in crisis situations, and certainly not be allowed to die because of preventable complications in childbirths. This still remains a distant goal in gender-imbalanced India. Women routinely receive poorer nutrition than men, suffering from anemia, and are less literate; more than one married woman in three has been subject to domestic violence, which is considered even by the majority of women as justified towards a disobedient wife (International Institute for Population Sciences and Macro International 2007); and in some states still the majority of girls marry below the legal age of 18 years, which reduces their capabilities to determine their own health and well-being. The lower value attributed to the female sex is a given in India, even though the position of women greatly improves when they age.

## 7.6 Discrimination against the Girl Child

India, along with the other "population billionaire" China, is infamous of being a hotbed of discrimination against the girl child in the form of sex-selective abortion: abortion of female fetuses after sex detection by ultrasound. The number of boys and girls is imbalanced, especially in the northern and northwestern parts of the country. The number of female children aged 0 to 6 is lower than that of boys, and the disparity in the child sex ratio has grown continuously since the 1960s (see Fig. 7.4), indicating discrimination against girl children. Child sex ratio among children 0–6 years of age has worsened during the last decade, 2001–11, so that in the latest census it stood at 914 girls per 1,000 boys.

It is a biological given that slightly more boys than girls are born, and in a situation where both sexes are treated similarly and health care is not very highly developed, the difference evens out by the age of 5. Boys tend to have more in-born abnormalities and thus their early mortality is slightly higher than that of girls. In parts of India, however, the disparity among 0–6-year-olds is so great that it cannot be explained away by natural causes. The child sex ratio is below 900 girls per 1,000 boys in Punjab, Haryana, Himachal Pradesh, Uttarakhand, Rajasthan, Uttar Pradesh, Maharashtra and Gujarat, which all are located in northern or western India. In the state of Haryana, the

**Figure 7.4.** Child sex ratio in the age group 0 to 6 years (girls per 1,000 boys) in India 1961–2011; the ratio has been constantly declining

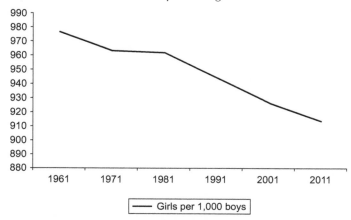

Source: Census of India (2011) (Office of the Registrar of India 2011b).

situation is the worst with only 830 girls to 1,000 boys in the 0–6 age group.[3] In southern and eastern parts of India, the disparity in sex ratio—at least for the time being—is slighter or absent. The most disturbing feature is that the shortfall in girls is mounting from decade to decade, and the number of areas suffering from imbalanced child sex ratios is also growing. This sinister phenomenon seems to spread geographically outwards from certain core and urban areas.

Previously, the dearth of girls in India was mainly due to their greater mortality but since the 1990s the abortion of female fetuses has become the dominant explanation for this imbalance. In Haryana and Punjab, which are among the most affluent areas in India, the sex of the fetus is commonly detected by ultrasound and the female fetus can be eliminated in all socio-economic groups. Families that already have a daughter, in particular, may consider the birth of another girl baby undesirable and be prepared to opt for eliminating the female fetus.

According to Jha et al. (2006), 30 percent of second and third girl babies are aborted, second daughters are especially rare in highly educated affluent urban families and about half a million female fetuses altogether are aborted annually. This rejection of girls is not linked to social disadvantage or lack of education; it is more common among better-off families and mothers with at least ten years of schooling. For example, the sex ratio at birth in the wealthiest areas of Delhi is more distorted than in slum areas. Tulsi Patel (2006) cites the ultrasound as a "must" among middle-class families in north India, not for health reasons but for detecting the sex of the fetus in order to rid themselves of unwanted daughters.

According to demographer Monica Das Gupta (1987), in Punjab where the sex imbalance was first established and is the worst, many families do not want even a single daughter in the family, even though in much of India the ideal family also has a daughter. In patrilineal families, the daughter leaves her family after marriage and the family line and inheritance follow from father to son. A daughter is seen as an economic and social liability. Financial security and care in old age is based on sons; whereas daughters have to be given dowries, comprising very substantial settlements in affluent families in order to secure a prestigious match. In much of north India, it is common to marry daughters "up" into a more prestigious or wealthy family of the same caste, and consequently it is not easy to find a suitable groom even if the daughter is accompanied by a handsome dowry. In the south, the situation is somewhat less problematic as isogamous marriages between status equals

3  In India, the sex ratio is usually expressed as a measure of females per 1,000 males, while elsewhere the figure is calculated on the basis of males per 1,000 or 100 females.

is the norm. South Indian women commonly have an economically active role in the family, thus they are not seen as an economic burden as much as in the northern Hindi-speaking areas where women usually stay at home and do not work even in the family farm or business. This different gender system is reflected in the fact that the southern parts of the country fare better than the north in sex-selective abortions and sex-specific child mortality. However, protecting the virtue and reputation of a daughter is considered troublesome to the family everywhere in India, and thus some parents want no girls at all. When a young man gets married, the daughter-in-law who moves into the household is expected to behave loyally like a daughter of the family.

The elimination of baby girls before birth is the greatest reason why in some areas in northern and western India there is a distinct majority of boys and young men. Even though the Central Government passed a law in 1994 making it illegal to determine the sex *in utero* through ultrasound or amniotic fluid tests, there are innumerable clinics all over India where women can have the sex of their fetus easily detected. As a result, a huge business in ultrasound facilities and abortion clinics has mushroomed in the country. This practice is difficult to curtail with legislation, because a doctor need not expressly state the sex of the fetus but rather indicate it with gestures or other signs: for example, particular kinds of Indian sweets signifying happy family events may be offered when a male fetus is detected. The first prosecutions against doctors in such sex determination clinics only occurred in 2006, after the law had been in force for 12 years.

Decision makers have realized this sinister phenomenon and some laws do exist to combat sex-selective abortion. However, the suggested administrative solutions like banning ultrasounds are at best cosmetic if they are not accompanied by action that addresses the socio-economic and cultural roots of preferring a male child. A number of studies in India, China and other starkly gender-biased societies have convincingly argued that periods of fertility decline, i.e. when the number of opportunities to have a son is effectively reduced, correspond with more masculine sex ratios and rising female disadvantage in survival, as parents manipulate the gender composition of their desired family size through prenatal sex-selection techniques (see Guilmoto 2010). Fertility decline in the face of unchanging social norms and attitudes in a patriarchal context serves to exacerbate discrimination against girls.

Some rays of light are visible, however: in Hyderabad, where the imbalance in sex ratios has been much less pronounced than in the northern and western regions, the local administration seems to have combated the problem with the help of strict enforcement of the demand that all patients attending ultrasound clinics be registered, along with successful registration of births. Fighting against the practice in the core areas such as Punjab and Haryana may demand different tactics, as the practice has become rooted in all echelons of society and the views of health personnel might accord with public opinion on the rightfulness of families to opt for eliminating female fetuses. Female fetuses are aborted particularly when they are second and third pregnancies in a family with only a daughter/daughters, and families may feel that they must secure themselves a son after having a daughter. However, this leads to imbalanced outcomes in the population as no boys are ever aborted to make sure a family has a daughter. Moreover, it has become common in some areas also to abort the first pregnancy in case it is a female. Families opting for sex-selective abortion are free riders who want to secure themselves the relative benefit of having sons while daughters are hoped to be delivered by other families.

In addition to the higher rate of female-fetus abortion, girl babies in India suffer from a higher risk of death than boys. The infant mortality rate, i.e. the death of children under one year old, of girls is greater than that of boys (49 per 1,000 compared to 46 per 1,000, according to the census figures in 2011), although the difference is closing up. This possibly reflects the fact that in conditions of widespread sex-selective abortions, fewer unwanted girls are born and consequently they receive better care. In other words, fewer girls are allowed to be born, but those that are born are more wanted and tend to survive. However, girl children still suffer from higher risk of death than boys across India, despite the fact that sex-selective abortions have become common in some areas.

Underlying these deaths is the poorer nutrition and health care given to girls: they are commonly considered tougher and stronger but less important than boys, and therefore their nutrition is not so diversified. When an illness occurs, a son is rushed to the doctor at once if it is at all possible financially. With a girl baby there might be a delay. Girls are cherished and loved, and their deaths are naturally not desired by most parents, but because they receive less attention and nourishment they are at greater risk. The question therefore is whether this is a matter of favoring boys rather than conscious discrimination against girls. For example, in Gopalapalli in south India, girls were seen as important members of the family, but because male babies were seen as fragile and vulnerable they were taken to the doctor for the slightest reason, unlike girls. There were smaller numbers of girls in the region than boys, although generally a woman's position was comparatively strong compared to elsewhere in India.

In some regions in India, girl babies are intentionally killed, but this practice is rare and for the whole of India it has no statistical significance. In the state of Rajasthan, it has been known that some Rajput sub-castes (traditionally soldiers and rulers) have killed girl babies since at least as early as the Middle

Ages, but over the last century this practice has been disappearing. On the other hand, the killing of girl babies in some areas in the southern state of Tamil Nadu is a new phenomenon, beginning in the 1970s and 80s, which has received much publicity, particularly since the BBC made a documentary that was broadcast internationally in the early 1990s. As a consequence of the publicity, a totally distorted picture of child killings as a common Indian custom was disseminated globally; in reality, however, infanticide is generally held to be as horrendous and unprecedented a deed in India as anywhere else. In the Tamil Nadu region where these killings have been happening, the locals nevertheless accept this manner of eliminating an unwanted girl as a way of avoiding economic disaster, as they would see it, and do not perceive any difference between an abortion and murdering a newborn. Shahid Pervez (2004), who has studied female infanticide in its newer Tamil Nadu form as well as more traditional Rajasthan forms, says that these phenomena do not become intelligible in the light of unambiguous economic or social explanations. The factors affecting the favoring of boys in these regions are similar to those present in the greater part of India, where girl babies are nevertheless *not* killed. Dowry problems, a patrilineal kinship system, women's restricted economic role and patriarchal cultural norms are almost omnipresent in India, but it is in very few regions that girl babies are killed.

If the current trend continues, by 2025 the disparity between males and females of marriageable age will seriously impede the chances of young men finding brides, especially in northwestern and western India. In India, marriage is universal and singledom very exceptional: less than 1 percent of women between 40 and 44 have never been married. So far the fact that there are fewer females than males has not affected chances of finding a wife: men usually marry women who are about 5 years younger (Sample Registration System 2007) and as each age group in northern India is still larger than the one before it, there are enough females to correspond to the demand for brides among males a few years older. This has in fact created a demographic situation where marriageable females outnumber marriageable males. But now, as fertility is dropping also in populous northern areas, at some point in near future the size of each new cohort will diminish and the "demand" for brides will not be filled by the "supply." If the social norm of the universal, endogamous and monogamous marriage retains its hold on India and the sex ratios continue to worsen as age cohorts diminish, the result could be socially discordant. The effect of the "marriage squeeze" is nevertheless class, caste and area specific. Economically poor men will most probably face the direst situation as the women of their groups will be in higher demand and will be able to choose.

Sometimes it is presumed, on an economic model, that the value of young women will grow in the future, when there is a dearth of them in society.

However, in starkly patriarchal societies the appreciation and status of women does not increase in such a situation. On the contrary, coercive practices like forced marriages, trafficking, wife capture, violence against women and growth in commercial sex services might emerge as a consequence of the difficulties in finding a wife in the traditional way. An international trade in women from less appreciated poorer countries and other Indian states might surface, as it has in South Korea and some parts of China where the sex ratio at birth has been skewed for a few decades. In India a strong emphasis on caste endogamy might make such a practice less attractive than in East Asia. Violence among young men and also sexual violence is predicted to increase, when large groups of young men are left without a chance of settling into married life (Hudson and den Boer 2004). Allowing sex-selective abortions to continue unchecked until the male–female sex ratio becomes so skewed that women become "valuable" will do nothing to improve their status or to empower them vis-à-vis men in Indian society, even if it may lead to lessening importance of the dowry system in some social groups.

Although the most extreme horror scenarios—such as predicting a war between China and India as sexually and socially frustrated youth directs its energies towards violence—seem unlikely, sex-ratio disparity in the population must have fundamental consequences. Demographer Christophe Guilmoto (2010) has presented projections of population structures which show how future population growth and marriage market will be affected by the combination of a declining overall fertility that narrows the base of the population pyramid, expected age difference at marriage between men and women, and the skewed sex ratio at birth. His calculations show that a marriage squeeze is bound to become acute in India in the coming decades, as it has done in China. Depending on how soon the skewed sex ratios return to normal, the surplus of marriageable men will vary between 10 to 25 percent. In 2030, an average cohort of prospective grooms would outnumber prospective brides by more than a million men each year. The imbalance is so huge in absolute numbers that no emigration from India nor the importation or regional mobility of brides is able to compensate for the lack of women. Society has to adjust to the fact that more men, most probably among the less privileged, will have to lead unmarried life.

## 7.7 Conclusion

Neo-Malthusian views stressing the pessimistic discrepancy between the growth of resources and growth of population have not come true even in India of fast population growth. The Green Revolution along with other innovations has helped to boost food production faster than doomsday prophets such as the biologist Paul R. Ehlrich have foreseen. Despite the sufficient production of food grains in India, a large part of the population suffers from hunger (see Chapter 8). The reasons for the lack of food have been political, both at a global level and nationally, rather than related to the productivity of agriculture or population growth as predicted by Nobel Laureate in Economics Amartya Sen (1982) in his excellent analysis of famines in developing countries.

Worries relating to population growth in India have arisen not only as a result of ecological reasons but because of economic and social development. Economists have quite differing views on the economic effects of population growth so that while some consider it an advantage, others argue it is a burden. A huge population is undoubtedly a liability for public administration and politics, because it makes the provision of basic services to everyone a very demanding project. As a growing part of the Indian population becomes able and willing to adopt a consumerist lifestyle, the repercussions could be devastating for the local and global environment. Development and adoption of environmentally friendly processes and techniques is needed as the Indian majority's justified quest for material security and well-being grows.

The fact that the population of India is set to increase by several hundreds of millions, even half a billion, does not necessarily mean there will be uncontrollable social difficulties, as this growth will be relatively slow and thus society will be given an opportunity to adjust. The most pressing issue facing India is food provision, and the crucial question of agricultural productivity and poverty reduction requires drastic attention from the Indian decision makers. The future of agriculture in India shows disquieting signs. Agricultural productivity will not be able to keep up with India's population growth nor the effects of global warming without radical innovations.

From a population and reproductive health point of view India's future is not unambiguously optimistic, but the situation is not hopeless either. Political parties, national organizations and lawmakers have started to work on the problems and some issues such as reproductive health policies and the services in some parts of the country have improved. The advances have, however, been far from sufficient in terms of gender equity. Women still suffer from a disproportionate burden of family planning as few alternative contraceptive methods to female sterilization have been made available to rural people. Domestic violence, unsafe abortions and home deliveries without qualified assistance, to name a few reproductive health shortcomings, are still too common. The most glaring gender injustice that has come to plague Indian society is sex-selective abortions. This will have a drastic effect on the whole society in the decades to come. The situation will improve only slowly because gender biases are considered legitimate by many people. The favorable development of reproductive health and respect for human rights in India depends not only on international pressure on national and state governments but also on the unswerving vigilance of women's and human rights organizations.

# Chapter 8

# BETWEEN POVERTY AND AFFLUENCE

Poverty and food deprivation are India's most serious problems. A great part of the population has to survive on insufficient nutrition, suffers from poor health, is illiterate and dies too young. By virtue of its huge population, India commonly takes the unfortunate first rank in global figures related to absolute poverty: the United Nation's World Food Program estimates that nearly half of the world's hungry live in India and according to World Bank, a third of the world's poor live in India. About 20 percent of the population is undernourished (von Grebmer et al. 2009a) and 32 percent lives under the new poverty line adopted in 2011, according to the Planning Commission of India (*The Hindu*, April 21, 2011). The worst-performing state, Madhya Pradesh, is at the same level as Chad and Ethiopia in terms of undernourishment and child mortality, while even the best-performing state, Punjab, is below the level reached by Vietnam or Honduras (von Grebmer et al. 2009b).

India's widespread poverty contrasts with the dynamics of its economy, which has been noticed in global business circles. Growth in GNP has been among the fastest and steadiest in the world. Nonetheless, economic growth per se is not enough to lift the masses from poverty. It is a recurrent question how this economic development will translate into improving economic standing of the underprivileged majority. Will the future of India be that of deepening economic polarization? Or will the growing wealth trickle down even to the lowest ladders? Economic development is an important side of development even if we here understand development more in terms of capacities than possessions. Without economic growth it is for example difficult to provide social, educational and health services for the benefit of the population. However, poverty is more than mere lack of resources; it is a relationship between the haves and the have-nots and speaking about poverty is to discourse about inequity. Poverty is also culturally experienced so that people in different societies and different cultural contexts do not have the same attitude to poverty.

## 8.1 Poverty—Absolute and Relative

Compared with other countries of the world, India is poor in terms of welfare despite its solid growth in Gross National Product (GNP). In the Human Development Index (HDI), produced by the United Nations Development Fund to compare development globally, India ranked 134th among the 187 participating countries in 2011. The HDI measures GNP per inhabitant, life expectancy and level of education. On the basis of GNP per inhabitant alone, India fares better than it does in the HDI overall. The situation appears similarly dismal in other comparative indexes such as the Global Hunger Index or Gender Gap Index: India's economic success has thus far failed to translate into social development and equity to the extent we could expect from other developing Asian countries.

Measurement of poverty and changes in the prevalence of poverty are important, if we are to understand how it is affected by certain social or economic measures. Poverty lines used for assessing the proportion of a population living in deprivation are more or less negotiated and arbitrary, and different indexes provide confusingly different results. Earlier official Indian poverty figures were based on the income needed for the minimum energy requirements of 2,400 kilocalories in rural areas and 2,100 in urban areas. Such a bare-minimum definition of poverty has faced considerable criticism: those who can ostensibly afford the minimum calorie intake have to cover other basic needs such as clothing, housing, health care, education and so on by cutting from the food budget. The consumption level of the majority of Indians is very low, and the major part of their earnings goes towards food. Still in 2005, about half of Indian households did not use shampoo and a quarter made do without such luxuries as washing powder (NCAER 2005).

It is incredible that the country has not yet faced rebellion despite the fact more than 200 million Indians live below the earlier established absolute poverty line, surviving undernourished and in abject poverty. In fact, we are witnessing a "silent famine," because the high mortality of the poor is due to exhausting physical labor accompanied by malnutrition which makes them susceptible to infections, and lack of financial means restricts their access to health care and drugs. Despite severe deprivation, most people have social networks that may be crucial in crisis situations. Monetary measurements of poverty are not able to take immaterial and material mutual help into account. Some commentators have raised doubts about the reliability of the surveys on economic poverty and consumption, stating that the poor do not necessarily disclose all their earnings or expenditure in surveys for tactical reasons. Nonetheless, the statistics on absolute poverty can be verified in other ways; for instance, physiological measures of poverty such as underweight and prevalence of anemia are also very high in India, 55 percent of women are anemic (International Institute for Population Sciences and Macro International 2007).

A new kind of poverty line was introduced by the Planning Commission in 2011, based on a cost of living index instead of caloric intake. This new poverty line takes into account expenditure required for education and health. Due to the new definition of the poverty line, the percentage of the population living below it rose substantially: according to the new definition, 37 percent lived in poverty in 2004 while the old poverty line implied that 27 percent were poor. Suddenly India had 100 million more poor. Skirmishes related to defining the poverty line bear high political relevance and are a graphic reminders of the controversial nature of statistical poverty estimates. The previous and undoubtedly very bare poverty line is still useful when assessing development in poverty reduction as it helps to highlight temporal changes. The new poverty line may, however, give a more realistic image of how many people face severe material deprivation. According to the provisional data of the Planning Commission, the proportion of Indians living below the new poverty line has decreased from 37 percent to 32 percent from 2004 to 2009 (*The Hindu*, April 21, 2011).

Poverty can both refer to relative poverty—economic inequality in society—and to absolute poverty or nutritional deprivation. The meaning of poverty depends partly on the degree of inequality in distribution of wealth in a society. If some live in abject poverty and others wallow in luxury, personal experiences of disadvantage are different than if wealth were to be distributed more equally. The Gini index is a standard mathematical means to examine the distribution of income, expenditure or wealth in societies. The number zero represents absolute equality in income distribution (all persons/households have equal earnings, expenditure or wealth) and the number 1 represents absolute inequality (one person/household has it all, others nothing). In this scale, India ranked lower than most European countries (in 2005, India's Gini index was 0.37), but better than in the USA (0.41), China (0.47) or Brazil (0.57) (UNDP 2008). In spite of inequalities in Indian society, the income distribution is more equal than in many other developing countries. The trends in the distribution of economic well-being measured using the Gini index are somewhat vague; from 1996–7 to 1999–2000, the index improved considerably in India, but since then it has worsened again, following a global trend. In India, it may be that per capita expenditure and income distribution is more equal than in China, but according to the Asian Development Bank, the distribution of *wealth* is clearly more unequal in India than in China. Moreover, social inequalities based on differences in education, health and caste hierarchy are so strong that Indian society is severely polarized.

One of the problems of setting the parameters of a poverty line is that they mostly ignore the meaning of social capital to human welfare. In India, the welfare of a family and individual does not depend merely on the available income or wealth. When poverty is measured in monetary value only, this leaves out of the picture the possibility of crisis assistance from family networks, reciprocating services with neighbors and friends and many other similar kinds of benefits. In the countryside, most families somehow survive despite having little cash, if they produce their own crops or utilize forest produce, as the *adivasis* commonly do. In everyday survival, the importance of family and kin networks is pivotal for all Indians, and for that reason those relationships have to be constantly maintained and invested in. On the other hand, among the chronically poorest families obligations may not be considered as strong as with the economically more secure: close relatives could be equally poor and thus unable to offer much financial help. This easily leads into a vicious circle of indebtedness to usurious moneylenders.

The most shocking feature of Indian poverty is child malnutrition. In 2002–7, close to half (44 percent) of Indian children below the age of five were suffering from serious or moderate underweight conditions (von Grebmer et al. 2009a). India is among the worst countries in the world in this respect. In comparison with China, the difference is huge: in China during the same time period, the percentage of undernourished children was 6 percent. From 1970, the percentage of undernourished children has gradually decreased by around 1 percent per year. If this pace does not accelerate, eradicating children's undernutrition in India will take half a century. According to the World Bank (2006), the ratio of undernourished children in India has reduced at a slower rate than in other countries in similar economic circumstances.

Children's nutritional deficiency is more common with rural children, girls, *dalits* and *adivasis*. More than three out of four preschool children suffer from anemia, reflecting inadequate food consumption. Anemia reduces learning capacity and is therefore pernicious for the individual and for the future of society as well. The cause of widespread low weight and anemia is not only the general poverty and shortage of food: even in households where the adults are not suffering from a lack of nutrition, children may suffer from growth problems. These may be the result not only of insufficient food but also repeated infections and inappropriate nutritional practices leading, for example, to a shortage of amino acids and vitamins in young children or insufficient solid foods for breastfed babies over 6 months old.

In the south Indian village of Gopalapalli in the mid-1990s, the low weight and stunted growth of children was visible and common. Children were usually fed boiled rice with a drop of oil and a sour sauce made from tart tamarinds (*caaru*), along with lentil stew (*pappu*). The children were unable to eat very hot-spiced curries and it was not deemed necessary to prepare separate milder food for them; consequently they very seldom ate vegetables or meat. Milk products, eggs and meat were the privilege of the better-off families in Gopalapalli, and they still are in rural India more generally, despite the fact that the ratio of per capita consumption of rice/wheat in the diet has relatively declined and the ratio of vegetables, meat and milk products has grown. Wheat and rice still continue to supply well over half of the total calorie intake of the average rural household (Chatterjee, Rae and Ray 2007).

## 8.2 Rural Origins of Poverty

More than two-thirds of Indians live in rural areas and consequently the core of the Indian poverty problem also lies in rural economy. In the countryside, wealth and poverty are connected with landownership and the productivity of agriculture. Landless laborers and marginal farmers depend on daily wages, and because work is available in abundance only during the high season, income is irregular. Around 30 percent of the Indian labor force are day laborers, and most of them suffer from seasonal shortage of income and thus of food. When plowing, sowing, weeding or reaping does not provide enough employment, landless laborers manage as they best can; moreover, work may not be available for all rural laborers even in the high agricultural season, leading to underemployment and seasonal migration. During the agricultural low season, in particular, day laborers' families may have to survive with only one square meal a day. Daily wages are so meager that it is difficult to save for a rainy day, although a rural family might manage somehow, provided income is regular and can be supplemented by produce from their own plot. Problems appear if sudden illnesses, poor harvests or natural disasters shake the household economy, drawing people rapidly into penury and indebtedness. In addition to seasonality and oversupply of labor, the main direct causes of rural poverty are indebtedness and landlessness. The importance of land reforms for poverty alleviation, even if they only provide a small plot, can be illustrated by the example of West Bengal which, unlike most Indian states, has successfully carried out land reform (see Chapter 9).

Earlier, before the monetary economy became all-encompassing, rural families lived in hereditary dependency relationships so that members of a worker family had a duty to be on call to serve their master family throughout the year and received as compensation the security of bare minimum maintenance from them. This somewhat balanced the seasonal changes in food supply, but simultaneously made the workers totally dependent on their masters as they could not take advantage of labor opportunities offered by others to improve their lot. These kinds of subjugating hereditary relationships often came to resemble serfdom, as the patrons commonly issued loans to the illiterate, *dalit* and other low caste workers who thus became objects of usury and exploitation (e.g. Breman 2007). Relations of bonded labor can still be found in some areas even if they are illegal, although today almost all rural workers receive their pay in cash without being attached personally to a certain master or family. They have been freed to cope on their own, to take advantage of what opportunities present themselves, but simultaneously have lost their prior basic survival security.

In areas where agriculture is productive and the land may produce three to four rice or wheat harvests a year with the help of irrigation, the economic situation of the day laborers also tends to be better, reflecting better employment opportunities. Increasing agricultural productivity in an ecologically sustainable and socially equable manner, including land reform, is a key issue in the elimination of poverty in India (see Chapter 7). In the past decades, the surplus labor force in rural areas has had to turn to casual seasonal work in rural towns and urban areas to try to survive. As the population grows and simultaneously agriculture needs less labor due to mechanization, an ever-growing proportion of rural laborers has to search for alternative sources of income. The development of the service and industrial sectors that can employ excess agricultural labor appears to be the only viable way to reduce poverty in India in the long run. Even if radical land reforms were implemented, the swelling of informal urban and semi-urban populations is inevitable. The situation can only be battled by the tandem development of the agricultural sector and growth of organized industrial production (Eshwaran 1994; Wood and Caladrino 2000).

Indian poverty has been traditionally predominantly rural with those living in urban spaces faring relatively better, but recently poverty has begun to urbanize; now in some states, the incidence of poverty is higher in urban than in rural areas, and in many states the previous advantage of living in urban areas appears to be fading (UNDP 2009). Urbanization is accelerating in India as everywhere but the pace is slower than the Asian average. One of the reasons for the lower prevalence of poverty in urban areas has derived from the fact that employment has not been as seasonally dependent as in agricultural areas. The latest surveys on the development of poverty in urban areas point out that the profile of poverty in India might be changing and thus will demand different policy measures in the future to those directed towards alleviating rural poverty. The key would be to create regular and decent sources of income for the urban poor (Breman 2009).

## 8.3 Coping with Poverty

For an outsider, poverty in India is an enigma: how is it possible that such a huge part of the population lives in extreme material misery, and yet no revolution seems to be brewing, nor is there even violent crime targeting the privileged? In spite of vast differences in wealth and welfare, the deprived rarely resort to political rebellion or delinquency in order to redistribute wealth from the affluent to the less fortunate. The existing social order appears to enjoy fundamental acceptance. Despite appearances, however, revolutionary political and military activity exists, especially in the poor, forested heartlands of the Deccan Plateau (see Chapter 4).

The commonly held view that the acceptance of poverty by the underprivileged reflects Hindu ideas of karma and predestination is not unanimously supported by anthropological research. The doctrine of reincarnation appears more as a justification of privilege among the better off than among the less fortunate (e.g. Arun 2007; Béteille 2002; Karanth 2004). In his novel *White Tiger*, author Aravind Adiga graphically describes one interpretation: that the poor remain loyal to their masters because rebellion, disobedience or disloyalty would lead to punishment not only of themselves but of their family and kin. India is a kin-based society where people prefer not to engage in contracts between labourers and employers purely as individuals: reliability is assessed on the basis of a person as a member of a kin group, even if the old type of pure patron–client relationships has eroded. However, individualized labor contracts between people without any prior ties are growing in importance, particularly in cities where the middle classes hire servants with whose families or villages they do not necessarily have a history of interconnectedness. It is a common complaint among the better off that servants have become unreliable and greedy and that patrons do not have the means to control and punish them as they used to (Dickey 2000; Säävälä 2010a). Explanations for the lack of rebellion, individual or collective, among the deprived are necessarily many.

Although otherworldly orientation among the Hindus hardly explains why poverty persists in India, there are undoubtedly some phenomena that derive from such a feature. Some choose poverty as their way of life; giving up possessions and sensual enjoyment in later life is appreciated particularly by Hindus. For example, holy Hindu renouncers, *sadhus*, will abandon ordinary material life and join monastic orders or groups of ascetics, owning nothing and living on daily alms and donations of food. According to Sanskritic Hindu traditions, relinquishing earthly life and dedicating oneself to spiritual ends is virtuous for older high-caste Hindu men, although during the house-holding life stage, a man should be engaged in earthly endeavors and material aspirations. Sometimes younger men and women and people from low castes and *dalits* also become ascetics although, apart from widows, such action is not considered as virtuous for them in the mainstream Vedic frame of reference. Modest material life was also idealized by Mahatma Gandhi as a model for every Indian. Abstaining from material comforts from time to time is a voluntary part of many married Hindu women's lives as they commonly choose to observe fasts on a certain day of the week or during certain phases of the moon, to earn personal spiritual merit and to ensure their husbands' longevity.

Hunger may be seen as desirable in certain situations and life stages, but the greater number of indigent Indians have never had the opportunity to choose between austerity and abundance. The majority of the poor consider their living conditions to be an undesirable and abysmal state that they are struggling to change. Living in continuous need is degrading. A south Indian rural woman fighting to earn her daily living described her situation quite indignantly when explaining why she was not thinking of having more than two children:

> We cannot afford to have many children, we are only potters. How could we fill all those stomachs? Our children are skinny. They never have good clothes. Would it be good to have ten like this? What? No. Those who have money can have many children; it looks nice, doesn't it? But we cannot. Therefore two is enough.

The humiliation following on from poverty—being unable to afford proper clothing or food for one's children—is pivotal for understanding the choices in the life of this woman. The inability to provide children material well-being is conceptualized as lack of love for the children, and feeding or literally giving rice is the most important symbol of care and affection. The material world and emotional ties cannot be separated in the thinking of the poor in India in the same way as for the affluent Westerner: lack of food is lack of love (Trawick 1992). Deprivation is pernicious for the maintenance of social attachments, because it weakens networks of giving and receiving. Hunger as a phenomenon itself can be seen as positive in particular voluntary situations, but if it means the inability to look after ones' near ones and provide for them, it is always humiliating.

The rural south Indian woman's comment above also illustrates the fact that she does not see her continuing poverty as a self-evident, irrevocable fate. She has opted for only two children in order to ease suffering in her family. Her statement shows consciousness of a present in which she can influence her life through her own actions and an alternative future in which her children might have a chance of ridding themselves of hunger and deprivation. If poverty is so absolute that people cannot fathom any alternative future, the poor have no motivation to limit the number of children born to them; indeed, they may even have many children in order to ensure that at least few survive and leave them to the mercy of destiny. In such a scenario, they cannot visualize any other kind of prospect for their children than their own present misery and inequality. If India is to reduce the number of people living in poverty, it is imperative that the horizon of their possibility and future expectations change. This is why India's poverty and its population problems are so tightly linked (see Chapter 7). Except in the highly populated core states in the north, this attitudinal change is already well under way. Research in the rural areas of Andhra Pradesh in south India in the mid-1990s demonstrated that notions of temporality—the relationship between the past, present and future—and feelings of entitlement to a better life for the children are central factors in people's willingness to adopt family planning (Säävälä 2001a).

## 8.4 Gendered Nature of Poverty

In India as in most developing societies, women carry the heaviest burden of poverty. The question is not only how many men versus how many women are living with very low income, but what poverty means for women and men when they are faced with such a situation. When adversity strikes, women are more handicapped as they find it more difficult to lift themselves from poverty than men. Women's opportunities and capabilities to act in situations of economic poverty are limited. These limitations derive from culturally defined gender bias which renders women of lesser value. Thus, women's poverty turns more easily into a chronic condition.

The limited opportunities to engage in gainful employment due to considerations of propriety are typical mechanisms that victimize women. In the case of widowhood, separation or any other marital misfortune, it is much harder for women to cope with their situation economically. The dependency of women on kin for support is so central for their survival that they cannot risk challenging gender norms too openly by, for example, finding gainful employment outside of the family sphere if the family opposed it. Women's wages are considerably lower and their private property rights, most notably access to arable landholdings, are limited in most regions. However, women may in some areas possess land and receive land as dowry. Legally they have similar right to inheritance as sons, but in practice women are expected to give up their share for their brothers. One of the most esteemed researchers on gender, poverty and environment in India, Bina Agarwal (2003) has noted that gender inequalities in access to private property and income security are found across most wealth and asset groups, even if in varying degrees.

Another side of gender bias and poverty is that of intra-household distribution of work, income, food and resources. Men and boys have the upper hand in food distribution which shows, for example, in widespread anemia among females and the higher rates of child mortality among girls. This means that even if a household is not living in a poverty condition, some of the household members, most commonly younger women and girls, may actually suffer from lack of resources, capabilities and means to improve their situation. Women's work is often invisible and underrated, and they are assigned the most time-intensive tasks that require constant engagement and leave little free time for other activities, such as collecting firewood and fodder or childcare. Thus, poverty cannot be spoken about only as a household matter; women in the most vulnerable groups, namely agricultural laborers, Scheduled Castes and Scheduled Tribes in the forested areas and drought-prone regions where we find the most chronic poverty (Mehta and Shah 2003) easily suffer the most if their family is hit by economic or social crises.

## 8.5 Has the Liberalization of the Economy Alleviated or Worsened Poverty?

When India's economic policy began to incorporate neo-liberal measures in the beginning of the 1990s, economists and sociologists had vastly differing prognoses about its effects on poverty. Many critical researchers were—and still are—convinced that poverty and inequality in society would inevitably increase. Meanwhile, the proponents of deregulation prophesied a so-called trickle-down effect, whereby the fruits of a booming economy would gradually percolate down from the well-to-do to the great masses of have-nots. Thus, as the national economy in India has grown rapidly in the last decade, has the growing wealth really filtered into the poorer sections of the population or has a small elite grabbed the best part of it? The issue is a very heated one among both academics and politicians. Predictably, this issue has turned out to raise rather different interpretations in economist and social scientist circles, depending on their ideological frame of reference.

Evaluating the effects of the new economic policy has proved to be rather difficult. Most researchers agree that neither dramatic impoverishment nor dramatic improvement has occurred, although poverty has slowly and continuously been declining in India. According to Angus Deaton and Jean Drèze (2002), the trend is a movement along a continuum in the same developmental direction initiated before deregulating policies were implemented. Decreases in poverty have neither radically accelerated nor slackened as a consequence of the economic reforms and it is difficult to differentiate the effects of economic reforms from many other transformations in society, for example legislation, technology, population age structure, the impact of the global situation or internal politics.

Deaton and Drèze describe how various dimensions of poverty changed in the 1990s, for better or worse. The laudable developments are that the proportion of those living in economic poverty is continually decreasing, the differences in welfare between urban and rural sections are narrowing and the literacy rate is rapidly increasing. At the same time, however, as the decline in infant mortality rate has slowed almost to a stop, landless laborers' wages are dragging behind other salaried groups and regional differences have increased. Southern and western India stand out as regions wherein poverty is rapidly declining; northern and eastern parts have generally not succeeded so well in this respect. The very thorough economic investigation made by Deaton and Drèze shows that the decrease in the ratio of Indians living in abject poverty had already started in the 1980s, before the reforms. Furthermore, welfare in a wider sense has increased in India: the most significant indicator of this is the increase in life expectancy which reflects better health and a lower risk of early death.

Many concerned scholars are of the opinion that globalization and economic liberalization are essentially harmful processes for the well-being of the lower socio-economic groups in developing societies. However, it is difficult to disentangle the effects of economic liberalization and globalization from a number of other social and political processes that are also already under way. Ruchira Ganguly-Scrase and Timothy Scrase (2009) have investigated the situation of the lower-middle classes in their qualitative study of West Bengal. Their conclusion is that the lower echelons of the middle classes have not been able to reap the benefits of the opening economy, unlike the upper-middle classes and the elite. They point out that those dependent on public sector employment may have actually lost their security due to the structural adjustment programs. Further, they argue that international capital has rarely challenged existing gender hierarchies in developing societies; instead it has harnessed them for its own benefit (Ganguly-Scrase and Scrase 2009, 77). However, the applicability of their qualitative study to a wider Indian reality remains in question. Their study is a good remainder that the consequences of liberalization are far from self-evident and they are differently felt according to social group, gender and region. In terms of gender differences, many scholars are convinced that globalization and economic liberalization have harmed Indian women's relative interests by making the female workforce more vulnerable through the creation of low-paid jobs (e.g. Kapadia 2002). Some empirical studies note, in turn, that the situation may bring some classes of women actually new and better opportunities, and that women workers feel that economic activity has improved their self-worth and domestic decision-making power (Mukhopadhyay 2003; Chakravarty 2004).

In India, hunger and poverty have not declined at the same pace as in other countries experiencing similar economic success. Moreover, high levels of hunger are seen even in states that are performing well economically. Economic growth rates do not automatically articulate with a reduction of hunger and child mortality, as shown in a study by the International Food Policy Research Institute (von Grebmer et al. 2009b). It remains to be seen how Indian society will manage to decrease hunger and poverty and redistribute the evident economic benefits of liberalization among poorer citizens, particularly to the most vulnerable, the children.

The government has not left the poverty problem to be solved by market forces alone, however. India has seen a plethora of programs aimed at trying to solve the problem of poverty. The most significant have been land reforms; the Public Distribution System which procures rice, wheat and other amenities from producers and sells them at subsidized prices to ration-card holders; free electricity to the farmers in many areas; and various work-for-food projects. These programs are not without their critics. The Public Distribution System, which allocates food in reduced price to ration-card holders, who are below poverty line, has been criticized for being wasteful partly due to the high number of fake cards (Mitra et al. 2010). Some state governments have started issuing electronic "smart cards" based on biometrics to improve the effectiveness of the system.

The government took on the task of eliminating extreme poverty in the 200 poorest areas with a work program called the Rural Employment Guarantee Program, executed in 2006. This program guarantees every household in these poorest areas paid public manual labor, such as road building, irrigation channel digging and so on, for at least for 100 days a year. Skeptics say that the program is inappropriate, wasteful of public funds and more likely to amass money in other pockets than those of the poor. It has also been said that it fails to facilitate the development of more employable skills among the poor, which could secure better pay. Nonetheless, advocates argue that this kind of program is the best possible way to decisively improve the standards of living of the most poverty-stricken people who do not have years to wait for economic improvements—their survival is determined here and now.

Economic reforms have been in practice in India for the past 20 years, opening the economy to global forces and foreign capital. Still, they have not managed to radically alter the situation of the poorest and a large part of the population remains in dire material deprivation, without the capacities to influence their situation. We cannot be certain what would have happened with regard to poverty in India if the economic reforms had not taken place, but we do know that during more than four decades of semi-planned economy following Indian independence, poverty, hunger, gender bias, social inequality and illiteracy failed to disappear despite a strong moral and political commitment among political leaders to address these problems. Assessing the impact of economic reforms on poverty and the economy more generally is a task that requires considerably further research and no simple conclusions can be drawn at this point. It may also be that economic liberalization reflects an intensification of very long-term processes of casualization of labor and widening income gaps (Sarkar and Mehta 2010) alongside new consumerist aspirations that create a feeling of unmet needs (Ganguly-Scrase and Scrase 2009; Säävälä 2010a).

It is to be hoped that if and when the productivity and efficacy of agriculture improves, industrial production and services will be able to accommodate the labor force released from agriculture. Growth in industrial production, on the other hand, needs a skilled labor force in addition to foreign capital. Therefore, raising the standard of basic education is central to improving the future welfare of India, from the point of view both of individuals and from that of the economic system as a whole (Wood and Caladrino 2000).

## 8.6 The Allure of Education

Literacy is a resource without which improvements in welfare can be ruled out. Because its population is so large, about 40 percent of the world's illiterate people live in India (Kingdon et al. 2004). In the census of 2011, the literacy rate (of persons 7 years and older) was 74 percent; of Indian women two in three could read and write. Literacy rates have improved during the last decade by 9 percentage points, and the improvement among women has been more pronounced than among men, thus narrowing the gender gap in literacy. Full literacy of the whole nation is still a goal for the future, but much progress has been achieved lately, especially since the start of the school meals program (see below). Nowadays primary school enrolment at the age of six is nearly universal, but the dropout rate remains high (Rustagi 2009). Among teenagers, particularly girls, attendance drops drastically at the secondary level. By classes 9 to 12, the attendance rate of girls falls to about 40 percent; while attendance in higher education is 11 percent (Mehrotra 2009).[1] The fast drop in the enrolment ratio of girls to boys after primary school is due to concerns about the safety and honor of maturing girls outside the domestic sphere and the need for their labor at home. In principle, the education of girls is appreciated, but this is not expressed in enrolment ratios. The national government has realized the importance of universal primary education and

---

1  The Central Government is targeting to increase the proportion of the age cohort in higher education into 21 percent by the year 2017 (*Chronicle of Higher Education*, July 7, 2009).

an all-India program called Sarva Shiksha Abhiyan (Education for All) was launched at the beginning of the millennium to improve educational facilities and to encourage parents to enroll all children in schools. Progress was initially slower than hoped, but the latest figures from the National Sample Survey are promising: only 4 percent of children at primary school age were not enrolled at school. However, as it has been noted in regional studies that children's non-enrolment is not necessarily reflected accurately in the official survey figures, these figures await the support of further surveys (Rustagi 2009).

People in India sincerely believe in the power of education. Parents invest huge amounts of money and effort in the education of their children, both among the better off and the less fortunate. The greater proportion of them go to basically free government schools, but anyone who can afford it tries to enroll their children in private English-language schools. Especially appreciated are convent schools managed by Christians, something which does not perturb Hindus and Muslims; no proselytizing is allowed to take place. Religious influence is only visible insofar as these schools may grant fee reductions to those with Christian backgrounds. This is one enticement for some less well-to-do, low-caste families to convert to Christianity.

Money alone does not guarantee admission to a private school, although the parents of new pupils have to make considerable donations and pay high tuition fees in schools of repute. Both the child applicant and the parents are expected to appear before a selection board and the family must come well-recommended and have good connections to speak for the child. It is difficult for those who come from the lower classes and castes to be admitted to prestigious schools, because their habitus and language speak of their humbler background and lack of cultural capital. It is also important to prepare children for the entrance examinations from early childhood. Most children commence school between the ages of five and six, but those who go to private schools start at the age of three or four, first attending the preschool where they are clad in school uniforms, acquire school discipline and learn to read amid play. The lower primary school consists of five classes, the middle school of three and the high school of four more. Those who aspire to higher education enroll in colleges, some of which are privately owned, while others are maintained by public funds. Lately private universities have also emerged in India, in addition to a high number of private colleges and other institutions of higher learning.

Teacher-absenteeism is a perennial problem in the Indian school system, particularly in small one-teacher rural village schools. If the teacher lives far from the school he or she might attend to her or his teaching duties irregularly. According to surveys, teacher-absenteeism is one of the reasons parents give for not enrolling their children in government schools or for allowing them to drop out; other reasons include the poor standard of teaching and children's lack of motivation to study (see Rustagi 2009). Despite some generally held suspicions, surveys reveal that reliance on child labor is rarely the reason behind parents neglecting to send a child to school. Even the poorest families are aware that education is the key to a better future. Sääväla's 2001 study of Gopalapalli shows that some important considerations dictating family planning are the requirements of children's future education. Parents in all economic categories want to educate their children as far as they can afford. In government schools, students do not wear uniforms, but still they have to be neatly dressed. In addition, there are books and materials to be bought, and, to ensure the child's success, supportive private tuition is a must. Even though the monthly expenditure is not excessive, for a poor family living on the verge of seasonal hunger such small regular expenses may be significant.

The style of teaching in government schools has so far received only minor attention, because the primary goal has been to improve school attendance and provide proper facilities—buildings, books and qualified teachers. In all Indian schools—excepting the most elite private institutions—the teaching is based on learning by rote. A good example of the results can be seen in the experiences of the 12-year-old daughter of Sääväla's rural landlady, who attended a private English-language school in a nearby small town. One day she asked Sääväla to test her geography knowledge. The girl could flawlessly repeat a whole chapter titled "Mountains in India" and when she was lauded for her good learning, she beamed. It was only after a few minutes that she very shyly asked in Telugu: "Elder sister, what is a mountain?" She could parrot information about mountains in English, but no one had bothered to explain the word itself, and she had not dared to ask her teacher. It was more important to rote-learn the whole chapter than to understand its contents. Similar learning practices are current in many colleges and universities, where it is not customary to encourage students to think independently. So far, Indian creative potentiality has remained underutilized.

Apart from the aim of securing universal primary education, which has recently showed promising developments, the main educational concern is the quality of secondary and higher education. In India, secondary education is largely academically oriented, while formal vocational training is scantily available and held at very low esteem. Higher education is popular compared to many other developing countries, with around one in ten students continuing on to obtain an academic degree; in China, for example, the corresponding figure is only 3 percent (Wood and Caladrino 2000). One of the problems of higher education, however, is that the standards of the colleges are so uneven: Singh (2003) estimates that perhaps only one in ten colleges is capable of providing appropriate scientific teaching. Some educational institutions are of a high international standard, such as the Indian Institutes of Technology, but the majority of degrees are received in institutions that fail to provide graduates with either academically viable skills or skills that are in demand. Private employers complain in the media that the bulk of graduates available in the labor market do not correspond to their expectations. As the Indian economy expands and the demand for highly educated personnel grows, the educational system faces new challenges in catering for the business environment.

## 8.7 The Revolutionary Midday-Meal Program

The midday-meal scheme is one of the most far-reaching developmental steps the present government has undertaken, in terms of education, poverty reduction and child nutrition. As early as the 1980s, some states had started distributing meals at government-run schools. Children in Tamil Nadu, for example, were given a simple meal in the middle of the school day. At the beginning of 2000, a group of national activist organizations kicked off a campaign called "Right to Food" to pressurize courts of law to intervene in hunger-related matters: although India produces enough food to fulfill the needs of all its citizens, many cannot afford to buy enough food to fulfill the basic nutritional requirements and are consequently underweight. The People's Union for Civil Liberties in Rajasthan initiated the "Right to Food Litigation" which demanded, among other things, that school meals be provided in government schools throughout the whole of India. Although a court ruling made it mandatory for the state governments to provide school meals, many states failed to do so. The Congress Party–led coalition government committed all state governments to organize midday meals in all schools in 2004. The Central Government finances the acquisition of the ingredients, while the state governments are responsible for arranging the necessary infrastructure and labor. In some states, private organizations and businesses have participated in the realization of the program. Within a few years the midday-meal scheme has become a more or less well-functioning practice almost everywhere. It has had a revolutionary impact on school attendance and has reduced dropout rates dramatically, improving learning results and gender equality in school enrolment.

Every government school and government-sponsored primary school is expected to engage a part-time cook who prepares a daily meal using ingredients found in the region. Although the meal is simple, the nutritional benefits for schoolchildren are remarkable: they receive at least one meal a day irrespective of the season or the income of their family. Many children of poor families used to come to school with empty stomachs, and before this scheme started, they used to return home at midday to eat, often not returning for the afternoon lessons. With a meal served at school, absenteeism lessens and learning capacity improves via the reduction of the anemia and undernutrition, which adversely affects cognitive potential. Food provision has enticed poor children, particularly girls, to attend school in much greater numbers than earlier; a study in Rajasthan, for example, shows that the number of students rose by 29 percent in single year, whereas in earlier years the increase had been mere 2 percent (Drèze and Goyal 2003). In the same study, a survey conducted in three different states indicates that nine out of ten parents of schoolchildren want the scheme to continue in the future.

The midday-meal scheme has had an impact not only on the nutritional status of children, but it has also affected caste relationships in a groundbreaking way. In some states, the governments have decreed that the cooks employed must be women from the Scheduled Castes. Traditionally, upper castes never eat food prepared by lower castes, especially by *dalits*, nor dine together with them. It is thought that impure elements are passed through food and thus eating together compromises one's higher status. When a meal is served at school, the children are expected to eat together irrespective of their communities. According to news reports, this revolutionary eating arrangement has, surprisingly, aroused very few open protests, although some traditionalist families have forbidden their children to touch the school meals and give them carry-along food from home (Drèze and Goyal 2003).

Although corruption undoubtedly exists in this government-funded project, as in all public programs, the midday-meal scheme has begun functioning relatively painlessly in a surprisingly short time. Newspapers have reported a few cases of misuse, in which the grain distributed by the Central Government for the purpose of the program has ended up in the wrong hands and on the black market, but generally speaking the program has had an impressive start. Drèze and Goyal (2003) examined the realization of the program in over 80 schools in three states and found that meals were almost universally available to children and that they were considered satisfactory by their parents, although weaknesses in the infrastructure, such as deficit roads and transport vehicles, variable availability of energy and especially too meager an allocation of finances, were causes of problems implementing the program in some locations. In most states, the daily allowance per child has been between R0.5–1 (1–2 euro cents), while the benefits accruing to the welfare of economically deprived and undernourished children have been enormous. It is difficult to imagine any other public scheme which could have achieved such far-reaching results with a comparable investment: the overall costs of the program in the whole Indian Union are equivalent to 13 percent of the country's defense budget. Some skeptics have suggested that the children might be exposed to health risks due to communal kitchens, but the meals are always freshly cooked from vegetarian ingredients so the danger of food poisoning or other epidemics is relatively small and, compared with nutritional and egalitarian benefits, insignificant.

Despite some shortcomings, launching the midday-meal program is one of the most significant socio-political achievements of the previous and current Central Governments, although its effects will only really become apparent in years to come. Encouraging school attendance and improving the nutritional status of school children will be reflected throughout society. In the new millennium, Indian children attend primary school more regularly than before, and for a longer period. Classrooms full of children also offer new challenges to teachers and motivate them in new ways.

## 8.8 Middle-class Escape from Poverty

The liberalization of the economy in India since the beginning of the 1990s has especially benefited the country's middle classes. The growth of information and communication technology has also brought well-educated and well-to-do Indians to the business centers of Euro-American metropolises, making India one of the most important producers of professionals in the business. India is different from many other developing countries in that it has a numerically and culturally strong middle class, which has its roots in colonial times. The middle classes have a definite say in the direction of India's future because they are economically active, innovative, politically determined and represent many cultural ideals which upwardly mobile sectors of the laboring classes try to emulate.

Assessing the size of the Indian middle class is as difficult and debatable as deciphering the number of "poor" in the country. There have been several estimations which differ according to which definitions and income cut-off points have been used. However, the size of the intermediate strata between those who depend on selling their labor power and those who have secured their economic existence by reliance on various forms of capital or decision-making positions, is somewhere between 150 and 300 million persons. The esteemed National Council of Applied Economic Research (NCAER) defines the middle class on the basis of household income and estimates its size to be much lower: according to them only about 6 percent of Indian households can be classified as belonging to the middle class (annual income minimum Rs 200,000 or 3,400 in 2005). The NCAER categorizes the Indian population into four groups: the rich, the middle class, the aspirants and the poor.

Although much is written and imagined in the media about the Indian middle classes, their number as defined by Western consumptive criteria is relatively small even if NCAER's "aspirants" are included. On the other hand, what the NCAER defines as "poor" does not refer to people who live in absolute poverty, but rather implies a relative limitation on consumptive possibilities. From a sociological point of view, it is artificial to classify people into different categories on the basis of income or consumption alone, although such classifications are useful when estimating changes in society. The proportion of indigents in India is shrinking, while the more affluent income classes are estimated to keep on growing strongly in the coming years. The second-lowest income class, which the research institute defines as "aspirant" households, is growing especially steadily. Market research institutions greatly exaggerated the growth of the buying power of the Indian middle classes in the 1990s, and many businesses which had invested in the production of consumer durables and marketing were bitterly disappointed in their unrealized expectations. The growth of middle-class incomes has been much more modest than the boldest had predicted. Since then, consumption projections concerning India have become more cautious.

The middle classes, or intermediate social strata, are not only an economic phenomenon defined by a certain level of income, however. Educational standards, values, lifestyle and aspirations influence whether people consider themselves or others to be middle class. In India, the term has different connotations than in the Euro-American context. An Indian middle-class family does not necessarily own a car, nor can they afford to travel abroad, so their relative level of consumption is noticeably lower than that of a Western European factory worker's family, for example. A car in India is a rather uncommon possession, with only 5 percent of households owning a four-wheeler in 2005. Typical consumer goods possessed by middle-class people include an electric mixer, a scooter, a color television and a gas cooker. However, the middle classes in India can afford the luxury of servants, which most middle-class Westerners cannot.

The roots of the Indian middle classes reach back to colonial times. The British rulers schooled the local elite, mainly the Brahmans, to take part in the governance of the country. They established English schools and some people had the opportunity to continue their studies in English universities as well. This so-called "old middle class" continued its life in independent India: arguably it comprised the leadership during the national awakening. The importance and role of the educated classes in the freedom struggle is still debated; some historians consider them central and others as less important vis-à-vis popular protest. In the early years of independence, the educated were necessary to the administration of the newborn state and in running the license economy, and educated people found employment mainly in the public sector. Entrepreneurs in the first decades of independent India were starkly divided: either they were petty bourgeoisie whose living standard was modest and education low, or industrial magnates. This polarized model of the business classes was due to the license system which put restrictions on industrial production. Regulations allowed only the extremes: small workshops could be established without license, and very large industrial conglomerates could afford to arrange the necessary manufacturing licenses by paying bribes and having the necessary contacts in the bureaucracy. Therefore, the Indian middle classes remained state-oriented up to the point of the economic reforms. During the new era, the old industrial elite faced the eradication of some of its privileges and new kinds of competition which partly marginalized it, forcing a total turnaround in business strategies.

Parallel to, and even rising past the old colonial Indian middle class, a new middle-class mentality representing an entirely new kind of ethos in the Indian context has emerged. Gurcharan Das (2002), a well-known columnist and former businessman, describes this new class as less hypocritical and more self-conscious than the old middle class. In the eyes of the older middle class, the new arrivals are seen in a very negative light, as smug upstarts; at the same time, middle-class people who come from humble backgrounds and low castes both admire those who have long-term middle-class traditions and accuse them of having become overtly Westernized and of abandoning the old Indian moral virtues. The women's sexual mores appear morally questionable to new middle-class eyes, and the interaction between generations is seen to be based on the wrong kind of equality.

In India, the social phenomenon that is the middle class is a multidimensional and internally divided field with a continuous struggle over not only concrete economic and social positions but social respect and its parameters at a symbolic level. Related to this, a debate rages over what should be called "genuine" Indian culture and tradition. The whole concept of the middle class and who should be considered as being part of it creates politically oriented civilizational struggles (Säävälä 2010a).

## 8.9 The Middle Classes and the Problem of Poverty

In spite of all the media hype, the "Westernization" in India is culturally insubstantial and centered on a small elite. Indeed, Indian sociologist Dipankar Gupta (2001) accuses the Indian middle classes of having adopted only a superficial layer of consumerism from the West, while leaving the deeper values of individualism, equality and anti-corruption untouched. He sees the middle class as a "Westoxicated," hypocritical and attitudinally conceited lot, who drape their traditional usages in the superficial garb of modernity. In Gupta's view, the followers of shallow Westernization who are in a hegemonic role in Indian society are not willing to work towards a more egalitarian India and thus the eradication of poverty appears unlikely.

Another well-known intellectual who has taken a critical stance on the cultural and social role of the new middle classes is Pavan K. Varma. In his widely read *The Great Indian Middle Class* (1998), he analyzes the transformations in the thinking of the middle classes in independent India, using newspaper reports as his source. According to Varma (1998), the middle class truly aspired towards a socially equal and secular nation at least up to the end of the 1980s. But the popularity of Hindu nationalism grew along with the economic reforms, and the expanding middle class concentrated more on ensuring their own riches and privileges than on strengthening the unified nation and removing poverty.

There is a similar pessimism in the writings of Gupta, Varma and many other scholars concerning the role of the new middle classes in the eradication of poverty: many see the middle classes as a politically reactionary, if not outright dangerous, social group. Actual empirical studies on the Indian middle classes are only now starting to emerge in greater numbers, and it is becoming more and more apparent that the middle classes do not form a unified social class or group (e.g. Fernandes 2006; Ganguly-Scrase and Scrase 2009). Indians themselves define the class by referring to education, English proficiency, regular income and a certain respectable way of life, and many different kinds of people see themselves as middle class: a high-school graduated office clerk with a low-caste background who has put his children into a private school is just as middle class as an affluent Brahman programmer in an IT company who can afford to go abroad for his holidays. Most likely these people see themselves as coming from different social strata, but there is also something that unifies them: they both greatly value higher education, and they want to see themselves as morally respectable representatives of the Indian nation—distinct from both the elite and the poor.

Transnational interconnectedness, reflecting the intensification of economic globalization, is currently deeply affecting India as well as most of the world. The increasing consciousness of difference that follows cross-border interaction has a peculiar cultural effect: instead of leading towards a dilution of cultural differences, it creates an awareness of divergent ways of life, and cultural identifications tend to become even stronger than before. Arjun Appadurai (1996), an American anthropologist and social theorist of Indian origin, refers to this globally visible tendency as "culturalism." Middle-class Indians are also more conscious than ever of being Indian: turning towards their own unique culture, deriving value from the ancient Vedas and sticking to religious rituals. Religion has seen a renaissance among middle-class Hindus: families who attended to religious practices less regularly a couple of decades ago are now performing them with enthusiasm. They are prepared to invest money and time in rituals, pilgrimages, visits to the temples and other sacred spaces, fasting and *kirtans* (religious song evenings). The Hindu identity of the middle classes has been reinforced, and some researchers, such as Varma, draw a direct line between this and the rise of extremist Hindu nationalism. In the thinking of the common man and woman, being middle class is identified as being of a caste Hindu background. Those who identify themselves as middle class, yet are Muslim, Christian, Sikh or *dalit*, etc., have to make a conscious decision about how much they want to emphasize their particularity.

People who describe themselves as middle class may dissociate themselves from the elite—the economic, political and cultural power holders—by alluding to their "Westernization" and moral depravation. Even though they themselves seek to purchase many of the same goods if they can afford them, they draw a distinct line between themselves and the affluent, who in their eyes lead a morally questionable life. The new middle classes relate to the West ambiguously: at times negatively, at times with admiration. This comes out nicely in a comment of a young lower-middle-class Hyderabadi man concerning women's way of dressing:

> Modern dress should be there but should not go beyond limits, should not be exposing. We are not rendered modern by wearing jeans and western clothes, but we should be modernised by nature, by *behaviour*, then only our moral purity shows. (Quoted in Säävälä 2010a, 126)

Closer examination of attitudes discloses that "Westernization" is associated with efficiency, hygiene and affluence, but also with selfishness, immorality and a mercenary mentality. The modern consumerist way of life is viewed in a positive light, whereas other Western values, particularly those organizing relations between men and women, individual and community, are not (Säävälä 2010a). Womanhood is in the center stage in defining middle class way of life as most of the central values touch upon women's roles as family members.

The middle classes are by definition in-between; as such, a definite line must also be drawn and maintained between people who include themselves in the category and the "poor." The disadvantaged are either viewed with distancing pity or their plight and suffering is brushed aside with references to habituation: the poor are supposed to be "used to" their poverty and unable to live in anything other than squalor. The caste-based way of thinking that allots different virtues, duties and rights (*dharma*) to each and everyone according to their birth status, makes it relatively easy to accommodate the class difference without needing to excuse one's own privilege (Säävälä 2010a). The new middle classes have varying attitudes to the role of the state and its political machinery in alleviating poverty, depending on their background.

Those who have managed to climb the social ladder with the help of the reservations for Scheduled Tribes, Scheduled Castes and Other Backward Classes in governmental jobs and seats in educational institutions tend to place more reliance on the actions of the state and national governments in battling inequality and poverty. Those who have improved their position by taking advantage of liberalized financial arrangements tend to have a very staunch belief in the free market and they often oppose public programs likely to increase public expenditure, citing them as wasteful and leading to corruption. The middle classes failed to solve India's poverty problem between independence and the end of 1980s, when pro-poverty alleviation and pro-state movements began to culminate more vigorously—and they are unlikely to solve it in New India either. The onus lies on the underdogs, the workers, the farmers and the underprivileged themselves to fight for their cause and pressure the political democracy to act for them.

## 8.10 Conclusion

Absolute, hunger-causing poverty is widespread but constantly decreasing in India and this decline will hopefully finally accelerate in the future, although thus far the pace of poverty reduction has been unpardonably slow compared to other developing Asian societies. India's greatest resource is its people. The creation of opportunities and innovations through better education would make all this valuable potential available for both the individual and the common good. The structure of the population is favorable to economic development and the dependency ratio of the elderly to the able-bodied will be kept in check for decades to come, unlike in most parts of the world. India could develop into a global center of production, like present-day China, and a hatchery of social, technical and scientific innovations if an improved standard of education for all and improvements in social equity could be guaranteed.

The proportion of Indians who can be called middle class is rising rapidly and the huge number aspiring to a better life is a politically unpredictable group if their hopes are frustrated. To the new middle classes, "the poor" represent a hopeless India: the attitude towards the less fortunate is negative and unsympathetic. Many new middle-class families have had to fight all their lives to get away from their humble backgrounds and once out of them they want to emphasize the distinction. However, while the attitudes of the better off towards the problems of poverty are often unresponsive, even cold-shouldered, there exists a political will towards removal of poverty. The parties do not represent only the well-to-do and the powerful, and they do try to arrange benefits and improvements to the voting masses, if sometimes with counterproductive or contradictory results like new caste-quota allotments and benefits to the farmers that appear useless from the perspective of the national economy. Finally, it appears that, as the new middle classes and business elite adopt an anti-welfare-state attitude, thereby stressing the benefits and power of the free market, constitutional democracy is possibly the only guarantee that poverty in India will be overcome in the coming decades.

# Chapter 9

# ECONOMY, LABOR AND PRODUCTION

India's economic growth has rested on a unique combination of its economic sectors. For the last few decades, India's fastest-growing economic domain has been its service sector which now makes up more than half of the gross national product. India's development, therefore, differs from that of China where industry has been the largest and fastest-growing economic domain.

**Chart 9.1.** Share (%) of gross domestic product in India per sector

|      | Agriculture | Industry | Services |
|------|-------------|----------|----------|
| 1991 | 31.4        | 25.9     | 42.7     |
| 1992 | 30. 3       | 25.6     | 44.1     |
| 1993 | 30.7        | 25.1     | 44.2     |
| 1994 | 30.0        | 25.2     | 44.8     |
| 1995 | 29.5        | 25.8     | 44.6     |
| 1996 | 27.3        | 26.9     | 45.8     |
| 1997 | 27.8        | 26.5     | 45.6     |
| 1998 | 26.0        | 26.4     | 47.6     |
| 1999 | 25.9        | 25.8     | 48.3     |
| 2000 | 25.0        | 25.3     | 49.7     |
| 2001 | 23.9        | 25.8     | 50.3     |
| 2002 | 24.0        | 25.0     | 51.0     |
| 2003 | 21.4        | 25.8     | 52.7     |
| 2004 | 21.7        | 25.6     | 52.7     |
| 2005 | 20.2        | 26.2     | 53.6     |
| 2006 | 19.5        | 26.4     | 54.1     |
| 2007 | 18.5        | 26.7     | 54.8     |
| 2008 | 17.8        | 26.5     | 55.7     |
| 2009 | 17.0        | 25.7     | 57.3     |
| 2010 | 14.20       | 28.0     | 57.8     |

Source: Interlink, www.interlinkre.com

Despite India's economic growth, the majority of workers lack secure contracts, benefits or social protection. 83 percent of the workforce in India, outside agriculture, worked informally during 1994–2000 (ILO 2002). Economic activities of even large companies may consist of both a formal and an informal workforce. Although the lines between formal and informal are increasingly blurred, the concept of informal employment generally refers to casual or insecure work with no welfare guarantees or protection by the employer or the state. Informal economy is also often defined as a type of economic activity that is not regulated or taxed by the state. Globalization and economic reforms have been accompanied by the swelling of the informal economy in many developing countries (ILO-WTO 2009). India's informal sector, too, has expanded through the restructuring of the public sector and the decentralization of production for global markets (Breman 2004; Joshi 2003; Parry et al. 1999; Chari 2004; De Neve 2005). Cross (2010) illustrates the interplay between new industry and informal economy by showing how even the special economic zones depend on the flexibility of labor: the terms of work within the special economic zone he studied in Andhra Pradesh, south India, were indistinguishable from any other sites of casual, informal and insecure labor. Similarly, Singh and Sapra (2007) note that within the garment industry, it is not easy to distinguish informal from formal labor, because formal units outsource work to smaller units in order to be able to compete.

## 9.1 Agriculture: Growth and Crisis

India has the second-largest arable area in the world after the United States. Agriculture, also part of the informal economy, employs 60 percent of the population, down from 70 percent in the early 1990s. The share of agriculture in overall GDP fell from 30 percent in the early nineties, to 14 percent in 2010. Agricultural growth slowed down considerably during the first decade of the reforms but reached later the government goal of 4 percent growth (Agricultural Trade Policy Analysis Unit 2007).

As in the West Bengali village of Janta, agricultural production has, almost simultaneously, experienced growth and crisis in India. Extreme poverty, which manifested itself as food scarcity, disappeared from Janta in the 1990s, reflecting the decrease of poverty in the entire state from 73 percent to 32 percent during 1977–2000 (Debroy and Bhandari 2006).

In Janta, affluent houses acquired television sets, motor cycles, tractors, jeeps and, from 2000 onwards, mobile phones. However, for most of the villagers the rise in living standards has meant small improvements in the quality of life. Daily laborers have prospered in that that they can now afford a more balanced diet, better-quality clothing, soap and oil. The villagers' understanding of the essentials of the standard of living is summed up by the Bengali expression *khaua makha pora*, which literally means eating, anointing the skin with oil and clothing.

The economic growth of rural West Bengal is often presented as an example of the benefits of land reforms because unlike most other states, West Bengal has distributed land to the landless. Although the allotted plots are too small to support even a small family, they bring additional income to daily laborers and increase the amount of arable land. Most researchers agree that the land reforms have, at least indirectly, contributed to agricultural growth by bridging the income gap. It has, however, been a new type of irrigation technology that has had the most decisive economic impact in the region. The inexpensive movable pump sets became common in the village during the 1990s allowing even small-scale farmers to grow several crops a year. The intensification of agriculture has provided landless laborers with considerably more employment opportunities than in earlier decades. Unlike in the Punjab, Haryana and western Uttar Pradesh, where the average farm size is bigger, the rise in productivity in West Bengal has raised the living standards of the rural majority because the intensification of agriculture has so far not led to large-scale, labor-displacing mechanization.

The rapid rate of improvement in the living standards of small-scale farmers stalled around the year 2000. Price ratios between produce and the cost of farming were most profitable around 1996–7, but since then the price of rice dropped, while the growing supply of vegetables decreased their market value. The Food Department subsidizes farmers by buying rice at a higher rate than market prices, but because the department buys rice through the rice-millers this subsidy does not fully reach the producers. By 2003, rice cultivation had plunged into a full-blown crisis. Only large-scale farmers could continue to make profits thanks to the higher rates of production and investments in side businesses.

Ghosh and Harris-White (2002) argue that the crisis has evolved from differences in the political control of agricultural price structures both within India and Asia. As a result of Central Government reforms, it is now possible to transport food grains between the various Indian states which, nevertheless, have retained the authority to decide on state subsidies. Due to the state-level differences in subsidies, cheap rice from Bihar now finds its way to West Bengal. The global liberalization of the rice market in turn has diminished West Bengal's farmers' previous markets in Bangladesh, Nepal and Bhutan because these countries are now able to import cheaper rice from other Asian countries.

Developments in Janta reflect what has happened to agriculture in all of India, except that growth in West Bengal started later than many other regions.

India started to develop its agriculture right after it gained independence. The land-leasing system created by the British was abolished in 1955, and a land ceiling was imposed in 1960.

The average farm size in India was about 1.4 hectares in the late 1990s and continues to shrink, as farms are usually divided on inheritance. Out of India's 116 million farmers, around 60 percent have less than 1 hectare and together they farm 17 percent of the land. The share of medium to large farms (above 4 hectares) is just over 7 percent of all holdings, but these account for around 40 percent of the land. Consequently, many of the small farms are subsistence holdings, with low investment and productivity growth (Agricultural Trade Policy Analysis Unit 2007).

India's dependence on agricultural imports in the early 1960s convinced planners that maintaining national independence, security and political stability required self-sufficiency in food production. The resulting policies led to a program of agricultural improvement called the Green Revolution, as well as a public distribution system and price supports for farmers. In 1969, prime minister Indira Gandhi nationalized 21 banks; in 1980, she required them to direct 40 percent of their credit towards agriculture and small-scale businesses. The government also initiated investments in agricultural sciences, rural administration and rural development projects (Debroy and Bhandari 2006).

India managed to get along with very few food imports in the 1980s and by the early 1990s, India was self-sufficient in food grain production. This "Green Revolution" dealt specifically with cultivation methods and entailed large farmers, in particular, adopting new irrigation methods, high-yielding hybrid seeds, fertilizers and pesticides in the main agricultural regions of India. The Green Revolution served to accentuate existing rural inequalities because its main target was the already progressive, wealthy farmers who were in the position to adapt to it. Regionally, the greatest improvements took place in the wheat-growing areas of Punjab. New farming methods led to increases in rice production and particularly in wheat production (Brass 1990).

The growth rate in agricultural GDP had risen gradually from 3 percent to 4 percent in the 1960s and 1970s, to 5–6 percent in the 1980s, to 6–7 percent following the financial reforms in 1991, but stalled and then declined sharply in the late 1990s to less than 2 percent (Debroy and Bhandari 2006). The vicious circle of rural indebtedness has intensified leading to tragedy: for the past decade, over 15,000 farmers commit suicide each year. The five most affected areas are Maharashtra, Karnataka, Andhra Pradesh, Madhya Pradesh and Chhattisgarh (National Crime Records Bureau 2010). The timing of the culmination of rural distress and discontent raises questions of the extent to which the economic reforms caused the crisis.

Investments in agriculture and rural infrastructure like irrigation, product development and research decreased from 1.92 percent to 1 percent during 1990–2003. Liberalization of the economy did not, however, entail cutting state subsidies to agriculture which mainly consists of subsidizing the sale of petrol and fertilizers. The GATT agreements did not presuppose the reduction of agricultural subsidies, because subsidies in India did not exceed the maximum standards (Kim 2006, 148). As oil prices have shot up, the government has increased both petrol subsidies as well as market prices. The greatest change for Indian agriculture has been the opening of the domestic market to imported goods as required by the GATT agreements.

India opened its agricultural economy to multinational companies at the same time as it terminated price regulation, except on wheat and rice which the State purchases for its grain bank and for public food distribution. Agricultural products now follow global market prices. As a result, income from the sale of products has often not kept up with rises in production costs. Indian producers now have to compete with countries which can afford to pay higher agricultural subsidies than India. Even though most Indian farm products are competitive in the world market and India still protects its production through relatively high import tariffs, import has superseded local production of some items. For instance, after the trade liberation India emerged as one of the greatest importers of cooking oil, despite the fact that India used to be self-sufficient in cooking oils (Debroy and Bhandari 2006).

As required by the World Bank's structural adjustment program, India opened its seed trade to multinational companies in 1998. The farmers had to replace the seeds they had saved from their own farming with purchased seeds, the cultivation of which require large investments in pesticides and fertilizers. Farming has become more capital intensive, which has led to a spiraling web of debt and bankruptcies because investments are no guarantee of good harvests. The cotton farmers who have invested in hybrid seeds marketed by multinational companies have been hit the hardest. The new varieties did not grow in India as expected, and the abundant subsidies paid by the US government to its cotton farmers have kept prices at an unbearable level for Indian farmers (Siva 2004).

But agriculture in India would be in crisis even without the economic reforms, because the Green Revolution never extended to the whole of rural India. Only about one-third of the arable land is irrigated. Both credit and insurance systems for farmers are still insufficient: in spite of official credit arrangements, many small-scale farmers have to resort to private moneylenders, because they do not fulfill the criteria for official credit. In most parts of India, the land has not been distributed to the landless as stipulated by the Central Government. The shortage of non-agricultural jobs in rural areas becomes more entrenched as small farms are fragmented into smaller units through inheritance. The weaknesses of the rural infrastructure add to the hazards of agriculture and entrepreneurship: the road network is insufficient and great parts of the rural areas are still without electricity. Many farmers cannot afford to have electricity, and the areas that do have it suffer from frequent power cuts because electricity production is not sufficient. Loss in production due to shortcomings in the distribution system is estimated at 20–25 percent (Debroy and Bhandari 2006).

Irrigation has increased agricultural production, but it has also lowered groundwater to a critical level in many areas where water-intensive crops such as rice and sugarcane are grown. Out of the 5,723 geographically defined areas of India, about 1,000 are in danger of drying out, whereas 20 years ago the figure was only 250. In Rajasthan, one of the most arid states, groundwater is in danger of running out in 80 percent of its areas. Even in Punjab, the state with the most effective farming system, 79 percent of its surface areas are at risk of drying out. In Haryana, the figure is 59 percent and in Tamil Nadu 46 percent (Sen Gupta 2006). As described in Chapter 11, depletion of groundwater can be prevented by recharging wells using harvested rainwater. Prime minister Manmohan Singh has warned the state governments not to provide cheap electricity to farmers for irrigation, but they are reluctant to raise the price of electricity for fear of losing votes (Sen Gupta 2006). Misuse and overuse of fertilizers together with irrigation have impoverished the soil: irrigation has increased salinity and fertilizers have led to nutritional imbalances (Debroy and Bhandari 2006).

Manmohan Singh, former finance minister in the government that started these economic reforms, believed at the beginning of the 1990s that agriculture would benefit even though economic liberalization did not directly concern agriculture. The escalation of the rural crisis has, however, made it clear that agricultural development requires special measures. The government coalition led by the Hindu nationalist party, the BJP, lost the election in 2004 mainly due to rural opposition. The Congress-led coalition government in turn committed itself to the development of rural areas. It has raised the Minimum Support Price at which it purchases rice and wheat from farmers considerably in past five years. The Central Government encourages state governments to promote agricultural diversity and contract farming. Cultivation of crops for bio-fuel is expected to help cultivate land not fertile enough for other crops.

However, the opportunities for the Central Government to develop agriculture are limited because state governments carry the main responsibility for agriculture. According to Ghosh and Harris-White (2002), who investigated the politics of the agrarian economy in Tamil Nadu, economic liberalization did not affect the state's agricultural policies. Political parties still safeguard their electorate with support packages for farmers, and the responsibility for agriculture is fragmented to various poorly coordinated sections of governance.

Despite large-scale distress among the rural populace, there is growth in areas where new methods have been successfully adopted and where farming methods are ecologically balanced. The worst-case scenario would be the widespread inability to improve agricultural production, leading to India's dependence on imports and to the intensification of the vicious cycle of rural poverty. This would have a major impact on the nation's economic development and increasingly drive people into the cities. The Central Government and the states are, however, likely to invest in rural development, and rural standards of living are likely to improve in spite of the difficulties because the majority of voters are rural. Any government seen to threaten rural economy is not likely to remain in power for a second term. In spite of the complexity of the problems, it is possible to increase production simply by bringing more arable land under ecologically sustainable irrigation.

The Central Government has increased its support for farmers but what has been largely still missing are the investments aimed at raising the agricultural productivity. One exception is Andhra Pradesh, which shifted its focus from information technology to developing agriculture. IT industries were encouraged in Andhra Pradesh under the aegis of chief minister Chandrababu Naidu (1995–2004), but he lost the election in 2004 due to the protests of rural voters. The Congress Party government led by chief minister Rajasekhara Reddy promised to invest in agriculture and especially irrigation projects. These irrigation projects were realized, but were saddled with corruption scandals.

The Central Government gave 30 million small farmers a loan waiver in 2008. Critics claim that the measure ignored those most in need, as only 20 million of the country's 110 million farmers are estimated to have bank loans, against the majority who are indebted to usurious private money lenders. Moneylenders are estimated to account for over 70 percent of loans to small farmers, at crippling interests averaging 30 percent (Raja 2008).

Nonetheless, rural economy shows some positive signs. Agricultural production grew at the rate of 4.5 percent during 2007–8. Largely due to unfavorable weather conditions the growth dipped to −0.1 percent in 2008–9. In 2009–10, widespread drought maintained the growth low, 0.4 percent, but largely thanks to favorable monsoon rains in 2010–11 the agriculture sector grew by 6.6 percent (Apco Worldwide 2011). According to NSS data from 2003–4, 62 percent of consumer expenditure in India comes from rural India (Bijapurkar 2008, 229). The rural economy is estimated to have grown on average 7.3 percent compared to 5.4 percent in the urban economy during the past 10 years.

Figures from the Central Statistical Organisation show that the rural economy accounted for 49 percent of India's GDP in 2000, which is a significant increase from 41 percent in 1981–2 and 46 percent in 1993–4 (India Knowledge@Wharton 2007). Much of this growth is driven by the rural non-farming sector: manufacturing, construction and trade, hotels and restaurants. The share of agriculture in rural economy has gone down from 64 percent in the early 1980s to 51.8 percent in 2000. Unlike upper-class urban India, rural India has not suffered much from the recession in export industries. Companies from Coca-Cola Co. to telecom provider Reliance Communications India Ltd have stated that rising sales in rural areas are driving their nationwide growth (India Knowledge@Wharton 2007).

The new work opportunities outside farming and in urban areas are predominantly available for men because women's mobility is restricted; consequently, Indian agriculture is feminizing. Women's work tends to remain invisible and unacknowledged in census data; nevertheless, women's share of rural workforce increased by 4 percent during 1991–2001 according to census information (Vepa 2007). In 2001, 33 percent of the cultivators and 47 percent of the agricultural laborers were women. In Andhra Pradesh, Gujarat, Karnataka, Madhya Pradesh, Maharashtra, Rajasthan and Tamil Nadu more than half of agricultural laborers are women, and women cultivators outnumber men in some states (Vepa 2007). Although Indian agriculture is largely viewed as male-centered activity, women have always formed a crucial part of the agricultural workforce. While culturally conceived ideas have relegated certain highly visible tasks, for instance plowing, as men's duties, much of the work of farming has been carried out by women. Low-caste women usually are able to participate in a greater variety of farming tasks than high-caste women.

## 9.2 Industrial Growth

Industries have not grown as briskly in India as in China to provide employment to the underemployed rural population. However, Indian industries have rationalized and improved profitability after the economic reforms.

In comparison to China, the growth of Indian industries has been burdened by the lack of suitably educated laborers and stringent labor laws. Particularly problematic for many employers is the law dictating that businesses employing more than 100 persons cannot fire an employee without permission from the local labor court. But Indians have also benefited from labor laws. The working conditions in India's special economic zones are not perfect, but workers' rights are not violated as blatantly as, for example, in China and Thailand, where workers are subjected to numerous hazards (Wilde and de Haan 2006).

The Government of India passed the Special Economic Zones (SEZ) Act in 2005 in order to attract investments, generate export revenues and create manufacturing jobs. In 2007, the government introduced a new piece of legislation, which extended its power to acquire land for SEZs. By 2009, India had 300 functioning SEZs and 560 had been approved. Companies enjoy many privileges such as tax concessions within the SEZs, and foreign companies can own 100 percent of their businesses. The Left front resisted the Central Government's attempt to leave the zones completely outside the purview of labor laws; nevertheless, state governments have the right to declare special economic zones as emergency services where workers do not have the right to go on strike. Labor union activities within the special economic zones are also restricted because outsiders are not permitted entry.

### 9.2.1 Conflicts over land acquisitions

Conflicts over the creation of special economic zones culminated in Nandigram in West Bengal, but land acquisitions have provoked large-scale protests also in other parts of India. The 1894 Act allows the government to acquire land for a "public purpose." It was originally devised to create a system of irrigation canals and roads, but in recent decades it has been used to buy land from reluctant peasant-farmers for private profit. Special economic zones and other new industries have tended to create few benefits, including jobs, in relation to the number of people they displace. Those who cannot prove their landownership by official documents such as through the registration of a title to property get little more than a pittance, and a large majority of those who are displaced due to land acquisition are unable to find an equivalent livelihood or other means of survival.

In 2009, the Supreme Court heard half a dozen cases against SEZs which could eventually lead to changes in India's policies and laws on the zones. In Orissa, India's largest steel project, POSCO, has been stalled since 2006 because of protests. Other major manufacturing projects have stalled due to land acquisition problems, including projects by Arcelol Mittal, Vedanta, Jindal Group, Tata Steel, GMR Energy and Nissan. Across India, nearly 200 proposed factories, railroads, highways, and other projects are held back due to land struggles. The association of Indian Chambers of Commerce estimates that investments worth $98 billion are stalled (Srivastava 2009). Local resistance led the government to withdraw the SEZ policy in Goa altogether in 2007; Goa no longer approves new special economic zones.

Although the present law states that landowners may lose their land rights in cases where the government has decided to acquire their land for a public purpose, in practice projects get stalled because politicians are reluctant to evict voters. States and companies have sought to offer terms and prices that landowners find acceptable and providing housing and job training for the displaced. For instance, JSW Bengal Steel paid farmers three times more that the price set by the government, as well as giving landowners company shares. In Pune, Maharashtra, villagers themselves created an industrial area raising their land value tenfold.

The pace of development of special economic zones has slowed down considerably. As of June 2009, 568 formal approvals had been granted for SEZ projects, but only half of these had acquired the necessary land. The Indian government is under growing pressure to formulate a humane rehabilitation policy for those displaced by land acquisitions. The Land Acquisition, Rehabilitation and Resettlement Bill was introduced in Lok Sabha in 2011, and it will be voted by the parliament after the public debate. If a new bill proposal is passed by the parliament, companies will be required to come to agreement with 80 percent of the landowners about the purchase of land after which the government could force the remaining landowners to sell at the market rate agreed by other landowners.

## 9.2.2 Upgrading the infrastructure

The Indian government's recent endeavors to improve infrastructure outside the SEZs shows that it realizes the need to make the entire economy, and not just the special economic zones, more favorable for industries and businesses. Decades of under-investment in roads, ports, airports and power has left the country—and even its fast-growing business hubs like Bangalore—crippled. Even in one of the richest states, Maharashtra, major cities lose power one day a week to relieve pressure on the grid. Whereas China was able to launch a massive upgrade initiative, building more than 40,000 km of expressways, India has just 6,000 km of such highways. India's new government has identified the rebuilding of infrastructure as a major way to induce growth and bridge regional divides. This includes the planned expenditure of $500 billion in 2007–12. Since the country's public debt stands at 82 percent of GDP, the eleventh-worst ranking in the world, much of the money for these new projects will have to come from private sources. Thus, the realization of these large-scale plans remains uncertain. The government expects that public and private organizations will invest in highways, power generation, ports and airports, and infrastructure will also be developed along the entire food distribution chain (Lamont 2009).

A recent McKinsey report (2009) concludes that India does not compare favorably with other countries in executing infrastructure projects, with difficulties stretching from the tendering process to project completion. Nevertheless, some major projects have been completed and others are on the way. Golden Quadrilateral—a $12 billion initiative spanning more than 4,800 km of four- and six-lane expressways connecting Mumbai, Delhi, Kolkata and Chennai—was announced complete in 2012. The first phase of a new subway in New Delhi was finished in late 2005 on budget and ahead of schedule. New airports are under construction in Bangalore and Hyderabad, with more planned elsewhere.

### 9.2.3 Growth during the global recession

Despite the land disputes and the global recession, India's industrial production increased in 2009 thanks to increased government spending and lower borrowing costs, which stoked the demand for cars, motorbikes and other consumer goods. Output at factories, utilities and mines rose 6.8 percent in July 2009 from 2008 (Bloomberg News, September 11, 2009).

The textile industry is India's largest, providing 30 percent of the country's export earnings and employing 35 million workers. During the last 5 years India's cotton production has risen by 57 percent. As in other developing countries, India's textile industry has benefited from the removal of textile trade quotas in 2005 as a result of the WTO agreement. Since 60 percent of the garments manufactured in India are exported, the textile industry has, however, suffered heavily because of the recession.

India is the world's tenth-largest steel producer, but apart from its largest and oldest company, Tata Steel, this industry has experienced economic difficulties because of Indian imports of cheap steel. Yet growth prospects for the industry seem promising because of the growing domestic demand. India was the only country to have recorded a positive overall growth in crude steel production, at 1.01 percent during the first quarter of 2009 (*Trade Chakra* 2009). The automotive industry in India has evinced vigorous growth thanks to the drop in interest rates, increasing domestic demand and the growth in exports.

## 9.3 Communication Superpower

India's radio, television, press and movie industries are the largest in the world, and India ranks fourth in the number of the Internet users. India was already the largest movie producer in the world in 1971, and 1,000 films are now produced in Indian film studios annually (Chakravarty 1993; Khanna 2003). Ten million people buy a movie ticket daily in India.

The spectrum of Indian films varies from Bollywood-type entertainment to art films. Song, dance and fantasy became the central elements of the Indian cinema already in the 1940s. In addition to Bollywood, the largest language groups—Hindi, Tamil, Telugu, Bengali, Marathi, Kannada, Odiya and Malayalam—support distinct major cinema industries and traditions.

The epics *Ramayana* and *Mahabharata*, classic Indian and nineteenth-century Parsi theatre, folk theatre, Hollywood and music television all have an influence on Indian cinema. In spite of Western influences and technology, Indian cinema has retained its distinct characteristics: it does not follow the realistic American cinematic tradition in its cinematography or narrative structure. The majority of films deal with romantic themes but they do not exclude topical issues: cinema both reflects and influences the culture and society. Despite their traditional elements, these films represent freedom and a certain novelty for most viewers. Although most films dilute conflicts, they also articulate problems and air conflicts.

Indian cinema is also an export product. Its themes and styles, deriving from Indian culture and society, enthrall surprisingly wide audiences round the world. Indian films are popular in South Africa, Southeast Asia, East Africa, Mauritius, the Caribbean Islands, the Near East, Great Britain, Canada, Australia, the United States and Eastern Europe (Gokulsing, Moti and Dissanayake 2004).

The growth of the press in India started in the 1970s after the termination of the emergency with its concomitant press censorship. There were 27,000 newspapers published in India in 93 languages in 2000 (Singhal and Rogers 2001, 54). Radio broadcasting started in India in 1923 and now serves two-thirds of Indian households. Commercial radio stations were permitted in 2000, and FM stations have captured new audiences in urban areas, although they are not allowed to broadcast news.

Television broadcasting commenced in India in 1959, in an experimental, educational format sponsored by UNESCO. Prime minister Indira Gandhi saw television as an important media for developing rural India—her critics accused her of harnessing the state television company, Doordarshan, for her own political purposes. Audiences grew slowly in the 1960s when Doordarshan had the broadcasting monopoly, but spread to rural areas when the SITE satellite television project began broadcasting educational programs to the villages of six states in the 1970s (Singhal and Rogers 2001, 54).

The demand for television sets grew rapidly in the 1980s when Doordarshan started to broadcast *Hum Log*, a soap opera about a middle-class family, and *Ramayana* and *Mahabharata*, the serialized versions of the two epics. The popularity of cable television increased in India after Iraq attacked Kuwait where many Indians were working as migrant laborers. During the war, Indians could follow developments from the international channels. To satisfy the demand for news of the conflict, Indian satellite television companies and news channels sprang up almost overnight. They sent programs to India from abroad via satellite, thus circumventing the law whereby only the Doordarshan had the monopoly to broadcast programs on Indian soil. In 1995, the Supreme Court overturned the government's claim that it owned the airways, declaring them to be public property.

India's media has become too vast and diverse for any ruling party to utilize it for its own purposes. Half of Indian households possessed television in 2007, and half of television owners had access to cable television. There are more than 400 private satellite TV channels permitted to uplink from India and more than 70 foreign satellite TV channels permitted to uplink from abroad and downlink in India. The educational programs of early television have been replaced by entertainment, news and educational programs disguised as entertainment. The great number of channels has segmented the audiences so that no one channel can dominate broadcasting as the Doordarshan used to do. The growth of the regional media has brought local issues into the limelight, while simultaneously bringing global issues even to the most remote villages (Govindassamy 2009).

The commercialization of the media has increased entertainment programs targeted at the middle and upper classes, which has resulted in less space for airing burning social issues. News channels aim to cut costs and maximize profits and this has led to the elimination of the traditional news reporting. Well-edited films have been replaced by chatting reporters and film fragments. Channels compete with scoops on scandals, showing live broadcasts of bureaucrats and politicians taking bribes. The media is also keen to air the concerns of civic organizations and no major problem or crisis can go unreported in India; the distress of farmers appears in the media regularly. Public discussions create pressure to provide solutions, as well as generating resolutions. As described in Chapter 11, media coverage of the health hazards caused by pollution led to the election victory of environmentalist politicians and the efforts to clean Delhi's air. The commercialization of the media exemplifies the growth of the domestic market and illustrates how advertising and brand creation have become prerequisites for sales promotion in India.

## 9.4 The Information Industries

About 0.2 percent of the Indian population works in the IT and outsourcing sector. This minority is often referred to as "the creamy layer"—a term that brings into focus the fact that the new affluence is concentrated in the hands of a small minority. The share of India's IT industry in the GDP increased from 1 percent in 1998 to 6 percent in 2010. The number of IT and outsourcing workers has increased from 300,000 to 2.5 million between 1999 and 2011 (Nasscom 2008). Reliable figures on the women's share of employment in India's IT sector are lacking, but women are estimated to comprise less than a third of workers. This share may increase in the future, as women constitute about 40 percent of all students currently enrolled in institutions of higher education (Donahue 2010). The Indian IT industries have managed to maintain growth despite the recession, albeit at a slower pace.

In spite of its rapid growth in the last decades, the history of the Indian IT sector did not start with the economic reforms. Both mathematics and programming have their roots in the long analytical tradition of Indian culture and philosophy, and especially the principles of modern mathematics which were developed in ancient India. The government started investing in defense and in nuclear and space technology in Bangalore during the Nehru regime. Bangalore, the capital of Karnataka, was chosen to be a center of technological development because at the time it was located outside the range of Pakistani missiles.

Electronics were Indianized because companies did not have foreign currency for imports, so they produced their own technologies. In 1977, the Janata government tightened its regulation of foreign companies, causing many multinational companies such as IBM to leave the country. Indian IT experts who had worked in these multinational companies and lost their jobs started their own companies serving the customers that the multinationals had deserted. The success stories of companies such as Wipro and Infosys and their founders have encouraged and symbolized an entire entrepreneurial ethic and spirit.

Azim Premji, the president of Wipro, discontinued his studies in the United States after his father's death, returning to India to take charge of the family company, Western Indian Vegetable Products Limited. Premji developed Wipro's food oil trade, but also took advantage of the growing demand for IT services by establishing Wipro Infotech. The company has made him the richest man in India (Singhal and Rogers 2001, 48–52).

Founder and former managing director of Infosys, Narayanan Murthy returned to India in 1975 from Paris where he had worked as a programmer. Murthy had wanted to become a Leftist politician and establish an orphanage. His future father-in-law, however, refused to allow his daughter to marry Murthy unless he had a job. So Murthy got a job in a small IT company. In 1981, he borrowed $250 from his wife in order to establish Infosys Technologies. The company started operating in a small flat which Murthy had bought with a loan, using his wife's jewelry as collateral. The company gradually attracted big companies as its clients, and Infosys became the first Indian company to be quoted in the US stock exchange in 1999 (Kumar and Sethi 2005, 52–63).

Prime minister Rajiv Gandhi reformed the sphere of information technology by reducing export duties and defining IT as an industry, which facilitated entrepreneurs' chances of acquiring credit. The economic reforms granted IT businesses a special status. Foreign companies operating in newly established technology parks were given tax concessions and 100 percent ownership rights.

The fast growth of Bangalore has become a burden on its infrastructure to the extent that many companies have sought cheaper locations and better infrastructure. New IT centers have developed in different parts of the country. Chennai has proved especially attractive thanks to its good infrastructure and short distance from both a harbor and Bangalore.

India is the world's most attractive outsourcing location thanks to the world's largest inexpensive, English-speaking workforce, undersea cables and abundant flight connections. Outsourcing business has grown annually at the rate of 60 percent during the last few decades. This sector employs about 1 million people at present and the number is estimated to swell to 2 million. In addition to call centers, Indian companies offer services in planning, architecture, management, legal services, accountancy and the development of medicines, health care and research.

The Indian IT industry has been able to offer high quality, productivity and the ability to meet deadlines. The best quality classification certificate in the world based on accuracy of programming has been granted to 74 companies, and 50 of them are located in India. Whereas the average answering time in a call center in the United States is 2.4 seconds, in India it is only 1.8 seconds (Gill 2005).

The extreme competitiveness creates pressures and an atmosphere of tension, which manifest in stress-related health problems among personnel (Nair 2006). Keeping one's national identity hidden has emerged as a new part of the work load: Indian call centers aim to train their workers in the American accent and lifestyle so that an American needing assistance cannot tell that he is being served from outside the United States. Because of the time difference, much of the call center activity takes place at night. The monotony of the work and scanty promotion prospects have led to a high rate of attrition among the workers. The annual turnover rates have been reported as high as 80 percent in the IT services sector and 100 percent for Indian call centers (Lacity et al. 2009). Both IT and outsourcing companies try to hold on to their workforce by arranging attractive leisure activities, so that the largest IT companies almost seem like holiday resorts with swimming pools, palm trees, gyms and shopping centers.

The growth of the Indian IT industry is restricted by the meager local demand for computers which are too expensive for most Indians to afford. Whereas the average American can buy a computer with the earnings from 12 days' work, the average Indian would need the earnings from 2 years. India's share of world programming markets is only 2 percent. Although India has the second-highest number of scientists in the world, this number also includes lower academic degrees and those from institutions of questionable standards due to the lack of resources. According to Gill (2005), the greatest weakness of the IT industry in India is that the majority of the workers have only a lower university degree. Whereas the United States produces 800 doctorates in information technology annually, India produces only 100. Consequently, most of the programming in India consists of routine tasks.

Although academic degrees are no guarantee of a job in India, the service sector is experiencing a shortage of suitable workers. Most Indian educational institutions direct their students to silently take notes during lectures and to learn by memorizing details, instead of teaching the skills required in the business world, like the art of conversation and voicing arguments, or how to make PowerPoint presentations in fluent English.

## 9.5 Conclusion

Agriculture and rural economy still employ large part of the population, and agriculture has to be able to feed the growing population. Thus, agriculture continues to be important for poverty reduction and economic growth. Despite the food self-sufficiency India has attained, agriculture continues to be faced with daunting problems. India's industries are hiring more underemployed rural people, although the shortcomings of the infrastructure like the power cuts and poor road networks hamper growth. The service industries, outsourcing businesses and IT industry still have promising prospects for growth. IT companies can increase productivity by expanding the share of development. To hold onto its leading position in the outsourcing trade, India has to improve its English-language teaching, as well as its entire higher education, and increase the number of fluent English speakers. Although there are no exact figures of English speakers in either country, a study by the British Council estimates that India may end up having less English speakers than China in the near future thanks to Chinese successes in boosting the learning of English within a much wider demographic, whereas in India it largely continues to be the privilege of a fairly elite group (Graddol 2010).

# Chapter 10

# NEW TECHNOLOGY:
# A SHORTCUT TO DEVELOPMENT?

New technologies hold the promise of offering an opportunity to accelerate development by leapfrogging to the latest high-tech solutions. Yet the GNP per inhabitant, for example of Karnataka, where one of India's foremost IT centers, Bangalore, is located, is lower than the average in India. An OECD study claims that the appropriation of IT technology by the poor can reduce poverty more efficiently than IT business itself, because the wealth created by IT companies is not evenly distributed (Batchelor et al. 2005). In comparison to many other developing nations, India has invested widely in using information technology for development.

Among the most ambitious ICT development plans in India is the National e-Governance Plan, which envisions providing all government services at computer kiosks all over India. Another large scale project, Unique Identity, launched in 2010, aims at improving access to state benefits by providing the poor with biometric identity cards. By 2012, 200 million members had added to store their fingerprints and irises to this voluntary database which will help them to claim their benefits (*Economist*, January 14, 2012).

In contrast to the large-scale state-led developmental plans, the actual motivations to use new technologies are diverse. The way middle-class Indians use sex-determination tests in order to abort female fetuses is a showcase example of how new technology may be used to reinforce aspirations which contribute to inequality. Another questionable form of technology use in India is surrogate motherhood. Couples unable to have a child can hire the womb of an Indian woman at a tenth of the cost of the same procedure in Western countries. Surrogate motherhood, until recently very rare, is a new form of profitable outsourcing, which poses many ethical questions. Not only does it expose women to health risks, but it poses difficult questions about the rights and emotions of the woman who has given birth to the child. Unlike in many other countries, womb-hiring has not been regulated in India but the Ministry of Health and Family Welfare has drafted a bill to control and monitor cases of surrogacy.

## 10.1 Limited Benefits of Computers

The Indian government embarked on computerization in 1986 when prime minister Rajiv Gandhi initiated NICNET, a network that connected the Central Government and the states through satellite networks. Thanks to this network, officers can directly access the information they require from databases without having to acquire all the information on paper.

Amul Milk Cooperative in Gujarat, which covers 70,000 villages, is a legendary example of the advantages of computerization. The farmers used to have to queue for so long to deliver milk that it could go sour. It took 10 days to get paid for the milk after the delivery. Now the milk is delivered onto digitalized scales which automatically measure fat percentage. The computer issues a slip for which the deliverer receives the payment instantly. Another success story of the adaptation of information technology is the computerization of the Indian Railways in 1999. Postal services are under computerization; and the archives of the Supreme Court and the handling of court cases have been computerized. Narayana Hrudayalaya, an institute specializing in heart diseases led by Bangalorean surgeon Devi Shetty has pioneered the diagnosis of rural patients via satellite. Both the state of Karnataka and the Indian Central Government have committed themselves to developing telemedicine, serving patients in remote areas directly from medical centers with the help of information technology, and 14 top-ranking Indian hospitals have been connected to rural health centers (I4D, May 2005).

Karnataka was the first state to computerize its land register, and many other states have since followed suit. Thanks to the computerized archives, farmers can now register their land and settle land disputes quickly without having to pay bribes, or at least not to the same extent as earlier. In the state of Andhra Pradesh, one can pay electricity, water and telephone bills and property tax in the Internet kiosks provided by the state. Citizens can also apply for and receive birth and death certificates, and various permits and passports through the Internet.

Several organizations and businesses offer Internet services for a fee in rural areas. The Kohlapur Cooperative has installed Internet kiosks in rural Maharashtra through which farmers can access information about farming, markets, health and education. E-Chaupal has opened Internet kiosks to foster the marketing of agricultural products in Madhya Pradesh, Andhra Pradesh, Karnataka and Uttar Pradesh. The farmers can now sell their products at the best possible price through the Internet without having to pay middlemen.

Computerized land registers and Internet payment systems have indeed improved governance in India by reducing officials' chances to demand bribes. As Kuriyan and Ray (2009) note, government-sponsored telecenters have also helped improve the general image of state governments by presenting them as clean and efficient. Yet, as in most developing countries, computers are still only accessed by a small minority in India. In fact, Sreekumar and Rivera-Sánchez (2008) argue that the performance of most ICT projects in rural India has been dismal. Computer kiosks are mainly used by the rural elites, and most of the projects have excluded women. ICT programs in general have been most successful in regions with higher agrarian prosperity and economic development, since increased access to market prices of agricultural commodities can benefit only those farmers that are not tied to wholesalers or moneylenders for buying seeds and fertilizers. Consequently, Sreekumar (2006) maintains that ICTs in rural India have served to reinforce existing social divides and even created new ones.

## 10.2 Internet Users are a Minority

Internet access and computer usage in India is hampered by the high price of computers, illiteracy, frequent power cuts, and the shortage of programs and relevant Internet sites in local languages. Yet, the lower-middle class has begun to embrace computers, driven by aspirations of a better future for the young through access to technology, and technology skills leading to technology jobs (Rangaswamy 2007b). Only 3 per 100 people in India had personal computers at home in 2007 (ITU 2009). It is difficult to get exact information on Internet use in India because many people use the Internet in public Internet cafes. Estimates vary from 1 in 10 Indians using the Internet regularly (Richardson 2009) to only 4 Internet users per 100 persons as estimated by ITU in 2007.

Indian youth has appropriated information technology more than the older generations. Middle and upper-class urban youth often use the Internet either at their homes or in Internet cafes without parental supervision, although parents usually control their children's social contacts carefully in other areas. Parents may consider browsing the Internet to be a useful hobby without being aware of how easy it is to establish contacts with strangers through the medium. Chat rooms in suburban areas are usually frequented by predominantly 18–22-year-old males who assume an online identity in order to meet new people. Visits to social-networking sites in India increased by 51 percent, from 13 million to 19 million visitors, during 2008, to 19 million visitors in December 2008 (Rangaswamy 2007a; Arora 2006; comScore 2008).

The number of broadband Internet subscribers was 0.37 per hundred persons in 2007 (ITU 2009); however, wireless technologies such as WLAN, edge and 3G have made the access to the Internet easier and more affordable in comparison to landline and broadband connections. The great majority of Indians are likely to access the Internet through their mobile phones, but so far the relatively high costs of both browsing and Internet-ready phones have stalled this growth potential. Approximately 9.3 million urban Indians used their mobile phones to access the Internet in 2009, a reach of approximately 3.3 percent of the urban population (Sinha 2009).

## 10.3 The Phenomenal Growth of the Mobile Market

Mobile technology obviates many of the obstacles of computerization: especially as low-end phones are much cheaper than computers. Calling requires neither literacy nor a constant source of electricity, and mobile networks are cheaper to build than landline networks. The rate of mobile phone sales in India has been record breaking ever since the introduction of mobile technology in 1995. India's teledensity has increased from less than 1 per 100 persons to 73 per 100 in the period 1991–2011.

The deregulation of the telesector opened up telephony for private operators, while the state continued to regulate and collect levies from the operator companies. Getting a landline connection used to take years under the old state monopoly. Mobile telephony made it possible to obtain a connection in merely a few minutes by buying a SIM card and talk time. Competition between mobile operators has driven the prices low, which in turn has helped to increase the subscriber base.

While the urban teledensity increased from 6 percent to 26 percent, the rural teledensity registered a mere increase from 0.4 percent to 2 percent between 1998 and 2005. The mobile revolution bypassed rural India initially because the state subsidized the building of landline networks instead of mobile networks, and the service provider companies found it more profitable to concentrate on urban areas instead of rural areas. But the building of mobile networks in rural areas has accelerated during the last few years thanks to the state subsidization of building of mobile networks, and operators turning their attention to the rural market after the likely saturation of the urban market in the near future (Kathuria et al. 2009). In 2011, rural teledensity in India reached 36 percent according to the Telecom Regulatory Authority of India.

## 10.4 Mobile Technology in the Village

During the author's fieldwork in a West Bengal village, Janta, in 1999–2000, the region's villages were not covered by a working phone system. One had to travel to town to make a call, but people seldom did so as the inadequate phone system meant they could not call other villages. By 2003, the district had just been covered by a mobile phone network, and there were four mobile phones in Janta and its two adjacent villages. By 2010, only 3 percent of the households in the village did not possess a phone.

Despite the initial low teledensity, phone services became available to the entire village thanks to public phones provided by service providers. These phones were placed in shops, whose owners made a small profit from operating them in return for ensuring that a person would be available to answer incoming calls. Callers usually came to use the phone equipped with a small piece of paper on which the phone number is written in Western numerals (as on the phone) and then had someone literate to dial for them. Calls were not made daily, but rather weekly or even monthly. Of the 100 calls recorded in 2005, 81 percent were made to relatives, 14 percent to business associates and 5 percent to friends. The majority of the calls (58 percent) were made to villages in the district—12 percent of the calls were to other districts, 16 percent to other states and one call was made to the United States.

During the period of low phone density, most calls were about organizing a phone call. In the village, a phone call could initiate a long chain of messages. One first needed to ask the person answering the neighborhood phone to deliver a message to the person to whom one wants to speak, asking that he or she should wait by the neighborhood phone at a specific time. Especially in the case of urgent matters, callers could simply relate their entire message to whoever has answered the phone, requesting this person to forward the message. Those answering the phone might also give information on behalf of the person with whom the caller would like to talk.

The public nature of the calls, as well as the collective manner of operating the phones, draws on village sociality and earlier patterns of communication. The social networks of rural West Bengal, India's most densely populated state, have always been well-knit. The nearest neighboring villages are almost adjacent to Janta and many people from Janta commute to Vishnupur (a town 12 kilometers from Janta) on a daily basis. Farmers sell vegetables in the marketplace, a few villagers have office jobs, college boys and girls attend school there and laborers go for work. Unlike many of the remotest villages in the district, Janta has good road connections. The villagers can commute by bike or bus to villages and cities farther away. Engine sounds rarely disturb the village's peaceful environment, although there were four cars, five tractors, and several motorbikes during the author's fieldwork. Janta also has a post office and daily mail delivery.

Village exogamy, women marrying outside their natal villages, is responsible for most of the connections between villages. Before the arrival of telephones, news of relatives in other villages, of women's natal families and men's in-laws, was conveyed via letter (by the literate part of the village) and visitors. Visitors brought with them other people's news (*khobor neua*) and delivered it to the relevant people in other villages, often on request. Phones have not done away with delivering other people's news, but they do give the villagers closer mutual interaction than before when there were fewer messages to deliver.

Visitor networks were often slow and even unreliable; consequently, villages were relatively isolated in comparison with urban areas. Women, for example, could not obtain news of a serious illness or the death of a close relative in time to view the body before the cremation and to participate in the death rituals. The inadequate communication infrastructure also contributed to villagers' considerable autonomy from state authorities and services. The more remote the village, the smaller the chances were of asking for or receiving help from outside in the case of emergencies and conflicts.

Since radios and television sets preceded phones in the villages, the villagers used to have better access to world news than to news of their relatives in other villages. Television viewing is not limited to television owners—usually middle- and large-scale farmers feel duty-bound to allow neighbors to watch their sets. Movies, mainly popular Hindi and Bengali movies (in the past on video tapes, but since 2000 on DVDs), are also shown daily in the village movie hall and in any neighborhoods that have acquired DVD players, where movies are shown in return for a small fee.

A chicken farmer who lived in the only neighborhood of the village that had electricity in 2003, was one of the first people in the village to obtain a mobile phone and shortly afterwards he also purchased a three-wheeler. These investments increased his monthly sales from 30 quintal to 150 quintal. He could soon invest in the village's first refrigerator, which he used for storing chickens. He also bought a color television and a DVD player and became the first villager to get cable television.

Car and tractor drivers purchased phones to help them stay in touch with customers and to call for help if they experience problems on the road. It did not take the local entrepreneurs long to realize that mobile phones help them extend their clientele. Thanks to mobile phones, micro-entrepreneurs can now keep in touch with their customers, even when they are on the road or transporting goods. As elsewhere in rural areas, farmers use phones to obtain information on prices. Agricultural produce can now also be sold by phone. Whereas deals were previously closed by signing a written contract well in advance of the products' delivery, sellers can now continue haggling with various buyers until it is time to deliver the products. Prices are settled by phone at the very last moment, which has decreased middlemen's profit and benefited the farmers. One other obvious economic benefit of phones is that that they help people save time. One does not need to be absent from work and travel to meet people in order to stay connected. This is especially important for daily laborers for whom a missed day from work may mean not being able to feed their family.

The diffusion of mobile phones in the village followed caste lines, with mainly upper castes buying phones until 2006. By 2010, calling charges had halved compared to charges in 2008, and Scheduled Castes had caught up with the higher castes in phone ownership. Public calling services were no longer offered in the village as there was no longer a market for them. Although the majority of the phones (81 percent) are classified as owned by the men of the families, I observed that phones are often kept in the house and shared by the entire family.

### 10.4.1 The kinship network

Villagers emphasize the usefulness of phones in reaching relatives in order to invite them to attend rituals such as funerals and weddings. Phones have become an especially effective medium for discussing marriage arrangements. People inform one another of arranged marriages, ask for information about potential brides and grooms, receive advice about marriage offers and deliver news of the acceptance or rejection of marriage proposals. The most decisive part of the marriage arrangement is when the groom's party comes to see the potential bride. The potential couple can see each other and afterwards usually give their opinion of the marriage proposal, although marriages are sometimes arranged without the bride and groom's opinions being taken into consideration. Phones help with the arrangement of these meetings, and make it possible for potential grooms to see more potential brides than was the case prior to the arrival of phones. Phones have also made it easier to express opinions about proposed marriage partners—rejection no longer needs to be conveyed face to face, but can be conveyed by phone. The increased exchange of information about potential spouses accentuates the dynamism of the marriage market along with the ensuing caste and class considerations.

Although the majority of calls are made within kinship groups, phones also serve to extend villagers' connections. Phones help villagers keep in touch with those relatives who have emigrated to other districts or abroad. According to a woman whose son works outside West Bengal, where they had only been able to talk about once a year before the arrival of the village phone, now they could speak to each other weekly (Tenhunen 2008b). Phones facilitate travelling and visiting: calls are made to discover relatives' whereabouts and to set up meetings and visits. Increased contact with villagers who have moved away has resulted in growth in the flow of information on employment opportunities outside the village.

The villagers perceive the ability to call for help as one of the phones' most crucial benefits. As one villager puts it:

> For example, if someone's father dies, the daughters are able to go there immediately and see the body before the cremation. And if a relative gets into trouble, I can go there immediately. When my daughter was very ill, I went with her to Vellore. She suddenly lost consciousness and I was

able to call a car immediately. This is the kind of convenience that we get from the phones.

In times of dispute, phones offer the possibility to obtain support from a larger group of relatives and friends than that available in one's immediate neighborhood. In extending and multiplying villagers' relationships, phones are conferring on village society much of the diversity of connectedness that is characteristic of urban living.

Increased connections to the world outside the village have also introduced changes to village politics, which used to entail villagers relying on the village leaders in times of crisis. Whereas 10 years ago, political disputes were settled in local village meetings, in 2010 even an informal meeting could be translocal. For instance, a young Bagdi man made phone calls to CPI-M leaders after someone had stolen rice from his field. The CPI-M leaders from Janta along with leaders from adjacent villages held several meetings which were arranged at a bus stand near the junction of two major roads connecting the adjacent villages. The new phone networks accentuate the dispersal of power beyond the village, as seeking help from outside the village during conflicts and crises has become easier. For instance, new *panchayat* representation and economic prosperity (new job opportunities and growing incomes among small and marginal farmers) have weakened the waning power of the dominant caste, the Tilis, and especially that of the wealthy.

### 10.4.2 Mobile phones and politics

Mobile phones have played a decisive role in organizing protests and strikes in West Bengal as in many other developing regions (Tenhunen 2011). Since mobile phones are relatively cheap and easy to use, low-income people in developing countries find them more accessible than the Internet with its e-mail and social-networking sites.

It is largely thanks to mobile phones that surprise police tactics did not work when they tried to subdue resistance against the setting up of the special economic zone in Nandigram (see Chapter 6). Villagers could effectively keep informed of the movement of the police contingent with the help of mobile phones. After the violence, 24-hour news stations broadcasted vivid reports of the conflict; in the past, before the liberation of television broadcasting, such events would only have merited a brief report in the newspapers.

Another type of West Bengali riot exemplifies how mobile technology can also be used to deliberately organize riots. Muslim extremists took advantage of the ruling Left's precarious situation after the violence in Nandigram by staging demonstrations against Bangladeshi feminist writer Tasleema Nasreen being allowed to reside in Kolkata. Rioters were called into the streets by text messages in a manner which seemed spontaneous but was later discovered to be part of planned activity (Siddiqui and Mondal 2007). Troops had to be deployed after the protests turned into riots, and the local government, which had once provided the author with asylum, forced her to leave the city.

Phones help both the opposition and the ruling party act more efficiently, but they are more important for newly emergent and growing organizations than for firmly established organizations such as the CPI-M. Unlike the former ruling party, opposition activists in the district of Bankura have used their phones for spontaneous activities such as organizing sudden strikes and reporting the ruling party's misdeeds. Opposition activists point out that phones help them react faster to events (Tenhunen 2011). News about local political disputes can be communicated upward through the party hierarchy, and party leaders can in turn coordinate political action and request news about action to be spread horizontally at lower levels. Vishnupur political activists, for instance, mention having used the phone to organize a protest because of the misuse of government money, which had been allocated for a rural work guarantee scheme (Tenhunen 2011). One of the top leaders of Trinamul notes that it used to take two months to arrange a general strike in the state, whereas nowadays such a strike can be arranged in just a few minutes with the help of text messaging.

Political activists, however, use phones more to organize party meetings and for political patronage purposes than to organize spontaneous demonstrations. Political activists and leaders receive calls from people in different types of trouble, and phones have made it feasible to react faster and to accomplish more in a shorter time-span than previously possible. Thanks to phones, patronage is now increasingly sought from other sources in addition to local leaders. It is now easier for villagers to skip the authority of a local leader and call a *panchayat* secretary, or someone higher in the party hierarchy, directly. Similarly, party activists can easily draw on diverse connections when settling disputes. An urban political activist, for instance, related how he could help a woman who had been raped by summoning the police, political leaders and doctors by telephone— while attending a family festival at a relative's house (Tenhunen 2011).

Political calls often involve translocal patronage in the form of development programs instituted by the Central Government. The execution of government programs, such as the rural work guarantee scheme, was the most common call topic for both the ruling party and opposition activists. One of the top leaders of the new ruling party, Trinamul, pointed out that phones make it possible for leaders to travel more than before. Earlier, political leaders had to stay at home to receive people; they can now be contacted anywhere. Mobile phones have freed the leaders to visit their constituency without having to neglect their other duties, which contributes to an increase in translocal political contacts.

Workers of the Trinamul Party office in Vishnupur frequently make calls to express support for their party members. CPI-M rule has not been solely based on violence, but coercive measures have been crucial for its electoral success (Gupta 2010). Since overt support for the opposition ran the risk of provoking CPI-M intimidation, phones offered the opposition a covert way of communication. Where the CPI-M sought to overpower the opposition through violent means, Trinamul has organized protection through phones, sending its cadres to protect its supporters, even if an attack is merely anticipated. A Vishnupur Trinamul leader emphasizes that without the protection offered through phones they would not have been able to increase their constituency (Tenhunen 2011). A consequence of this greater readiness for action is that violence has escalated in West Bengal. As Gupta (2010) notes, all parties have become equipped with violence.

Phone use builds on earlier political patterns and culture, but has made politics faster, more heterogeneous, and translocal. Not only can activists connect more promptly with their supporters and voters, but they can also communicate more efficiently with different organizations, both horizontally (e.g. other activists, organizations such as the police and communal elected bodies, etc.) and vertically (e.g. with their leaders and subordinates). Incidents that appear to be spontaneous reactions to the ruling party's misdeeds often originate in communication between different levels of party hierarchies followed by the horizontal spreading of information both within and outside the party. Even pre-organized protests may appear spontaneous because organizations can initiate protests quickly and spread the word more broadly using mobile phones. Although translocal political calls mainly take place within pre-existing networks, the use of phones in combination with information provided by the private television stations extends the information sharing networks.

### 10.4.3 Gender of calling

In Janta, all the mobile phones were purchased by men, and all the shops in which the public phones were placed belonged to men. However, in many houses women are in charge of delivering news and operating the phone because their husbands need to be on the road to purchase stocks or sell products. When men travel they often leave their personal mobile phone at home making calls on the road from public phones or use other people's phones.

Phones have increased communication between women and their natal families, although in 2005 women formed only a minority of the callers: 29

percent of the sample of 100 calls. By 2010, 40 percent of callers were female, among callers of 27 mobile phone-owning households whose calling patterns were surveyed. The women's increased contact with their natal village and female relatives in other villages is part of broader changes in the village's gender relationships, the most pronounced of which are the increase in education for females, women becoming visible in formal politics and a few high-caste women taking up white-collar jobs.

Phones, like television sets and DVD players, help women extend their sphere unobtrusively and without overtly moving out of the home. Since natal families continue to be the major source of support for women if they are mistreated in their in-laws' house, fall ill or face starvation, women identify the improved communication systems as playing a major role in advancing their position. Besides such criteria as a potential groom's personal characteristics and the condition of his house, unmarried girls pay attention to whether the house has a motorcycle or bicycle, is close to good bus connections and whether it has a phone.

Phones have not been adopted by a stagnant society, but by a changing rural society and culture influenced by political reforms, the introduction of new agricultural methods and the women's movement. My observations of the economic impact of phones support earlier research on the benefits of phones for small-scale businesses in such diverse locations as Tanzania, Egypt, South Africa, Bangladesh, urban India and Thailand (Bayes 1999; Loyola 2005; Coyle 2005). In all of these places, phones are associated with a form of social logistics characterized by an increased multiplicity of social contacts and greater efficiency of market relationships. At the same time, the appropriation of phones draws from local cultural change and intensifies it; phones amplify cultural patterns but they do so selectively (Tenhunen 2008b). Instead of travelling, visiting and having long face-to-face discussions, phones reinforce the practice of brief conversations. As keeping in touch becomes more frequent and casual, the meanings of relationships change. The type of sociality phones encourage depends on the number of phones: as the phone density increases, villagers share phones in smaller circles than before.

## 10.5 The Potential of Developmental Applications of Mobile Technology

The building of rural networks is speeding up rural cultural and social changes, but more policy measures and services could harness mobile technology for more efficient poverty reduction. Developmental applications of mobile technology have proved one of the most promising ways to encourage development, but India has been slow in putting these into practice on a large scale. For instance, in Kenya m-pesa, a mobile banking system introduced in 2007, had become the largest financial service in the country by 2009. There is a growing interest in m-banking in India; however, current banking regulations do not allow m-banking.

Using mobile technology to provide farmers with accurate and detailed forecasts help them to save their crops from storms and allow them to sow their seed during ideal conditions. Reuters pioneered the launch of the first service to provide information on weather and markets for farmers in India over mobile phones in 2006. Some other organizations like Tata Indicom have followed suit, but still only a small minority of farmers are offered information services through SMS.

Rubber farmers and dealers in Kerala track commodity prices in real time through the Rubber Board's SMS service system. In Maharashtra, a mobile application allows farmers to remotely access their irrigation pumps, which eliminates the need to travel long distances to check how they are functioning. Nokia's Life Tools application provides information on weather and markets, as well as educational content, but its use is limited to one service provider and requires a relatively high-end phone (Banks 2009).

Voxiva Company has deployed a phone- and web-based data collection and disease-surveillance system in Tamil Nadu. The "Health Watch" program makes use of existing communications infrastructures (i.e. mobile phones, fixed-line phones and the Internet) to allow health workers in remote areas to reports of incidences of disease outbreaks to health officials in real time. TeleDoc uses mobile phones to connect village-based health care workers with doctors in urban areas for remote diagnosis and treatment in Haryana. Many more health applications are currently being developed in India and elsewhere (Vital Wave Consulting 2009).

As many pilot projects prove, it is possible to use mobile technology to set up electronic marketplaces, banking systems and labor banks, as well as delivering information on education, health issues and women's concerns by phone. Yet, large-scale developmental applications of mobile technology are still absent in India. The technology is already there but the problem remains of how well the various stakeholders involved—telemarket, states, service providers, NGOs and industries—will cooperate to provide developmental applications in affordable ways.

## 10.6 Conclusion

Although new technologies are often associated with development, their use does not necessitate an entry into ultra-modern society and way of life. Technologies are used as part of cultural and social processes. They can facilitate diverse impacts—depending largely on whose terms and how the technology is made available. Unlike computers, mobile telephony has not been celebrated as a tool of transparent governing by states and major development agencies although mobile phones are used for safeguarding the transparency of how public funds are used even without any special applications. The overwhelming attention given to computers by states and development discourses has hindered the acknowledgement and harnessing of the potential of those technologies perceived as more mundane than computers—such as mobile phones and radios. Similar to computer kiosks in rural India, mobile phones encouraged inequality in rural India because large-scale farmers and small-scale businessmen reap the most economic benefits of these technologies. However, phones are more accessible than computers—the divides they create may prove more transitory and easier to bridge than other digital divides.

# Chapter 11

# GROWTH BURDENS THE ENVIRONMENT

The relationship between development and environmental problems is ambiguous. While industrialization and urbanization entail economic growth, they tend to increase pollution. However, increase in affluence can enhance the resources to abate pollution. The environmental Kuznets curve hypothesis maintains that pollution tends to increase with economic growth and then decline with the appropriation of better abatement technologies (Ghosh 2007). The crucial question for India is whether it will be able to follow the curve and invest its new wealth in protecting the environment.

India's water supplies are meager in relation to the population, and climate change is likely to complicate the problem. A growing economy and consumption are manifesting themselves in the worsening of the pollution of air and water. The air in urban areas is highly polluted and so are the main rivers of India. The percentage of pollutants in the air in 60 percent of Indian cities exceeds one and a half times the permissible limits. According to the Centre for Science and Environment, the noxious emission from cars increased eightfold when the Indian economy doubled during 1975–95 (Roychowdhury et al. 2006). The same organization estimates that more than one million people die because of pollution annually, and tens of millions suffer from various pollution-related health hazards. Cleaning up the air and water could strengthen economic growth because pollution and environmental degradation incur huge health expenses.

A growing economy and rising population aggravate environmental problems but their local main cause is administrative. Human settlements are often allowed to mushroom without proper planning or control. Sewage plants, for example, are useless if houses are not connected to the sewage system or if machinery does not work due to power cuts. The technology meant for cleaning the water or air is often in poor condition because officials do not have sufficient maintenance funds, while corruption also hinders attempts to deal with pollution.

Although India has comprehensive environmental legislation and administration, Indian democracy has proved weak in the face of environmental challenges. Environmental laws and ambitious programs remain largely unexecuted and state-owned enterprises and power plants may even be found among the worst polluters. Political decision makers lack the courage to intervene in the activities of the worst offenders such as large businesses. Neither are they very keen to regulate the smaller polluters, who comprise the majority of the electorate (Narain 2002). India lacks policies for transportation, private participation in abatement measures, as well as the economic incentives which would motivate citizens, industries and governmental units to reduce pollution.

Environmental problems entail an often unacknowledged gendered dimension: an increase in women's time and energy spent in fuel, fodder and water collection and an adverse effect on the health and nutrition of household members in general. Consequently, women's participation in environmental projects is important both for improving family welfare and promoting gender equity (Agarwal 1995). Women from various strata of society have played an active part in the India's vibrant environmental movement. The women of rural Uttarakhand pioneered the Chipko movement in 1970s to protect trees. Eminent philosopher, environmental activist and eco feminist, Vandana Siva's thinking has been influenced by the Chipko movement. Grassroots activist and social worker Medha Patkar has helped shape both domestic and international environmental policies through her work with people living under the threat of displacement by large dam-building projects. Sunita Narain heads a Delhi-based influential Centre for Science and Environment which has skillfully influenced decision makers through research and information sharing activities.

Despite its lingering problems, India's administration and civil society have developed promising solutions to its environmental challenges. One such example is Surat, a city of 3.9 million people situated 250 kilometers north of Mumbai. It is known for its textile industry and diamond trade, but in spite of its burgeoning economy it was also famous for its squalor. Garbage disposal in Surat, as in many towns which are small by Indian standards, was poorly organized. The unhygienic conditions led to the spread of disease, and the worst happened in 1994: after heavy rains and floods the town was struck by an epidemic which was classified as plague, although the claim was never ascertained. People fleeing the contagion were allowed to enter other towns in India only after a medical examination and many business establishments had to close their Surat branches. The epidemic soon had an effect on the economy of the entire country: exports became suspect, Indian planes were banned from foreign air space, and the Bombay Stock Exchange plummeted (Rattanani 1999).

It did not take long to bring the epidemic under control, but the town itself was cleaned up only after Suryadevra Ramchandra Rao was appointed head of Surat's municipal corporation in 1995. Rao initiated the steps that transformed Surat into the country's second-cleanest town (after Chandigarh). Officials spared no one who violated environmental regulations and the most powerful culprits were tackled first. In a town where only 40 percent of the daily garbage was cleared, the figure is now close to 97 percent. In the slum areas, 75 percent of the streets were paved, and several health clinics were established in the town. Morbidity fell amazingly by 65 percent in three years. Yet much work still needs to be done. Only 37 percent of houses are connected to the sewage system. The sewers remain open; emissions from factories still pollute rivers and many slum areas lack flushing toilets (Rattanani 1999). Surat's development is exemplary; however, most towns and cities of India have yet to repeat what Surat has managed to do.

## 11.1 Efforts to Clean Up the Air

India's capital, Delhi, with its 16.7 million inhabitants is the second-largest metropolis by population in India and one of the most polluted cities in the world. In the twenty-first century, Delhi emerged as an exemplar in environmental protection. Delhi's air became easier to breathe and visibility improved thanks to the decrease in smog in 2002–4. The carbon monoxide content of the air decreased by almost 50 percent and particle content by 38 percent during 1998–2004. In the 1990s, the pollution in Delhi's atmosphere exceeded the WHO standards by five times, and 70 percent of these contaminants originated from automobiles (Roychowdhury et al. 2006). Air purification programs were initiated by the Centre for Science and Environment in Delhi, which began by publishing pamphlets with titles like "Death by breathing" and printing posters which graphically illustrated the effects of pollution by showing two pairs of lungs: one healthy, the other with the black spots typical of an average Delhi resident. The campaign evoked media interest, and politicians were pressured to take a stand on pollution. The environment emerged as the key issue of the state elections in 1998, and Congress Party candidate Sheila Dixit, who promised to tackle the pollution problems, won the election (Jain 2004).

In 1996, the Centre for Science and Environment sued the state of Delhi for neglecting the implementation of environmental regulations. The Supreme Court ordered the administration to take steps to clean up the air through stricter emission limits, the phasing out of old vehicles and the gradual conversion of public transport to the use of compressed natural gas (CNG). Many powerful organizations, especially in the automotive industry, opposed the change by playing down the harmful effects of diesel vehicles.

The natural gas distribution system was still inadequate in 2002 when the conversion took place, which led to traffic chaos, but after its initial difficulties the Delhi public transport service made the shift and emissions were significantly reduced. The growing number of private vehicles still threatens air quality, however, and in 2007 Delhi was again discussing measures to increase visibility and decrease smog. The number of private vehicles has increased by 157 percent in the past decade, and the number of high-polluting diesel cars by 425 percent. In 2009, Delhi's air was reported to have reverted back to being as polluted as it was before the use of CNG as the fuel for public transportation. Delhi now has more vehicles than Mumbai, Kolkata, and Chennai combined (*Hindustan Times*, November 8, 2009).

Like some of its neighboring countries, India possesses large reservoirs of natural gas, and new pipelines are under construction. Where natural gas is not available, public transport is still being made to rely on less polluting fuels. Kolkata and Delhi have their underground transport systems and Mumbai is building one (Roychowdhury et al. 2006).

Public transportation also now runs on natural gas in Ahmedabad, Kanpur and Lucknow. Ahmedabad, Chennai, Hyderabad, Mumbai, Pune and Kolkata have all been able to improve their air quality. However, as the air quality has improved in some big cities, it has started to deteriorate in the smaller towns, where air quality is not even regularly monitored. In 2003, the worst polluted towns in India were Ahmedabad (Gujarat), Kanpur (Uttar Pradesh), Solapur (Maharasthra), Lucknow (Uttar Pradesh), Delhi, Jaipur (Rajasthan), Kolkata (West Bengal), Tiruvananthapuram (Kerala), Dehradun (Uttaranchal) and Kota (Rajasthan). The amount of air-born particles exceeds the permissible limits in 57 percent of Indian towns according to a survey by the magazine *Down to Earth* (2006).

## 11.2 Towards Renewable Energy

As a country rich in bio-fuel resources—wind and hydro energy, solar energy, bio-mass and bio-gas—India has remarkable possibilities to reduce its dependence on oil and coal. India has a ministry for renewable energy which aims to increase the share of renewable energy from 5 percent to 25 percent. India's wind power industry has grown into the fourth largest in the world and the largest among developing nations.

In 2009, India launched an ambitious mission to increase its solar power hundredfold in the next 13 years. The first phase will focus on solar thermal energy, and on promoting off-grid systems to serve populations without access to commercial energy. In the second phase, competitive solar energy will be offered throughout the country. The mission plans to provide solar lighting systems to cover about 10,000 villages and hamlets. It will also set up standalone rural solar power plants in Lakshadweep, Andaman and Nicobar Islands and the Ladakh region of Jammu and Kashmir (*Hindustan Times* 2009b).

At present, India produces about a third of its energy from oil, most of which it imports. Consequently, the Indian economy is vulnerable to fluctuations in oil prices. India has oil fields in Maharasthra, Gujarat and Assam, and it has activated its search for more.

Over half of India's energy is still dependent on its large reserves of coal; consequently, the country is the second-fastest growing and third-largest producer of greenhouse gases. Like China, India is reluctant to accept restrictions on greenhouse gas emissions, because the per capita emissions of both countries are significantly smaller than those of the Western countries (Loikala et al. 2006).

**Chart 11.1.** Top-ten annual energy-related $CO_2$ emitters for the year 2009

|  | % of total global emissions | Tons of CHG per capita |
|---|---|---|
| China | 23.6 | 5.13 |
| US | 17.9 | 16.9 |
| India | 5.5 | 1.37 |
| Russia | 5.3 | 10.8 |
| Japan | 3.8 | 8.6 |
| Germany | 2.5 | 9.2 |
| Iran | 1.8 | 7.3 |
| Canada | 1.8 | 15.4 |
| Korea | 1.8 | 10.6 |
| UK | 1.8 | 7.5 |

Source: International Energy Agency (2011).

## 11.3 Shortage of Clean Water

Kolkata, the third-most populous metropolitan area in India (14.1 million), struggles with substantial pollution problems, but it has also pioneered environmentally by designing a spectacular way to treat its waste water. Kolkata's sewage and waste is treated in the world's biggest biological waste treatment system without expensive or energy consuming technology: it is filtered through the city's eastern wetlands so that nature's own eco-system decomposes organic waste, producing nutrients for agriculture and fisheries. Before the expansion of Kolkata, the nearby ponds were filled with tidal waters from the sea, and abundant fish lived in the ponds. The raising of the estuary areas and rampant construction of houses, however, gradually prevented tidal flow from accessing the ponds. The city started to direct its waste water to the wetlands in 1930s, and fish returned to the ponds. It was not until the 1980s that researchers began investigating how the waste water becomes clean enough to support marine life. It was discovered that the bacteria growing in the ponds due to abundant sunlight and lush algae growth efficiently decompose organic waste providing nutrients for fisheries (Ghosh 1998).

Kolkata is a megacity of 13 million inhabitants, which produces 600 million liters of waste water and 2,500 tons of solid waste every day. The waste water flows through underground sewers to pumping stations on the eastern side of the city from where it opens out into the sewers of the wetlands. Solid waste too is brought here and finally used by 254 fisheries and farms after treatment. Although the wetland area is protected, the city's expansion is posing a threat to its existence. The state government has had to demolish illegal buildings from the area repeatedly. The latest danger to the wetlands is a planned new highway which would bisect the protected area and facilitate illegal building (Mitra 2006).

India has invested huge sums of money in cleaning its main rivers, but so far efforts have not proved as successful as Kolkata's achievements with domestic sewage. Sewage plants have not produced the desired results because much of the waste water does not reach them—most dwellings are not connected to any sewage system. In 2009, India had over 600 million people without access to a toilet (Deen 2009). Furthermore, water treatment facilities in India have not been able to remove traces of heavy metals. Since polluted rivers are the major sources of municipal water for most towns and cities that spring up along them, residents are exposed to unknown quantities of pollutants through the water they consume (Agarwal et al. 1999, 59). Sewage plants are, moreover, hampered by their poor maintenance and frequent power cuts (Agarwal et al. 1999).

Religious ceremonies also contribute to the pollution of rivers which are considered holy. Any river water, and particularly that of Ganges, is believed to have a purifying effect; bathing in it cures impurity and delivers bathers from sin. Hindus mostly cremate their dead and scatter the ashes in rivers. Since not everyone can afford to buy firewood for a cremation pyre, bodies are sometimes illegally thrown directly into rivers. Statues of gods and goddesses, which are elaborately painted with synthetic colors containing heavy metals like lead and zinc, are immersed in the rivers after the rituals. Flowers and other offerings to gods, often in plastic bags, as well as animal carcasses, are also thrown into the rivers. In many places, it is customary not to burn the dead bodies of holy men, newborn babies or those who have died of infectious diseases before throwing them into the river (Agarwal et al. 1999).

India's environmental administration now aims to have waste water treated before it reaches the rivers. New technological solutions have become available as India has lowered its custom duties on imported technology. The environmental organizations emphasize that tackling pollution requires entirely new solutions. For instance, instead of building expensive, water-consuming flush toilets, India should encourage the building of eco-toilets.

Thanks to the rising affluence, more Indians can now afford to make a pilgrimage to the Himalayas, to the source of the Ganges, which is believed to be the birth place of Hindu gods and goddesses. Mountain areas are suffering from the increasing influx of visitors, because more trees have to be felled in order to build accommodation for tourists and for use as firewood. As the forested areas have shrunk, the rain and snowfalls which sustain the glaciers have diminished, and the melting glaciers supply less water, thereby threatening the flow of the Ganges (Lak 2005). Gangotri glacier has, however, slowed its retreat from 20 meters a year during 2000–2003 to 12 meters after the Uttaranchal state government started to successfully control the flow of tourists (Aron 2009).

India's groundwater resources are meager, and rainfall is limited to short periods. Half of the total rainfall occurs in a period of 15 days, and 90 percent of the rivers flow only for four months out of the year. South Asia has thousands of years-old methods of dealing with water scarcity, but these techniques decayed during the colonial era because the colonial state was more interested in building large-scale sewage systems and dams than preserving and developing the ancient water harvesting systems.

Independent India has not been able to provide adequate water supplies to all its citizens. Consequently, citizens have resorted to their own solutions; both urban and rural households dig their own wells. Water has also become a marketable commodity as rich and poor alike often have to purchase water. Digging wells has helped to secure drinking water as well as water for irrigation but the problem remains that groundwater is becoming scarce. Electric pumps have accelerated the problem, enabling the extraction of far more groundwater in a shorter period of time than it was possible to draw by hand over hundreds of years. In many areas, the farmers have pumped the groundwater to a critical level and in some areas exhausted it with the help of free electricity provided by some state governments. Out of the 5,723 geographically defined areas of India, groundwater is at a critical level in over 1,000 (Sen Gupta 2006).

As the groundwater levels have sunk, digging wells has become more expensive. Those who can afford to dig deep have started selling water, and in many cities, water is already heavily rationed: it is available only during certain hours, or people may have to queue for hours to get their daily ration. Shortage of water has led to water disputes. The landowners have a right to dig wells on their own land irrespective of the level and availability of groundwater. Consequently, neighbors often have to compete for water by deepening their wells. Corporations and even states are also involved in water disputes. When Coca-Cola started to pump water into their Kerala factories, the water situation in the region deteriorated to the extent that the residents organized themselves in protest. The right of Coca-Cola to pump water was solved by the Supreme Court, which ruled that the company had to shut its factories and provide water to people affected by the water shortage they had helped to cause.

Tamil Nadu has accused Karnataka of not allowing the water of the Cauvery River to flow into Tamil Nadu as agreed by the states. When the chief minister of Karnataka had the flow of water into the Tamil Nadu territories blocked, thereby countermanding a Supreme Court ruling, clashes flamed up between the people of the two states. Karnataka is also involved in a water dispute with another neighboring state, Andhra Pradesh. A recent dispute over the use of the Yamuna River among the states of Delhi, Haryana and Uttar Pradesh was resolved by conferences involving three state chief ministers as well as the Central Government. This approach was adopted only after prior intervention by the Supreme Court failed. Not all disputes have happy endings, however: for example, the larger dispute between Karnataka and Tamil Nadu over the waters of the Cauvery has lingered on for decades (Richard and Singh 2001).

State governments dominate the allocation of river waters. Since rivers cross state boundaries disputes are inevitable. The Inter-State Water Disputes Act of 1956 was legislated to deal with conflicts, and included provisions for the establishment of tribunals to adjudicate where direct negotiations have failed. However, states have sometimes refused to accept the tribunals' decisions. Even courts have been ignored in water disputes. The Central Government has sometimes intervened directly as well, but in the most intractable cases, such as the sharing of the Ravi-Beas waters among Haryana, Jammu and Kashmir, Rajasthan and Punjab, central intervention has been unsuccessful. An unambiguous institutional mechanism for settling interstate water disputes does not exist. Water conflicts in India are increasing and spilling into other issues. Although many of the conflicts are successfully resolved, India lacks a mechanism and platform for dialogue and contestation between different stakeholders (Joy et al. 2008).

## 11.4 Controversial Dams

The Central Government of India has alleviated the water shortage by capturing the energy of the rivers and storing water for consumption by building dams. Dams have swallowed millions of peoples' homes and their construction is becoming more controversial. As the population grows, so does the number of people who have to be relocated, but vacant land is getting scarcer. States have only recently started to compensate for the loss of land by land instead of cash, but the new land can seldom compensate for what people have lost. Most of the people who lose their homes as a result of dam building are *adivasis*, tribals who get part of their livelihood from gathering forest products. As they are not compensated for their loss with forest land, they lose their livelihood due to the relocation.

Kerala's Silent Valley project was the first dam project which the Central Government, under Indira Gandhi, had to give up in 1983. Since the proposed dam would have destroyed India's only untouched rainforest, international environmental organizations supported the campaign against the dam construction. Since then, four other dam projects have been discontinued due to their ecological impact and opposition provided by the environmental movement. A number of ongoing dam projects are being carried out amid protests.

The biggest prevailing controversy surrounds the Narmada project, which was initially supported by the World Bank. The Narmada originates in the central state of Madhya Pradesh and empties into the Arabian Sea after flowing through Maharashtra and Gujarat. The plan is to build 30 large, 135 medium and 3,000 small dams on the Narmada which would turn the river into a chain of lakes. The movement against the project began in 1984, when a citizens' organization led by Medha Patkar exposed the poor planning of the project: its ecological impact and expenses were grossly underestimated and benefits from irrigation overestimated.

The World Bank withdrew from the project in 1993, but the dam is still under construction. The state governments have tried to win over the protesters by tempting them with lucrative relocation plans, but the protestors continue to gather to demonstrate and go on hunger strikes at the sites of dam construction and in Delhi. The Supreme Court gave the go-ahead for the construction of the dam in 2000 ruling that its height could be raised to 90 meters and no higher. This is far below the proposed height of 130 meters, but higher than the 88 meters sought by the anti-dam activists (Agarwal et al. 1999).

Since free water and electricity have led to water overuse, the World Bank has recommended water pricing as a way to guide people to use water more efficiently. Many state governments have tried to improve the water supply by cooperating with private entrepreneurs and water has become a marketable commodity which is often sold more cheaply to companies than to private consumers. Opponents of commercialization argue that the sale of water leads to it becoming available to the rich and the big companies at the expense of neglecting the poor.

In recent years, environmental bodies in India have been developing solutions to tackle the water shortage by drawing on ancient methods. Because 43 percent of the annual rain and snowfall does not reach the rivers and groundwater, rainwater harvesting has great potential in India. Delhi, Bangalore and Chennai now require the building of water harvesting systems into all new constructions. Some drought-prone states like Gujarat and Rajasthan have successfully employed communal water harvesting methods in rural areas.

Water is a renewable resource in a country like India where it rains heavily during the monsoons. Water shortage, in turn, is a result of human action: water is allowed to become polluted, and investments in the harvesting and distribution of water have not been sufficient. A report by the International Water Management Institute notes the alarming trends in water scarcity but also sees real possibilities in preventing the crisis from escalating if India invests in recharging groundwater, distributing water-saving technologies and increasing crop productivity (Amarasinghe et al. 2007).

## 11.5 Climate Change as a Threat to Agriculture

Global warming due to emissions of greenhouse gases adds to India's environmental challenges. The greenhouse effect refers to the warming produced as a result of greenhouse gases in the atmosphere which trap heat. By 2000, industrialization had increased the atmospheric carbon dioxide content by 31 percent, methane by 151 percent and nitrous oxide by 17 percent since 1750. Global temperatures have risen by 0.6 degrees in the last 100 years, and India's temperature has risen by 0.3–0.6 degrees since 1860 (IPCC 2001).

Many factors, however, influence the climate: temperatures have always varied periodically, and climatic systems can counterbalance changes. Moreover, climatic phenomena vary in different layers of the atmosphere and in different parts of the world. Climate change does not progress irrevocably. It is influenced by human action: the worst predictions will not materialize if emissions can be radically reduced. Worst affected by climate change are countries like India where large parts of the population depend on agriculture. Global warming has already affected the rainfall in India, increasing it in some places and decreasing it in others.

If the melting of the Himalayan glaciers continues, the water in Ganges will first increase and later decrease, threatening the water supply of 400 million people who live in the delta regions in India. They will have to increasingly rely on groundwater and monsoon rains. Authoritative report by IPCC, an international scientific panel overseen by the United Nations, asserted in 2007 that Himalayan glaciers are receding faster than in any other part of the world and the likelihood of them disappearing by the year 2035 and perhaps sooner is very high if the Earth keeps warming at the current rate. However, in 2010 IPCC admitted the prediction had been based on an unsupported estimate, an interview with an Indian glacier scientist who now denies having given the estimate (Rosenthal 2010). Other studies have offered different estimations but they all confirm the increase in melting speed (D'Monte 2009).

Global warming influences the vegetation both directly and indirectly through increasing weeds and pests. Particularly sensitive to the variation in rainfall is rain-fed farming, which constitutes 65 percent of the cultivation in India. The effect of climatic change on agricultural production is worst in the coastal regions, but it may also reduce the harvests in the most productive regions like Punjab, Haryana and western Uttar Pradesh (Sanghi, Mendelsohn and Dinar 1998). Warming has already been reported to have decreased harvests in Punjab where rises in the temperature have decreased yields by making harvests develop too quickly. Researchers have estimated that for every 0.5 degree (Centigrade) increase in winter temperature, the harvest is advanced by at least a week, and the yield falls by about 0.45 tons per acre, which equals a 10 percent drop in wheat production across Punjab, the main wheat producing area of India (Sharma 2009).

India has a densely populated 7,500 km-long shallow coastline, which has been estimated to be one of the most vulnerable areas if the sea level rises due to climatic change: floods would wipe out coastal areas and salt water would flow into arable land. The rise in sea levels would thus increase freshwater shortages, causing havoc to coastal habitation. Such coastal livelihoods as agriculture, fishing and tourism would be affected.

A recent study by University of British Columbia predicts that India could lose up to 40 percent of its fish populations in 50 years as a result of global warming. Some fish species move to cooler waters from the coastal waters. Monsoon variations, frequent droughts and severe storms kill fish in freshwater bodies inland affecting breeding patterns (Thakur 2009).

Satellite pictures of the Sunderbans in West Bengal from 50–60 years ago show that islands have submerged. Scientists have recently reported on notable sea ingress and erosion along the Mahabalipuram and Cuddalore coasts and on the Lakshadweep islands. They warn that almost India's entire extensive coastline, especially the deltaic regions, is in danger of being eaten away by the sea (Bakshi 2009).

## 11.6 Conclusion

Environmental problems in India decelerate economic growth. Finding solutions in water harvesting, conversion to renewable fuels, better sewage treatment and the prevention of air pollution can stimulate growth.

Although neither India's Central Government nor the states have succeeded in protecting the environment as stipulated by law, many successful Indian projects illustrate how civil society can force the government to take better care of the environment. As the problems with sewage plants illustrate, solutions have to take into consideration the concerns of local communities. Reducing emissions is both a technological and a social challenge. Creating economic incentives for private citizens, companies and municipal authorities to curb their polluting activities could help turn the positive examples of pollution reduction into mainstream practices.

# Chapter 12

# CONCLUSION

For many, India represents the spiritualized East, a salvation from, and the opposite of, the materialism and emptiness of Western life. For others, it embodies extreme disparity and misery—and for others still, it is the herald of new technologies. The picture of India often reflects the observer's own interests, which tends to distort understanding of how Indians experience their lives and what they strive for. This book has drawn from various sources in order to present diverse social and cultural factors which affect India's future. In spite of its long cultural heritage, India is not an unchanging and eternal realm of the spirit; and India can still be India without poverty and disparity. In the following pages, we sum up the specificities of India's development, as well as its main challenges, strengths and opportunities.

## 12.1 Growth Continues

Although affected by the global economic slowdowns, India's economic growth has continued far faster than that of Western economies. This growth alone does not, however, solve India's problems. Affluence does not automatically trickle down to the poor as some protagonists of economic reforms assume and hope for.

India is growing more unequal, although the situation is still better than in China or the USA. Yet poverty has decreased since the 1980s: Dyson et al. (2004) estimate that the ratio of poor will fall to about one tenth of the population by 2026, provided that the economy continues to grow at same rate as it did in the 1990s. Shortcomings in education, social security and health care hamper growth prospects and development, although there is slow improvement. The Manmohan Singh government, which came to power in 2004, was the first coalition government to increase government spending on education, health care and infrastructure.

Private consumption has contributed to growth to a greater degree in India than in China. Rural India represents the largest future market in the world, and already many products have higher sales in the countryside than in towns. Although the share of agriculture in the Indian economy has declined to less than 14 percent, agricultural development plays a crucial role because India's urbanization has been slow in comparison to the rest of Asia: by 2030, India is expected to have 41 percent of its population living in cities and towns.

It is probable that both the Central Government of India and the state governments will continue to invest in rural development, and that rural standards of living will rise, because the rural population continues to represent the majority in the electorate. Any government daring to impair rural living standards cannot hope to remain in office. Indeed, the Congress government secured its electoral victory in the parliamentary elections of 2009 through its rural-work guarantee scheme and loan waivers for farmers.

Rural protest is also forcing the Indian government to reformulate its land policies for industries. Industries have not grown as briskly in India as they have in China, in terms of providing employment to underemployed rural populations. However, they have rationalized operations and improved profitability since the economic reforms. The Indian government has sought to boost new industries through the creation of special economic zones (SEZ). However, SEZs have tended to create few benefits, including jobs, in relation to the number of people they displace. Farmers may be compelled to sell their land to make way for an SEZ, but the price paid is often well below the market rate. Consequently, hundreds of building projects are stalled due to local protest all across India.

IT-related businesses have contributed greatly to India's economic growth; nevertheless, this field employs only a tiny minority of the workforce. Adopting information technologies for socially productive purposes, therefore, has greater beneficial impact for the majority of Indians than the IT business sector. Both state and local governments have computerized their services with varying degrees of success, and many civic organizations provide computer kiosks for developmental purposes. Information technologies can help bridge the gap between the government and its people, as well as reduce officials' opportunities to command bribes. However, due to the frequent power cuts, illiteracy and the high price of computers, by far the most common form of information technology in India is not the computer but the mobile phone. As in other regions without prior access to electronic information technologies, the appropriation of mobile technology has multiplied relationships and improved the efficiency of small-scale businesses in India.

## 12.2 Incremental Transfer of Power

Although democracy may serve to stall radical changes and reforms, it is India's strength and advantage. Unlike China, India has a functioning judiciary and banking system, as well as freedom of speech. Civic organizations frequently criticize governments and take advantage of the Right to Information Act in order to force officials to account for their actions. The vigilance of citizens guarantees that undemocratic practices can be changed in India in spite of social disparities. Due to the extensiveness and heterogeneity of print and electronic media in India, glaring social and political problems cannot remain hidden from public attention. However, the growing commercialization of the media constantly increases entertainment content, weakening the significance of mass media as agents of social awareness and improvement.

India's economic reforms have transferred power away from officials to the actual economic and political decision makers. The constitution of the Indian political elite has changed largely thanks to caste-based political mobilization and women's increasing political participation, while power has shifted to coalition governments from the single-party governments like that of the Congress Party, which were able to rule India autocratically up to the 1990s. The relative ease of the democratization has to do with its incrementality: in most regions upper castes still dominate due to their better education and social standing.

The division of power between the Central Government and state governments is sometimes seen as occasioning dissension in many fields, but it also promotes development. Many of the reforms of the Central Government— like the midday-meal program and the expansion of caste quotas—have been introduced and tested in individual states before their extension nationwide. The biggest stumbling block of the coalition governments as well as state governments has been their inability to reduce the budget deficits, a failure which limits badly needed investments in infrastructure, education and health care. Another crucial shortcoming is the insufficient political will to combat corruption. However, the main source of instability both in foreign relations and domestic politics is the extremist Hindu movement and the tensions it creates between the Hindus and the Muslims. As the second-largest party, the Hindu Nationalistic Party has a real chance of increasing in power to the point of being able to form a government.

In its foreign policy, India emphasizes economic interests over ideological objectives, but its interests in Asian economic cooperation and South–South interaction carry on Jawaharlal Nehru's visions of Third World global influence by virtue of the cooperation between nations in the sphere. Economic growth has underscored India's international importance. Deepening Asian economic integration could shift the focus of the world economy increasingly towards Asia and India. India's strained relationship with its two neighbors China and Pakistan, however, hampers the prospects of economic cooperation in Asia.

## 12.3 Local Values and Meanings Prevail

Indians can influence their own destiny not only through political action but also by changing their everyday culture. Deep-rooted cultural meanings are changing, albeit slowly. Concepts of the person and his or her relation to the community, relations between men and women, basic values, ideals and conceptions of human nature—these are all changing. The transformations are a consequence of the internal dynamics of society: when subjugated groups are able to alter their position, they change both the role and cultural meanings attached to social hierarchies. The former Untouchable Hindus, who have improved their economic position, provide a good example of this: in their ritual life they emphasize auspiciousness more eagerly than principles of ritual purity, an interpretation of Hindu life that is producing new views of the values upon which a respectable position in society may be based.

The changes are partly similar to what is happening elsewhere in the globalizing world: the similarity of available consumer goods and means of communication is clearly observable everywhere. Regardless of these superficial similarities, however, Indians live their life according to their own values, adapting to global forces in locally meaningful ways. Marrying according to the wishes of the family, performing religious ceremonies, maintaining personal eating habits and appreciating a distinct kind of entertainment, for example, are accentuated amid globalization. The more that people from different cultures interact, the more importance they often place on their own cultural identity; the "Westernization" of Indians is often only skin-deep, remaining at a level of consumption as a thin, superficial veneer of worldly goods. Similarly, growing prosperity does not necessarily mean empowerment for subjugated groups and women: for instance, the distortion of the sex ratio—with all this implies—is greatest in the well-to-do states of Punjab, Haryana, Maharashtra and Gujarat, which have experienced fast economic growth.

## 12.4 Regional Patterns of Population Growth

India's population will continue to grow in the following decades to become the largest in the world, bypassing China. Providing basic services like education and health care to such a huge population is an enormous task requiring vast resources. In this respect, India's problems are similar to those faced by many developing countries; only its massive size provides India's problems with unprecedented magnitude. The population, however, not only consumes resources but it also creates them and the most densely populated areas of India are by no means its poorest regions. Population growth will decelerate in the near future, although the yearly increase will remain formidable for decades, despite the fact that women are giving birth, on average, to a much smaller number of children than before. The explanation lies in the age structure: a large proportion of the total population consists of women of childbearing age. Regional differences in childbearing patterns will prevail in India so that the population of the northern Hindi-speaking areas will continue to grow even after the rest of the country has reached a more stable situation. As the same northern area is beset with many other economic and social problems, the geographical polarization of the country may prompt unpredictable political consequences.

The effects of the increasingly imbalanced sex ratio of the population may also have untoward consequences for gender relations. The number of male children is already significantly greater than female children in the northwestern parts of the country. The principal cause for this is the induced abortion of female fetuses which is practiced in order to secure the birth of the desired son or sons. However, this is a regional, not a nationwide problem; most of the country is relatively unaffected by the imbalance in the sex ratio at birth and sex-selective abortions, although the practice seems to be spreading outwards from the core areas. In some parts, especially in Punjab and its neighboring areas where the practice has been popular since the early 1990s, it is increasingly difficult for young men to find a bride. In India, marriage preferably takes place endogamously within one's own caste; consequently, wives brought in from other castes or ethnic groups would experience degradingly negative reactions—the Chinese practice of importing brides from economically poorer nations or regions to compensate for fewer local women is not likely to work in India. Instead of "raising the value of daughters" who are in high demand as brides, the worsening sex ratio may in a male-dominated society lead to a vicious cycle. The fewer females in society, the less willing people may be to have daughters at all, as protecting young women against kidnapping, sexual abuse and other threats to their honor—and thus the family's—become more demanding.

## 12.5 Environmental Challenges

Population growth, among other factors, may accentuate the water shortage. However, India has plenty of rainfall, and climate change is even strengthening monsoon rains in some regions; water is a renewable resource. Water shortage, is manmade: water has been allowed to become polluted in some areas, and in others there has not been sufficient investment in its collection and distribution systems. Nevertheless, the water problem is crucial. Agriculture has to be able to feed the growing population, and agricultural growth is possible only by improving irrigation systems and bringing more arable lands under irrigation in sustainable ways.

Industrial growth and concomitantly expanding consumption aggravate India's pollution and environmental problems causing extra expenditure and slowing down the country's economic growth. Therefore, new methods of rainwater harvesting, renewable energies, waste disposal and air cleaning could benefit the economy. Although India has not been able to protect the environment as stipulated by international environmental laws, civic environmental movements have, in many case, been able to force the government to initiate protective measures.

The global warming caused by increases in the emission of greenhouse gases brings additional challenges. India has a 7,500 km-long, densely populated, shallow coastline. It is estimated to be one of the world's most vulnerable areas should sea levels rise as a result of the climate change. Furthermore, because the temperature changes affect vegetation, agricultural areas are among those most likely to suffer. For example, as a consequence of the melting of the glaciers in the Himalayas, the water of the River Ganges is likely to first increase and later diminish. There are 400 million people living in the river delta whose water supply and welfare will be affected by such a contingency.

India has seen tremendous upheavals during the two decades we have been conducting research in India. Things we never thought possible have materialized: former Untouchables and women have risen to become political leaders, voting is computerized, midday meals are available for all school children, and baby girls are commonly aborted among the middle classes. Although all changes have not been constructive in the well-being of Indians, in spite of the still prevalent corruption, poverty, disparities and violations of human rights there have been clear improvements. As so many who are working with India would agree: India does not cease to amaze.

Since the economic reforms, India has risen in international prominence both economically and politically, while Indian diaspora is extending India's cultural influence across its borders. But whether this century will be India's depends on how India can meet its challenges in fighting poverty, solving its environmental problems, educating its youthful population and providing equal welfare to its citizens. Global, national and local political action will influence the extent to which economic growth in India will pay social dividends to improve the capabilities of women, the poor, uneducated, *dalits* and other vulnerable groups and lead to development.

# REFERENCES

Agarwal, Anil, Sunita Nara in and Srabani Sen. 1999. *The citizens' fifth report. Part I: National overview*. New Delhi: Centre for Science and Environment.

Agarwal, Bina. 2003. Gender inequality, cooperation and environmental sustainability. In *Inequality, collective action and environmental sustainability*, ed. Jean-Marie Baland, Samuel Bowles and Pranab Bardhan. Princeton: Princeton University Press.

————. 1995. *Gender, environment and poverty interlinks in rural India: Regional variations and temporal shifts, 1971–1991*. United Nations Research Institute for Social Development. Dp 62. Online: http://www.unrisd.org/unrisd/website/document.nsf/d2a23ad2d50cb2a280256eb300385855/e9df658745ec6c3080256b67005b6798/$file/dp62m2.pdf (accessed March 27, 2012).

Agricultural Trade Policy Analysis Unit. 2007. India's role in world agriculture. *European Communities*. Online: http://ec.europa.eu/agriculture/publi/map/03_07.pdf (accessed March 27, 2012).

Amarasinghe, Upali A., Tushaar Shah, Hugh Turral and B. K. Anand. 2007. *India's water future to 2025–2050: Business-as-usual scenario and deviations*. Colombo: International Water Management Institute.

Andelman, David A. 2007. Special Report: The world's most corrupt countries. *Forbes*, April 3. Online: http://www.forbes.com/2007/04/03/corruption-countries-nations-biz-07caphosp-cx_da_0403corrupt.html (accessed May14, 2012).

Andersen, Walter K. 2010. The US engagement with India: Reviving the momentum. *India Quarterly: A Journal of International Affairs* 66, no. 1: 13–33.

Apco Worldwide. 2011. Indian agriculture: The view from the ground up. Online: http://www.apcoworldwide.com/content/PDFs/Indian_Agriculture032011.pdf (accessed March 27, 2012).

Appadurai, Arjun. 1996. *Modernity at large*. Minneapolis: University of Minnesota Press.

————. 1986. Is Homo hierarchicus? *American Ethnologist* 13, no. 4: 745–61.

Aron, Sunita. 2009. A ray of hope for Gangotri. *Hindustan Times*, November 21.

Arora, Navneet. 2006. *Increased flirtation of adolescents with computers: A change in primary relationships*. All India Sociological Conference. December 27. Chennai.

Arun, C. Joe. 2007. From stigma to self-assertion. *Contributions to Indian Sociology* 41, no. 1: 81–104.

Aura, Siru. 2006. Agency at marital breakdown: Redefining Hindu women's networks and positions. In *Culture, power and agency: Gender in Indian ethnography*, ed. Lina Fruzzetti and Sirpa Tenhunen. Kolkata: Stree.

Azam, Khalid M. and P. K. Pradhan. 2005. Fertilizer pricing strategy in the Indian market. In *Rural marketing: Thrust and challenges*, ed. M. Rahman Samiuddin, Anjila Saxena and Harsh Dwivedi. New Delhi: National Publishing House.

Bagchi, Amaresh and John Kurian. 2005. Regional inequalities in India. In *The politics of economic reforms in India*, ed. Jos Mooji. New Delhi: Sage.

Bajpaee, Chietigj. 2008. The Indian elephant returns to Africa. *Asia Times Online*, April 25. Online: http://www.atimes.com/atimes/South_Asia/JD25Df02.html (accessed March 27, 2012).

Bakshi, Amba Batra. 2009. The sea's teeth: Is coastal India going under—east first? *Outlook*, September 28. Online: http://www.outlookindia.com/article.aspx?261877 (accessed March 27, 2012).

Balwantray, Mehta, Bhawan Vidya and Moth Masjid. 2006. Corruption in trucking operations in India. Transparency International India.

Banerjee, Abhijit et al. 2002. Strategy for economic reform in West Bengal. *Economic and Political Weekly*, October 12.

Banks, Ken. 2009. Mobile database, kiwanja.net. Online: http://kiwanja.net/ (accessed March 27, 2012).

Basu, Amrita. 1996. Caste and class: The rise of Hindu nationalism in India. *Harvard International Review* 18, no. 3: 28–31.

Batchelor, Simon, Nigel Scott and Nigel Taylor. 2005. *Background paper: The contribution of ICTs to pro-poor growth*. Dac Network on Poverty Reduction. Online: http://www.oecd.org/officialdocuments/publicdisplaydocumentpdf/?cote=DCD/DAC/POVNET%282005%298&docLanguage=En (accessed May 15, 2012).

Bayes, Abdul. 1999. *Village pay phones and poverty reduction: Insights from a Grameen Bank initiative in Bangladesh*. Bonn: Centre for Development Research.

BBC News. 2009. Profile: Jayaram Jayalalitha. Online: http://news.bbc.co.uk/2/hi/south_asia/4762593.stm (accessed May 14, 2012).

Bellamy, Carol. 2005. Comment. In *India rising: Emergence of a new world power*, ed. Tarun Das, Colette Mathur and Frank-Jürgen Richter. Singapore: Marshall Cavendish Business.

Béteille, Andre. 2002. *Caste, class and power: Changing patterns of stratification in a Tanjore village*. Delhi: Oxford University Press.

————. 1991. *Society and politics in India: Essays in a comparative perspective*. London: Tanjore Athlone Press.

Bhagawati, J. N. and T. N. Srinivasan. 1993. *India's economic reforms*. New Delhi: Ministry of Finance.

Bijapurkar, Rama. 2008. *We are like that only: Understanding the logic of consumer India*. Delhi: Penguin.

Bloomberg News. 2009. India's industrial production rises for seventh month. September 11.

Borooah, Vani and Sriya Iyer. 2004. *Religion and fertility in India: The role of son preference and daughter aversion*. Cambridge Working Papers in Economics no. 436, University of Cambridge.

Bose, Sugata and Ayesha Jalal. 1998. *Modern South Asia: History, culture, political economy*. Delhi: Oxford University Press.

Bowring, Philip. 2006. Maoists who menace India. *International Herald Tribune*, April 18.

Brass, Paul. 1990. *The politics of India since Independence*. New Delhi: Cambridge University Press.

Breman, Jan. 2009. Myth of the global safety net. *New Left Review* 59 (September–October). Online: http://www.newleftreview.org/?page=article&view=2800 (accessed March 27, 2012).

————. 2007. Wage hunters and gatherers; the labouring poor in India. *The Jan Breman omnibus: Of peasants, migrants and paupers*. New Delhi: Oxford University Press.

_____. 2004. *The making and unmaking of and industrial working class: Sliding down the labour hierarchy in Ahmedabad, India.* Delhi: Oxford University Press.

Bruns, Bryan, G. Lamar Robert and Chongchit Sripun Tiam-Tong. 1996. *Village telephones: Socioeconomic impacts and implications for rural futures.* Online: http://www.cm.ksc.co.th/~bruns/rurtel.html (accessed March 27, 2012).

Caldwell, John C. 2006. Will HIV/AIDS levels in Asia reach the level of Sub-Saharan Africa? *Asia-Pacific Population Journal* 21, no. 1: 3–9.

Caldwell, John C., Bruce K. Caldwell, Pat Caldwell, Peter F. McDonald and Thomas Schindlmayr. 2006. *Demographic transition theory.* Dordrecht: Springer.

Cecchini S. and M. Raina. 2002. Village information kiosks for the Warana Cooperatives in India. World Bank. Online: http://web.worldbank.org/WBSITE/EXTERNAL/TOPICS/EXTINFORMATIONANDCOMMUNICATIONANDTECHNOLOGIES/EXTEGOVERNMENT/0,,contentMDK:20486701~isCURL:Y~menuPK:702592~pagePK:148956~piPK:216618~theSitePK:702586,00.html (accessed March 27, 2012).

Centre for the Study of Developing Societies. 2007. State of the Nation Survey (New Delhi).

Chakravarty, D. 2004. Expansion of market and freedom of expression: Women and the electronic media. *Economic and Political Weekly* 39, no. 45: 4910–16.

Chakravarty, Sumita S. 1993. *National identity in Indian popular cinema 1947–1987.* Austin: University of Texas Press.

Chandrasekhar, C. P., Jayati Ghosh and Anamitra Roychowdhury. 2006. The "demographic dividend" and young India's economic future. *Economic and Political Weekly,* 9 December.

Char, Arundhati. 2011. *Male involvement in family planning and reproductive health in rural Central India.* Acta Universitatis Tamperensis, 1687. Tampere: Tampere University Press.

Char, Arundhati, Minna Säävälä and Teija Kulmala. 2009. Male perceptions on female sterilization: A community-based study in rural Central India. *International Perspectives on Sexual and Reproductive Health* 35, no. 3: 131–8.

Chari, S. 2004. *Fraternal capital: Peasant workers, self-made man, and globalization in provincial India.* New Delhi: Permanent Black.

Chatterjee, Indrani, ed. 2004. *Unfamiliar relations: Family and history in South Asia.* New Brunswick, NJ: Rutgers University.

Chatterjee, Partha. 1993. *The nation and its fragments: Colonial and postcolonial histories.* Princeton: Princeton University Press.

Chatterjee, Srikanta, Allan Rae and Ranjan Ray. 2007. Food consumption and calorie intake in contemporary India. Online: https://editorialexpress.com/cgi-bin/conference/download.cgi?db_name=NZAE2007&paper_id=72 (accessed March 27, 2012).

*Chronicle of Higher Education.* 2009. India pushes higher-education expansion with 40% budget increase. July 7.

Ciotti, Manuela. 2006. In the past we were a bit "Chamar": Education as a self- and community engineering process in northern India. *Journal of the Royal Anthropological Institute* 12, no. 4: 899–916.

Cohen, Stephen. 2001. *Emerging power: India.* Washington, DC: Brookings Institution Press.

comScore. 2008. India's social networking market sees global brands gain prominence in 2008. Online: http://www.comscore.com/Press_Events/Press_Releases/2009/2/India_Social_Networking (accessed March 27, 2012).

Coyle, Diana, ed. 2005. *Africa: The impact of mobile phones.* Vodafone Policy Paper Series, no. 2 (March). Online: http://www.vodafone.com/assets/files/en/AIMP_09032005. pdf (accessed March 27 2012).

Cross, Jamie. 2010. Neoliberalism as unexceptional: Economic zones and the everyday precariousness of working life in South India. *Critique of Anthropology* 30, no. 4: 355–73.

D'Monte, Darryl. 2009. Beating retreat. *Hindustan Times,* November 23.

Das Gupta, Monica. 1987. Selective discrimination against female children in rural Punjab, India. *Population and Development Review* 13, no. 1: 77–100.

Das, Gurcharan. 2002. *India unbound: The social and economic revolution from Independence to the global information age.* New Delhi: Penguin.

Das, S. K. 2005. Reforms and the Indian administrative service. In *The politics of economic reforms in India,* ed. Jos Mooij. New Delhi: Sage.

Das, Veena and J. P. S. Uberoi. 1971. The elementary structure of caste. *Contributions to Indian Sociology* 5: 33–43.

Datta, Bishakha, ed. 2000. *And who will make the chapatis?: A study of all-women panchayats in Maharashtra.* Kolkata: Stree.

Deanton, Angus and Jean Drèze. 2002. *Poverty and inequality in India: A re-examination.* Centre for Development Economics Working Papers, no. 107. Delhi School of Economics. Online: http://www.cdedse.org/pdf/work107.pdf (accessed March 27, 2012).

Debroy, Bibek and Laveesh Bhandari. 2006. *Rapid growth of selected Asian economies. Lessons and implications for agriculture. Part II. Indian agriculture and scenario for 2020.* Online: http://www. fao.org/docrep/009/ag088e/AG088E07.htm#part2.5.1 (accessed March 27, 2012).

Deen, Thalif. 2009. INDIA: When toilets were as scarce as hen's teeth. IPS, August 19. Online: http://ipsnews.net/news.asp?idnews=48143 (accessed March 27, 2012).

De Neve, G. 2005. *The everyday politics of labour: Working lives in India's informal economy.* Delhi: Social Science Press.

Dickey, Sara. 2000. Permeable homes: Domestic service, household space and vulnerability of class boundaries in urban India. *American Ethnologist* 27, no. 2: 462–89.

Donahue, Asmaa. 2010. *International adolescent girls, cornerstone of society: Building evidence and policies for inclusive societies.* Background Paper 5th UNICEF-GPIA. New York City. The New School, April 26–8.

Donner, Henrika. 2008. *Domestic goddesses, maternity, globalization and middle-class identity in contemporary India.* Aldershot: Ashgate.

*Down to Earth.* 2006. Smog now envelopes India's smaller cities. November 19. Online: http://www.downtoearth.org.in/full6.asp?foldername=20030831&filename=news& sec_id=4&sid=26# (accessed March 27, 2012).

Doyal L. and I. Gough. 1991. *A theory of human need.* London: Macmillan.

Drèze, Jean and Aparajita Goyal. 2003. The future of mid-day meals. *Frontline,* August 2. Online: http://www.hinduonnet.com/fline/fl2016/stories/20030815002208500.htm (accessed March 27, 2012).

Dumont, Louis. 1970. *Homo hierarchicus: An essay in the caste system.* Chicago: Chicago University Press.

Dyson, Tim. 2004. India's population: The future. In *Twenty-first century India: Population, economy, human development, and the environment,* ed. Tim Dyson, Robert Cassen and Leela Visaria. Oxford: Oxford University Press.

Dyson, Tim and M. Moore. 1983. On kinship structure, female autonomy and demographic behaviour in India. *Population and Development Review* 9: 35–60.

*Economist.* 2012. India's identity scheme: The magic number. January 14.

Engqvist, Jonatan Habib and Maria Lantz, eds. 2008. *Dharavi: Documenting informalities.* Stockholm: The Royal University College of Fine Art and Architecture.

Erikson, L. 2003. Snakes in Bombay: A case study of British/Indian outsourcing partnership. *The Milestone* 4: 1–3.

Eshwaran, Mukesh. 1994. *Why poverty persists in India.* New Delhi: Oxford University Press.

Fernandes, Leela. 2006. *India's new middle class: Democratic politics in an era of economic reform.* Minneapolis: University of Minnesota Press.

Forbes, Geraldine. 1999. *Women in modern India.* New Delhi: Foundation Books.

Frank, Katherine. 2002. *Indira.* New York: HarperCollins.

Fuller, Christopher and Haripriya Narasimhan. 2007. Information technology professionals and the new-rich middle class in Chennai (Madras). *Modern Asian Studies* 41, no. 1: 121–50.

Ganguly-Scrase, Ruchira and Timothy J. Scrase. 2009. *Globalization and the middle classes in India: The social and sultural impact of neoliberal reforms.* London: Routledge.

Ghosh, Dhrubajyoti. 1998. The Calcutta wetlands: Turning bad water into good. Change Makers. Online: http://www.changemakers.net/journal/98october/ghosh.cfm (accessed March 27, 2012).

Ghosh, P. K. and B. Harriss-White. 2002. A crises in the rice economy. *Frontline* 19, no. 19: 14–27.

Ghosh, Nilanjan. 2007. Air pollution in India: The post-liberalisation era. In *Indian cities in transition,* ed. Annapurna Shaw. Delhi: Orient Longman.

Gill, S. S. 2005. *Information revolution and India – A critique.* Delhi: Rupa & Co.

Gokulsing, K. Moti and Wimal Dissanayake. 2004. *Indian popular cinema: A narrative of cultural change.* London: Trentham Books.

Government of India. 2008. *Report on the conditions of work and promotion of livelihoods in the unorganised sector.* New Delhi: National Commission for Enterprises in the Unorganised Sector, Government of India.

Government of Madhya Pradesh. 2002. *The Bhopal document. Charting a new course for dalits for the 21st century.* Bhopal: Government of Madhya Pradesh.

Govindassamyat, Manoj. 2009. 150 more TV stations entering India, I&B ministry wants to cap numbers. MoneyMint, October 11.

Graddol, David. 2010. *English next India: The future of English in India.* British Council. http://www.britishcouncil.org/learning-english-next-india-2010-book.pdf (accessed July 25, 2012).

Guha, Ramachandra. 2007. *India after Gandhi: The history of the world's largest democracy.* New Delhi: HarperCollins.

Guilmoto, C. Z. 2010. Longer-term disruption to demographic structures in China and India resulting from skewed sex ratios at birth. *Asian Population Studies* 6, no. 1: 3–24.

Guilmoto C. Z. and Isabelle Attané. 2005. *The geography of deteriorating child sex ratio in China and India.* International Union for the Scientific Study of Population, 25th International Population Conference, Tours, France. Online: http://iussp2005.princeton.edu/download.aspx?submissionId=51524 (accessed March 27, 2012).

Guilmoto C. Z. and S. Irudaya Rajan, eds. 2005. *Fertility transition in South India.* New Delhi: Sage.

Gupta, Dipankar. 2001. *Mistaken modernity. India between worlds.* Delhi: HarperCollins.

————. 2000. *Interrogating caste. Understanding hierarchy and difference in Indian society.* Delhi: Penguin.

Gupta, Monobina. 2010. *Left politics in Bengal: Time travels among Bhadralok Marxists.* Delhi: Orient Blackswan.

Gupta, Prashant, Rajat Gupta and Thomas Netzer. 2009. *Building India: Accelerating infrastructure projects*. McKinsey & Company report. New Delhi: Magnum Custom Publishing.

Gupta, Smita. 2009a. BSP at the crossroads. *Economic and Political Weekly*, June 27.

_____. 2009b. Worry lines on the map. *Outlook*, December 28.

Gupta, Sunanda. 2012. Innovative technology for maternal and child care. Paper presented in the International Conference in Millennium Development Goals Related to Reproductive Health: Status, Challenges and Future Directions, March 18–21, 2012, Mumbai, India.

Hancock, Mary. 1999. *Womanhood in the making: Domestic ritual and public culture in urban South India*. Boulder: Westview.

Hansen, Thomas Blom. 1999. *The saffron wave: Democracy and Hindu nationalism in modern India*. Princeton: Princeton University Press.

Harriss-White, Barbara. 2002. *Development, policy and agriculture in India in the 1990s*. Queen Elizabeth House Working Paper Series. Online: http://www3.qeh.ox.ac.uk/pdf/qehwp/qehwps78.pdf (accessed May 15, 2012).

*Hindustan Times*. 2009a. Delhi air thick with pollution. November 8.

_____. 2009b. India unveils ambitious solar power mission. November 23.

Hodgson, An. 2007. The rise of second-tier cities in India. *Euromonitor International*, October 6. Online: http://www.euromonitor.com/The_rise_of_second_tier_cities_in_India (accessed March 27, 2012).

Hohethal, Annika. 2003. English in India: Loyalty and attitudes. *Language in India*, vol. 3, May 5. Online: http://www.languageinindia.com/may2003/annika.html#chapter5 (accessed March 27, 2012).

Hudson, Valerie M. and Andrea M. den Boer, 2004. *Bare branches: The security implications of Asia's surplus male population*. Cambridge, MA: MIT Press.

I4D. 2005. Taking health care to rural areas. *Information for Development*, May. Online: http://www.i4donline.net/may05/satellitetech.asp (accessed March 27, 2012).

International Energy Agency (IEA). 2011. *$CO_2$ emissions from fuel combustion: Highlights*. Paris, France: IEA.

International Institute for Population Sciences (IIPS) and Macro International. 2008. *National family health survey (NFHS-3), India, 2005–06: Andhra Pradesh*. Mumbai: IIPS.

_____. 2007. *National family health survey (NFHS-3), 2005–2006: India*, vol. 1. Mumbai: IIPS.

International Labour Organization. 2002. *Women and men in the informal economy: A statistical picture*. Geneva: ILO Employment Sector.

International Labour Organization and World Trade Organization (ILO). 2009. *Globalization and informal jobs in developing countries*. Geneva: International Institute of Labour Studies and Washington: Economic Research and Statistics Division. Online: www.ilo.org/public/english/bureau/inst/download/globalinform.pdf (accessed March 27, 2012).

*India Daily*. 2009. Bihar no. one in agriculture growth, Punjab at 14th place! December 28. Online: http://www.indiadaily.org/entry/bihar-no-one-in-agriculture-growth-punjab-at-14th-place/ (accessed March 27, 2012).

India Knowledge@Wharton. 2007. Does urban development drive rural growth in India? 20 September. Online: http://knowledge.wharton.upenn.edu/india/article.cfm?articleid=4224 (accessed March 27, 2012).

IPCC. 2001. *Climate change 2001*. Cambridge: Cambridge University Press.

ITU. 2009. ICT eye. Online: http://www.itu.int/ITU-D/icteye/DisplayCountry.aspx?code=IND (accessed March 27, 2012).

Jaffrelot, Christophe. 2006. *India's silent revolution: The rise of the low castes in North Indian politics.* Delhi: Permanent Black.

———. 1999. *The Hindu nationalist movement and Indian politics 1925 to the 1990s.* Delhi: Penguin.

Jain, Sonu. 2004. Smog city to clean capital: How Delhi did it. Climate IMC, March 20, 2006. Online: http://www.climateimc.org/en/breaking-news/2006/03/20/smog-city-clean-capital-how-delhi-did-it (accessed May 15, 2012).

James, K. S. 2008. Glorifying Malthus: Current debate on "demographic dividend" in India. *Economic and Political Weekly,* June 21.

Jeffery, Patricia, Roger Jeffery and Andrew Lyon. 1989. *Labour pains and labour power: Women and childbearing in India.* London: Zed Books.

Jeffrey, Robin. 2010. *Media and modernity: Communications, women and the state in India.* New Delhi: Permanent Black.

Jha, Prabhat et al. 2006. Low male-to-female sex ratio of children born in India: national survey of 1.1 million households. *Lancet* 367, no. 9, 506: 211–18.

Joshi, C. 2003. *Lost worlds: Indian labour and its forgotten histories.* Delhi: Permanent Black.

Joy, K. L., Paranjape Gujja, Goud Vinod Suhas and Shruti Vispute, eds. 2008. *Water conflicts in India: A million revolts in the making.* Delhi: Routledge India.

Kapadia, K., ed. 2002. *The violence of development: The politics of identity, gender and social inequalities in India.* London: Zed Books.

Karanth, G. K. 2004. Replication or dissent? Culture and institutions among "Untouchable" scheduled castes in Karnataka. *Contributions to Indian Sociology* 38, nos. 1–2: 137–63.

Kathuria, Rajat, Mahesh Uppal and Mamta. 2009. An econometric analysis of the impact of mobile. *India: The impact of mobile phones. Moving the debate forward.* The Policy Paper Series, no. 9. Vodafone Group.

Khan, M. E. 2012. Conditional cash transition: Will it help in achieving the goals? Paper presented at the International Conference on Millennium Development Goals Related to Reproductive Health: Status, Challenges and Future Directions, March 18–21, 2012, Mumbai, India.

Khanna, Amit. 2003. The business of Hindi films. In *Encyclopaedia of Hindi cinema,* ed. Gulzar et al. New Delhi : Encyclopaedia Britannica (India).

Kim, Chan Wahn. 2006. *Economic liberalisation and India's foreign policy.* Delhi: Kalpaz Publication.

Kim, Sun Bae et al. 2007. India's urbanization: Emerging opportunities. *Asia Economics Analyst* 7, no. 13. Online: http://www.goldmansachs.com/our-thinking/brics/brics-reports-pdfs/india-urbanization.pdf (accessed May 10, 2012).

Kingdon, Geeta, Robert Cassen, Kristy McNay and Leela Visaria. 2004. Education and literacy. In *Twenty-first century India. Population, economy, human development, and the environment,* ed. Tim Dyson, Robert Cassen and Leela Visaria. Oxford: Oxford University Press.

Kumar, Rajendra. 2004. *Social, governance, and economic impact assessment of information and communication technology interventions in rural India,* unpublished thesis, MIT department of Urban Studies and Planning.

Kumar, Rajesh and Anand Kumar Sethi. 2005. *Doing business in India: A guide for Western managers.* New York: Palgrave Macmillan.

Kumar, Rajesh et al. 2006. Trends in HIV-1 in young adults in south India from 2000 to 2004: A prevalence study. *Lancet* 367: 9517, s. 1164–72.

Kuriyan, Renee and Isha Ray. 2009. Outsourcing the state? Public–private partnerships and information technologies in India. *World Development* 37, no. 10: 1663–73.

Lacity, Mary C., Vidya V. Iyer and Prasad S. Rudramuniyaiah. 2009. Turnover intentions of Indian IS professionals. In *Information systems outsourcing: Enduring themes, global challenges, and process opportunities*, ed. Rudy Hirschheim, Armin Heinzl and Jens Dibbern. Berlin, Heidelberg: Springer.

Lak, Daniel. 2005. *Mantras of change: Reporting India in a time of flux.* Delhi: Penguin.

Lamont, James. 2009. Infrastructure delays to cost India $200bn. *Financial Times*, August 12.

Leahy, Joe. 2008. India needs to triple energy capacity to meet demand. *Financial Times*, June 4.

Loikala, J., et al. 2006. *Opportunities for Finnish environmental technology in India.* Helsinki: Sitra.

Loyoloa, Joseph. 2005. Inter-city marketing network for women micro-entrepreneurs using mobile phone: Social capital brings economic development I4D. *Information for Development*, July. Online: http://www.i4donline.net/feb05/intercity_full.asp (accessed May 14, 2012).

Mahadevia, Darshin. 2005. From stealth to aggression: Economic reforms and communal politics in Gujarat. In *The politics of economic reforms in India*, ed. Jos Mooij. New Delhi: Sage.

Mahapatra, B. P. 1990. A demographic appraisal of multilingualism in India. In *Multilingualism in India*, ed. D. P. Pattanayak. Clevedon: Multilingual Matters Ltd.

Manian, Ranjini. 2007. *Doing business in India for dummies.* New Delhi: Wiley India.

Mehdudia, Sujay. 2011. Poverty rate declines from 37.2% to 32%. *The Hindu*, April 21. Online: http://www.thehindu.com/todays-paper/tp-national/article1713579.ece?css=print (accessed March 27, 2012).

Mehrotra, Santosh. 2009. Indian higher education: Time for a serious rethink. *International Higher Education* 56 (Summer). Online: http://www.bc.edu/bc_org/avp/soe/cihe/newsletter/Number56/p5_Mehrotra.htm (accessed March 27, 2012).

Mehta, Aasha Kapur and Amita Shah. 2003. Chronic poverty in India: Incidence, causes and policies. *World Development* 31, no. 3: 491–511.

Mencher, Joan. 1975. The caste system upside down. *Current Anthropology* 15, no. 4: 469–93.

Mendelsohn, Olivier and Marika Vicziany. 2000. *The untouchables: Subordination, poverty and the state in modern India.* Cambridge: Cambridge University Press.

Mitra, Maureen Nandini. 2006. West Bengal's wetlands under threat. *Down to Earth*, November 20. Online: http://www.downtoearth.org.in/Full6.asp?FolderName=20060 915&FileNAme=news&sid=3&sec_id=4 (accessed March 27, 2012).

Mohan, Raja S. 2005. *Crossing the Rubicon: The shaping of India's new foreign policy.* Delhi: Penguin.

Mooij, Jos, ed. 2005. *The politics of economic reforms in India.* New Delhi: Sage.

Moorhouse, Geoffrey. 1983. *Calcutta. The city revealed.* London: Penguin.

Mukhopadhyay, S. 2002. Status of women under economic reforms: The Indian case. In *Tracking gender equity under economic reforms: Continuity and change in South Asia*, ed. R. Sudarshan and S. Mukhopadhyay, New Delhi: Kali for Women.

Nair, Saju K. 2006. Emerging health problems in a new profession: A study of software executives. All India Sociological Conference. December 27. Chennai.

Nandy, Ashis. 1983. *The intimate enemy: Loss and recovery of self under colonialism.* Delhi: Oxford University Press.

Narain, Sunita. 2002. Changing environmentalism. *Seminar* 516. Online: http://www.india-seminar.com/2002 (accessed March 27, 2012).

National Crime Records Bureau. 2010. Accidental deaths and suicides in India.

Nasscom. 2008. Annual report: National Family Health Survey. Online: http://www. nasscom.org/upload/Annual_Report07-08.pdf (accessed March 27, 2012).

Naujoks, Daniel. 2009. *Emigration, immigration, and diaspora relations in India.* Country Profiles, Migration Policy Institute. Online: http://www.migrationinformation.org/Profiles/ display.cfm?ID=745 (accessed March 27, 2012).

Navlakha, Gautam. 2006. Maoists in India. *Economic and Political Weekly,* June 10.

Nayar, Lola. 2009. Bilateral trade: Bazaar ping-pong. *Outlook,* November 16.

NCAER. 2005. *The great Indian market. Results for the NCAER's market information survey of households.* National Council of Applied Economic Research, New Delhi. Online: http://www.ncaer. org/downloads/PPT/TheGreatIndianMarket.pdf (accessed March 27, 2012).

Nussbaum, Martha C. 2000. *Women and human development: The capabilities approach.* Cambridge University Press: Cambridge.

Office of the Registrar General, India. 2011a. *Maternal & child mortality and total fertility rates. sample registration system (SRS).* July 7. Online: http://www.censusindia.gov.in/vital_ statistics/SRS_Bulletins/MMR_release_070711.pdf (accessed March 27, 2012).

Office of the Registrar General and Census Commissioner, India. 2011b. *Provisional population totals paper 1 of 2011 India Series 1.* New Delhi. Online: http://www.censusindia. gov.in/2011-prov-results/prov_results_paper1_india.html (accessed March 27, 2012).

_____. 2006. *Population projections for India and states 2001–2026. Report of the technical group on population projections constituted by the National Commission on Population.* New Delhi. Online: http://nrhm-mis.nic.in/UI/Public%20Periodic/Population_Projection_Report_2006. pdf (accessed March 27, 2012).

Pai, Sudha. 2005. Populism and economic reforms: The BJP experiment in Uttar Pradesh. In *The politics of economic reforms in India,* ed. Jos Mooij. New Delhi: Sage.

Pande, Amrita. 2009. "My body pays the monthly bills": Embodied labor and the politics of surrogacy in India. Paper presented in Gendering Asia Network Conference: Gender, Mobility, and Citizenship. University of Helsinki. May 29.

Parry J., J. Breman, and K. Kapadia, eds. 1999. *The worlds of indian industrial labour.* New Delhi: Sage.

Patel, Tulsi 2006. *Sex-selective abortion in India.* New Delhi: Sage.

Pervez, Shahid Muhammed. 2004. Post-colonial understandings of female infanticide in north and south India. Unpublished paper.

Planning Commission. 2012. *Press note on poverty estimates, 2009–10.* Online: http:// planningcommission.nic.in/news/press_pov1903.pdf (accessed March 26, 2012).

Price, Pamela. 2000. Da Sonia Gandhi ble politiker. In *Nærbilder av India: Samfunn, Politikk og Utvikling,* ed. Hanne Kathinka Frøystad, Eldrid Ingebjørg Mageli and Arild Engelsen Ruud. Oslo: Cappelen Akademisk Forlag.

Purfield, Catriona. 2006. Mind the gap—Is economic growth in India leaving some states behind? *International Monetary Fund Working Paper.* Online: http://www.imf.org/external/ pubs/ft/wp/2006/wp06103.pdf (accessed May 15, 2012).

Radhakrishna, R., Prafulla Ketkar and Aisha Sultanat. 2005. *Alternate approaches to security: National integration governance non military challenges.* Delhi: Institute of Peace and Conflicts Studies.

Raja, M. 2008. $15bn loan waiver reaps harvest of anger. *Asia Times Online,* March. Online: http://www.atimes.com/atimes/South_Asia/JC11Df01.html (accessed May 15, 2012).

Ramesh, Randeep. 2006. Inside India's hidden war. *Guardian Unlimited*, May 9. Online: http://www.guardian.co.uk/india/story/0,1770612,00.html (accessed March 27, 2012).

Rangaswamy, N. 2007a. ICT for development and commerce: A case study of internet cafes in India. Paper presented at the 9th International Conference on Social Implications of Computers in Developing Countries. Sao Paolo, Brazil.

————. 2007b. The aspirational PC: Home computers and Indian middle class domesticity. Unpublished paper prepared for Microsoft Research India.

Rattanani, Jagdish. 1999. Hearts and minds: A city mired in indifference stages a remarkable turnaround. CNN Asia Now. Online: http://edition.cnn.com/ASIANOW/asiaweek/features/asiacities/ac1999/data/improved.surat.html (accessed May 15, 2012).

Rao, Ursula. 2010. Making the global city: Urban citizenship at the margins of Delhi. *Ethnos* 75, no. 4: 402–24.

Ray, Himanshu Prabha and Edward A. Alpers. 2007. *Cross currents and community networks: The history of the Indian Ocean world.* Delhi: Oxford University Press.

Rawkins, Paul. 2006. India's public finances: Do they matter? *Deutsche Bank Research,* January 13. Online:http://www.dbresearch.de/PROD/DBR_INTERNET_DE-PROD/PROD 0000000000195414/India%27s+public+finances%3A+Do+they+matter%3F.pdf (accessed March 27, 2012).

Rawls, John. 1971. *A theory of justice.* Oxford: Oxford University Press.

Richard, Alan and Nirvikar Singh. 2001. *Inter state disputes in India: Institutions and policies.* Department of Environmental Studies and Department of Economics. University of California, Santa Cruz.

Richardson, Ben. 2009. Can India boost internet usage? BBC, May 26. Online: http://news.bbc.co.uk/2/hi/business/8067930.stm (accessed May 15, 2012).

Rosenthal, Elisabeth. 2010. Regret on Himalayan glaciers estimate. *New York Times,* January 20.

Roubini, Nouriel. 2009. Are there bright spots amid the global recession? *Forbes,* June 8. Online: http://www.forbes.com/2009/08/05/recession-china-india-qatar-poland-brazil-opinions-columnists-nouriel-roubini.html (accessed March 27, 2012).

Roychowdhury, Anumita, Vivek Chattopadhya, Chirag Shah and Priyanka Chandola. 2006. *The leapfrog factor: Clearing the air in Asian cities.* Delhi: Centre for Science and Research.

Rustagi, Preet, ed. 2009. *Concerns, conflicts, and cohesions: Universalization of elementary education in India.* New Delhi: Oxford University Press.

Säävälä, Minna. 2010a. *Middle-class moralities. Struggles over belonging and prestige in India.* Hyderabad: Orient Blackswan.

————. 2010b. Below replacement-level fertility in conditions of slow social and economic development: A review of the evidence from South India. *Finnish Yearbook of Population Research* 45: 45–66.

————. 2001a. *Fertility and familial power relations: Procreation in South India.* Curzon: Richmond.

————. 2001b. Low caste but middle class: Some religious strategies for middle-class identification in Hyderabad. *Contributions to Indian Sociology* 35, no. 3: 293–318.

Sachs, Jeffrey and Anathi Ramiah. 2002. Understanding regional economic growth in India. *Asian Economic Papers* 1: 3.

Sample Registration System. 2009. *Special bulletin on maternal mortality in India 2004–06.* Office of the Registrar General, Vital Statistics Division, Government of India.

————. 2007. *SRS Baseline Survey Report 2004.* Office of the Registrar General, Government of India.

Sanghi, A., R. Mendelsohn and A. Dinar. 1998. The climate sensitivity of Indian agriculture. In *Measuring the impact of climate change on Indian agriculture*, ed. A. Dinar. World Bank Technical Paper, no. 402. Washington, DC: The World Bank.

Sardar, Ziauddin. 2008. *Balti Britain: A provocative journey through Asian Britain*. London: Granta.

Sarkar, S., and B. S. Mehta. 2010. Income inequality in India: Pre- and post-reform periods. *Economic and Political Weekly* 45, no. 37: 45–55.

Savarkar, Vinayak Damodar. 2003. *Hindutva: Who is a Hindu?* New Delhi: Hindi Sahitya Sadan.

Sen, Amartya. 2005. *The argumentative Indian: Writings on Indian history, culture and identity*. New York: Penguin.

———. 1999. *Development as freedom*. New York: Alfred A. Knopf.

———. 1982. *Poverty and famines: An essay on entitlements and deprivation*. Oxford: Clarendon Press.

Sen Gupta, Somini. 2006. Thirsty giant India digs deeper, but wells are drying up. *New York Times*, September 30.

Sengupta, Shuddhabrata. 2006. Sound is an image. *Outlook*, October 16. Online: http://www.outlookindia.com/full.asp?fodname=20061016&fname=JMobile+phones+New+%28F%29&sid=1 (accessed March 27, 2012).

Shah. A. M. 2010. *The structure of Indian society: Then and now*. New Delhi: Routledge.

Sharma, Amit. 2009. A warm winter, an empty harvest. *Hindustan Times*, November 21.

Siddiqui, Imran Ahmed and Pronab Mondal. 2007. Planned with precision – Police see plot behind eruption. *Telegraph*, November 23.

Sikand, Yoginder Singh. 2004. *Caste in Indian Muslim society*. Online: http://stateless.freehosting.net/Caste in Indian Muslim Society.htm (accessed March 28, 2012). Originally published in *Asianists' Asia*, ed. T. Wignesan. Centre de Recherches sur les Etudes Asiatiques: Paris.

Singh, Amrik. 2003. Academic standards in Indian universities: Ravages of affiliation. *Economic and Political Weekly*, July 26.

Singh Dheeraj, M. L. Meena, M. Chaudhary, H. Daya and A. Dudi. 2009. Small farms, a way to prosperity: A case study of a small farmer from Pali, India. 111 EAAE-IAAE seminar "Small Farms: Decline or Persistence." University of Kent, Canterbury, UK, June 26–7.

Singh, Navsharan and Mrinalini Kaur Sapra. 2007. Liberalization in trade and finance: India's garment sector. In *Trade liberalization and India's informal economy*, ed. Barbara Harriss-White and Anushree Sinha. New Delhi: Oxford.

Singhal, Arvind and M. Everett Rogers. 2001. *India's communication revolution: From bullock carts to cyber marts*. New Delhi: Sage.

Siva, Vandana. 2004. The suicide economy of corporate globalisation. *Countercurrents*. Online: http://www.countercurrents.org/glo-shiva050404.htm (accessed March 27, 2012).

Sivaramakrishnana, K. C., Amitabh Kundu and B. N. Singh. 2008. *Handbook of urbanization in India*. 2nd edn. Delhi: Oxford University Press.

Sondhi, Sunil. 2009. *Combating corruption in India: The role of civil society*. The 18th World Congress of International Political Science Association, Elokuu 2000, Quebec, Canada. *South Asia Intelligence Review*. Online: http://www.satp.org/ (accessed March 27, 2012).

*South Asia Intelligence Review*. 2009. Online: http://www.terrorism.net/component/content/article/68-terrorism/5051-south-asian-intelligence-review-oct-19-2009 (accessed March 27, 2012).

Spolsky, R. 1978. *Educational linguistics: An introduction*. Rowley, Mass: Newbury House.

Sreekumar, T. T. 2006. ICTs for the poor: Civil society and cyberlibertarian developmentalism in rural India. In *Political economy & information capitalism in India: Digital divide, development divide and equity*, ed. G. Parayil. New York: Palgrave.

Sreekumar, T. T. and Milagros Rivera-Sanchez. 2008. ICTs and development: Revisiting the Asian experience. *Science, Technology and Society* 13, no. 2: 159–74.

Srinivas, M. N. 1989. Some reflections on the nature of caste hierarchy. *Contributions to Indian Sociology* 18, no. 2: 51–67.

Srinivasan, T. N. and Suresh D. Tedulkar. 2003. *Reintegrating India with the world economy*. Washington, DC: Institute for International Economics.

Srivastava, Mehul. 2009. What is holding India back. *Businessweek*, October 19.

Stern, Robert W. 1993. *Changing India*. New Delhi: Foundation Books.

Suri, K. C. 2005. The dilemma of democracy: Economic reforms and electoral politics in Andhra Pradesh. In *The politics of economic reforms in India*, ed. Jos Mooij. New Delhi: Sage.

Tenhunen, Sirpa. 2011. Culture, conflict and translocal communication: Mobile technology and politics in rural West Bengal, India. *Ethnos* 76, no. 3: 398–420.

———. 2009. *Means of awakening: Gender, politics and practice in rural India*. Kolkata: Stree.

———. 2008a. Gift of money: Rearticulating tradition and market economy. *Modern Asian Studies* 42, no. 5: 1035–55.

———. 2008b. Mobile technology in the village: ICTs, culture, and social logistics in India. *Journal of the Royal Anthropological Institute* 14, no. 3 (September): 515–34.

———. 2003a. Culture and political agency: Gender, kinship and village politics in West Bengal. *Contributions to Indian Sociology* 37, no. 3: 495–518.

———. 2003b. *Secret freedom in the city: Women's wage work and agency in Calcutta*. Quebec: World Heritage Press.

Thakur, Joydeep. 2009. Fish move north to beat the heat. *Hindustan Times*, November 21.

Thakurta, Paranjoy Guha. 2009. Can India's economy overtake China? *BBC*, October 3. Online: http://news.bbc.co.uk/2/hi/8273464.stm (accessed May 15, 2012).

Tiwari, G. 2008. Interplay of love, sex and marriage in a polyandrous society in the high Himalayas of India. In *Intimacies: love and sex across cultures*, ed. W. R. Jankowiak. New York: Routledge.

Trade Chakra. 2009. Steel industry. *Trade Chakra*. Online: http://www.tradechakra.com/indian-economy/industries/steel-industry.html (accessed March 27, 2012).

Trawick, Margaret. 1992. *Notes on love in a Tamil family*. Berkeley: University of California Press.

Uberoi, Patricia. 2006. *Freedom and destiny: Gender, family, and popular culture in India*. Delhi: Oxford University Press.

UNDP. 2009. *India: Urban Poverty Report 2009*. Ministry of Housing and Urban Poverty Alleviation and UNDP. New Delhi: Oxford University Press.

———. 2008. *Human Development Report 2007/2008*. Fighting climate change: Human solidarity in divided world. United Nations Development Program.

———. 2006. *Human Development Reports*. Online: http://hdr.undp.org/statistics/ (accessed May 15, 2012).

United Nations, Department of Economic and Social Affairs, Population Division. 2011. *World population to reach 10 billion by 2100 if fertility in all countries converges to replacement level*. World Population Prospects: The 2010 Revision, press release, May 3. Online: http://esa.un.org/wpp/Other-Information/Press_Release_WPP2010.pdf (accessed March 28, 2012).

_____. 2009. *World population prospects: The 2008 revision, highlights.* Working Paper No. ESA/P/WP.210. Online: http://www.un.org/esa/population/publications/wpp2008/wpp2008_highlights.pdf (accessed March 27, 2012).

van der Veer, Peter. 1994. *Religious nationalism: Hindus and Muslims in India.* Berkeley: University of California Press.

Varma, Pavan K. 1998. *The great Indian middle class.* New Delhi: Penguin.

Varshney, Ashutosh. 2000. Is India becoming more democratic? *Journal of Asian Studies* 59, no.1: 3–25.

Vepa, Swarna Sadasivam. 2007. The feminization of agriculture and the marginalization of women's economic stake. In *Gender, food security and rural livelihoods,* ed. Maithreyi Krishnaraj. Kolkata: Stree.

Verma, Gita Dewan. 2003. *Slumming India: A chronicle of slums and their saviours.* Delhi: Penguin.

Vishwakarma, Rajesh Kumar. 2012. Future scenario of foodgrains: A case study for gap between demand and supply. Indiastat, February–March, 2012. Online: http://www.indiaagristat.com/article/40/rajesh/article40.html (accessed March 27, 2012).

Visaria, Praveen. 2002. Population policy. *Seminar* 511. Online: http://www.india-seminar.com/semframe.html (accessed May 24, 2012).

vitalanalytics.in. 2009. Urban mobile phone users in India: What do they access the Internet for. *Plugged In,* August 10. Online: http://www.pluggd.in/mobile-internet-users-in-india-297 (accessed March 27, 2012).

Vital Wave Consulting. 2009. *Health for development: The opportunity of mobile technology for healthcare in the developing world.* Washington, DC and Berkshire, UK: UN Foundation/Vodafone Foundation Partnership.

von Grebmer, Klaus et al. 2009a. *Global hunger index: The challenge of hunger: focus on financial crisis and gender inequality.* Bonn, Washington DC and Dublin: International Food Policy Research Institute.

_____. 2009b. *India state hunger index: Comparisons of hunger across states,* ed. Purnima Menon, Anil Deolalikar and Anjor Bhaskar. Washington, DC, Bonn and Riverside: International Food Policy Research Institute, Welthugerhilfe and University of California, Riverside.

Wilde, Joseph and Esther de Haan. 2006. *High cost of calling: Critical issues in the mobile phone industry.* Centre for Research on Multinational Corporations. Amsterdam. Online: http://www.somo.nl/html/paginas/pdf/High_Cost_of_Calling_nov_2006_EN.pdf (accessed March 27, 2012).

Witsoe, Jeffrey. 2011. Corruption as power: Caste and the political imagination of the postcolonial state. *American Ethnologist* 38, no. 1: 73–85.

Wolpert, Stanley. 1989. *A new history of India.* New York: Oxford University Press.

World Bank. 2006. *India: Malnutrition report.* Online: http://web.worldbank.org/WBSITE/EXTERNAL/COUNTRIES/SOUTHASIAEXT/0,,contentMDK:20916955~pagePK:146736~piPK:146830~theSitePK:223547,00.html (accessed May 24, 2012).

Wood, Adrian and Michele Caladrino. 2000. When other giant awakens: Trade and human resources in India. *Economic and Political Weekly,* December 30.

Yadav, Yogendra. 1999. Politics. In *India briefing: Looking back, looking ahead,* ed. Bouton Marshall and Philip Oldenberg. Armonk, NY: M. E. Sharpe.

_____. 1996. Reconfiguring on Indian politics: State assembly elections, 1993–95. *Economic and Political Weekly,* January 13.

Yardley, Jim. 2009. Maoist rebels widen deadly reach across India. *New York Times,* October 1.

# INDEX

Lightning Source UK Ltd.
Milton Keynes UK
UKHW012137180121
377089UK00012B/276